RETRAIN YOUR
BUSINESS
BRAIN

OUTSMART THE CORPORATE COMPETITION

Donalee Markus, Ph.D.
Lindsey Paige Markus, M.A., and Pat Taylor

Dearborn™
Trade Publishing
A **Kaplan Professional** Company

This publication is designed to provide accurate and authoritative information in regard to the subject matter covered. It is sold with the understanding that the publisher is not engaged in rendering legal, accounting, or other professional service. If legal advice or other expert assistance is required, the services of a competent professional person should be sought.

Vice President and Publisher: Cynthia A. Zigmund
Acquisitions Editor: Jonathan Malysiak
Senior Managing Editor: Jack Kiburz
Interior Design: Lucy Jenkins
Interior and Cover Design: Scott Rattray, Rattray Design
Typesetting: the dotted i

Published by Dearborn Trade Publishing
A Kaplan Professional Company

Printed in the United States of America

03 04 05 10 9 8 7 6 5 4 3 2 1

Library of Congress Cataloging-in-Publication Data

Markus, Donalee, 1945-
    Retrain your business brain: outsmart the corporate competition / Donalee Markus, Lindsey Paige Markus, and Pat Taylor.
      p. cm.
    Includes bibliographical references and index.
    ISBN 0-7931-7015-X (7.25x9 paperback)
    1. Organizational effectiveness. 2. Decision making. 3. Problem solving. 4. Creative thinking. 5. Puzzles. I. Markus, Lindsey Paige, 1976- II. Taylor, Pat, 1952- III. Title.
HD30.23.M3687 2003
650.1—dc21

2003005945

DEDICATION

In fond memory of my beloved parents,
Nate and Rose Weinstein

My father taught me how to make everyone feel special.
My mother taught me empathy and love.
Together, my parents nurtured my creativity, gave me confidence, and taught
me tolerance, perseverance, and how to bring out the best in all people.
Without these gifts I would not have found my passion.

I offer this work as my contribution.
The exercises and teachings are accurate and honest accounts of my
clinical experiences.

A C K N O W L E D G M E N T S

This book is all about learning, growing, and changing. My personal journey to develop complex paper-and-pencil puzzles for high-functioning adults in-volved similar types of discovery, exploration, and risk taking. Twenty-one years ago when I spoke of creating new neural connections, audiences were sparse and skeptical. How can I ever thank those who have supported my work with partic-ipation and kind words of encouragement?

From each and every client I have learned new ways to access the mysterious "black box"—the brain. And from these client experiences I would communi-cate to my brilliant instructional designer, Pat Taylor, the types of exercises that could strengthen weaker skill areas. Pat and I joke that we share a brain, but I cannot imagine that I am her intellectual equal. She amazes me with her ability to translate my requests for cognitive behavioral changes into paper-and-pencil exercises. Her biggest pleasure is creating exercises that stop me cold in my tracks. I relish our weekly dynamic sessions. Many days Pat appears dreary-eyed and sleepless, because she insists on forgoing sleep to give our projects her very best. Pat's talent, skill, and devotion are unparalleled. This book was made possible by her efforts.

I am particularly indebted to Dr. Jeri Morris, a neuropsychologist who patiently educates and reeducates me about the neuroanatomy of the brain. Jeri has helped me to refine my treatment and tools. We've collaborated on many projects, and I have become a stronger clinician through her guidance and teach-ings. She is not only a wonderful colleague but also a great friend.

No one encouraged me to write this book more than Amy Wax. "Self-publish!" she proclaimed. "You have a moral responsibility to spread the word." A success-ful eight-time author of The K&W Guide to College for Students with Learning Disabilities, Amy has been an outspoken source of encouragement and referrals and has become a wonderful friend. In addition, her husband, Howard, has taken it upon himself to plan the most spectacular events and getaways, so that I can complete projects and celebrate their completion. He is the ultimate concierge.

I am terrible at marketing and PR! Fortunately, Amy Falk and her wonderful team work diligently to communicate my work to a larger audience. She has the uncomfortable job of pushing the donkey (me!) uphill, yet she continues with strong determination to market Learning How to Learn and Designs for Strong Minds. I feel fortunate to have Falk & Associates representing me!

Dr. Deborah Zelinsky, a talented developmental optometrist, has tutored me in neuroanatomy, the visual systems, and sensory integration. Debbie and I confer about patients and share information. We collaborate to ensure our clients benefit from our coordinated efforts. She keeps me abreast of everything she learns from literature to conferences. Her teachings have been invaluable in helping me to understand the mind-eye connection. Thank you Alice Nixon for opening my world to the science of color and sound. I am exploring the brain's interpretation of light and color as I complete this book.

I could listen to Dr. Richard Kaufman talk about psychiatry and biochemistry for hours. Richard takes the time to share treatment protocol and biochemical intervention. He patiently explains, teaches, and answers all of my questions, and he never makes me feel like I am imposing on his valuable time.

When I first received a phone call from Chris Williams, director of training and development for NASA, in June of 1996, I thought it was a joke. People always thought I was out there, and now NASA was calling me for training! Chris is one tough cookie. She researched my credentials and references and visited me in Chicago to experience Designs for Strong Minds. Who would have guessed that she would become my strongest advocate. She fought government bureaucracy and educated NASA on the value of mental agility. Everyone is anxious to connect the dots since NASA scientists have participated in the program. Chris's brilliance and persistence have facilitated a win-win consulting relationship with NASA for over six years.

Many talented people have contributed time and energy to consult in the effort to advance the concepts of brain plasticity with the unselfish goal of benefiting the greater population. Thank you Carol Naughton of Naughton and Associates, Cliff Primer of Set Point Graphics, Dima Taranov and Dina Pastel of Kukubla Designs, and Inna Pastel for your support and commitment to this work. Web designer Lee Ann Holt and writer Karen Rosenthal were also very generous and put forth their very best efforts to create an outstanding Web site. Karen, thank you for always being available to put your magic touch on my muddled prose. And kudos to Lee Ann for never being too busy to clean up a cluttered design—Microsoft will just have to wait!

I am the chaos agent, but no one would know that because I have the BEST office manager! Karin Zaverdinos is the most organized person ever—she even has files for files. She is extremely bright, a talented writer, and so personable. She makes me look good!

A special thanks goes to Stanley Meadows, who has provided me with exceptional legal counsel in exchange for homemade osso bucco and wild mushroom risotto. I thank my mother for my culinary skills, which have facilitated my friendship and meetings with Stanley.

It is no secret that I've been pioneering for 21 years. My life has lost much of its balance during that time. I owe a special gratitude to my understanding friends who recognized my passion and gave me the space to pursue my dreams. They phoned to say hello, invited me to functions and events, and never made me feel guilty when my work prevented me from participating. Thank you Dolores and Dr. Ralph Barnett, Barbara and Dean Becker, Robin and Bob Berman, Paula and Howard Bernstein, Diane and Mickey Brown, my dear cousin Karen and Mel Burke, Karen and Alan Carney, Andrea Biel and Dr. Mimis Cohen, my dear cousins Marla and Dr. Michael Finger, Nancy and Dan Gooze, Dahlia and Dr. Daniel Graupe, Krystina and Wally Kaszubski, Chris and Dr. Frank Maggio, Lauren Mangrum, Jean and Stanley Meadows, Judy Prager, Anne and Neal Rosen, my dear Aunt Dolores and Mike Rubin, and Janet and Jack Teisch—for recognizing and accepting that I'm just "a little bit eccentric" and for respecting my journey. Unfortunately, one of my biggest supporters, my cousin and friend Alan Finger, didn't live to see this book come to fruition, but his encouragement and love helped me get here. There are so many more wonderful family, friends, and clients to mention—I hope you all know how special you are to me.

My sisters, Cheri Friedman and Candace Weinstein, want to read every paper I write and want to do every puzzle I create. Candace lives in California but is in constant communication and always sends me articles and promotional ideas. Cheri lives nearby and diligently tries to bring socialization and exercise into my life. "Balance!" she proclaims and whisks me off for a fast walk. Cheri would do anything for me. Although she runs a successful interior design business, she pilots my programs and accompanies me when I need help at a seminar. Most important, Cheri, her sons Brian and Bradley, and their lovely wives, Julie and Jolie, always know how to make me laugh! My brother Mark Weinstein phones constantly to keep track of my personal and professional experiences. He is always anxious to give legal advice. My sisters and brother are not only my best friends but also a constant source of inspiration and encouragement for my work.

My nieces and nephews participated in my after-school classes. Initially, the decision to participate was made by their parents. But when they elected to return to see me as adults before graduate school, it was a vote of confidence that has allowed me to share a very special relationship with each and every one of them. Thank you Brian and Bradley Friedman, Jonathan and Jeffrey Finger, and Jennifer and Tiffany Finger.

My mother-in-law, Ida Markus, at 89, participated in my study on "Brain Plasticity in the Aging Brain." She was a wonderful subject and has always encouraged my pursuit.

Heartfelt gratitude to Bruce Wexler, who while working on another book with Jean Iversen, took the opportunity to mention my work and *Retrain Your Business Brain*. I know it took real courage for someone who didn't originally embrace "the dots." The rest is history. And to Jean Iversen, formerly of Dearborn Trade Publishing, what a risk taker you are! I know this opportunity was made possible because of you and Bruce, and I cannot thank you both enough. Jon Malysiak inherited *Retrain Your Business Brain* in January 2003. Not only did he have to quickly integrate into a new work culture, but he was confronted with puzzles to solve, new ideas, and research related to brain agility in an adult population—talk about information overload! Jon attacked the challenge with tremendous energy. He is always in constant communication and works to make my daughter, Lindsey, Pat, and me comfortable with Dearborn's decisions. Jon is a great advisor and a wonderful team member.

Finally, it is to my husband Norman and my four loving children, Rodrick, Lindsey Paige, Brent, and Gavin, that I owe the greatest debt. They have always respected my passion for my work. They are quick to go to the grocery store, prepare meals, drive siblings, answer phones, collate programs, or assist in a class or seminar. They perform these tasks with a smile and with love.

All of my children are born teachers; they have all learned to mediate. I have watched them bring out the best in friends, clients, and each other. Rod teaches me daily about people; he can crystallize their soul and spirit. Everyone is comfortable working with Rod. He has the amazing ability to turn a volatile situation into something manageable. He truly has a gift with people. Brent's passion is in landscape architecture, but he confided that he would always be available to help me. He just loves being involved in growth and change, whether with landscapes or people. Brent's twin brother Gavin I lovingly refer to as the conduit. We jokingly call him the CTO, because he makes everything happen from computer programs to Web site designs. He even accompanied me to the University of

Pennsylvania to help translate mediation to computer-related programming. Gavin works with his heart and soul on every project.

Last, but not least, my favorite (and only) daughter, Lindsey Paige, has been working with me full-time for the past two years. She is constantly telling me that I am not tough enough, and it is often difficult to identify which one of us is the boss. I watch her enhance my systems and "kick up" my entire operation. She has developed a private practice in Chicago and co-presents at corporate seminars. She makes out-of-town meetings truly an adventure, and I feel so lucky that she has joined my practice. She is also the coauthor of this book. My children have all supported and generously given their time and energy to encourage my dream. Could any mother ask for more?

My wonderful husband, Norman, has always unselfishly made all of my dreams come true. He has provided financial and emotional support for all of my graduate and postdoctoral work. Because my office is out of our home, he periodically peers in to witness the progress my students are making. Norman's patients arrive with questions regarding face-lifts and *other* cosmetic procedures, and he somehow ends up discussing my work and sends them to our Web site <www.designsforstrongminds.com>. His intellectual insight and uncompromising standards have made him my harshest critic and most challenging audience. He is responsible for my constant pursuit of excellence. I couldn't ask for a more loving and supportive partner and friend.

How could I neglect to mention Dee Dickinson, New Horizons for Learning <www.newhorizons.org>, who has encouraged me since 1988 to write this book and share my work on enhancing brain agility? Dee has always been a staunch supporter. Though our respective schedules leave little time to keep in touch, on receiving a draft of the book, she immediately went into high gear with ideas for promoting the work and spreading the word.

C O N T E N T S

....

CHAPTER 4

CHAPTER 5

CHAPTER 6

CHAPTER 7

CHAPTER 8

Verbal Mental Agility 145

CHAPTER 9

Connecting the Dots 169

CHAPTER 10

Categories 209

CHAPTER 11

Decoding a System 229

CHAPTER 12

Getting the Results You Want 253

INTRODUCTION

This is not a typical business book. Though its goal is to help you and even your organization gain a competitive edge, it doesn't go about helping you achieve this goal by offering advice about strategic planning, global marketing, or e-commerce. Instead, it provides you with numerous visual puzzles. You may be familiar with this type of puzzle from your school days or various intelligence tests. They ask you to find the next image in a progression of images or to connect the dots or to figure out what's wrong with this picture. At first glance, these puzzles may seem completely irrelevant to the organizational challenges you're facing.

Upon closer inspection, however, you'll discover that the skills required to work effectively on these puzzles are the same ones you need to work effectively. When a critical mass of people in an organization develop the mental agility these puzzles confer, they make the organization more innovative, better at decision making, and significantly more productive. Many books offer compelling strategies to provide change within the organization. This book takes a much different approach—my focus is on you, the individual. Without changing the individuals within the organization, the organization artificially limits its ability to change and grow. In addition, I have designed the book so that you can pass these insights on to others in your organization.

The puzzles in this book have been selected from among the more than 10,000 that I've developed to stimulate and enhance mental agility. The people who have benefited from them include not only corporate employees but entrepreneurs, doctors, lawyers, students, and senior citizens. To help you understand the validity of the theory behind these exercises, I'd like to share how I came upon it and translated the theory into practice.

MY PUZZLE DEVELOPMENT JOURNEY

I began my working life as a teacher. Armed with a B.A. and M.A. from National Louis College of Education, I taught classes in elementary schools, high schools, and colleges. I loved teaching, but I always felt there had to be a more effective way to do it.

As a Ph.D. candidate at Northwestern University, I was searching for a way in which I could help people change, and I found it when I came across an article by Paul Chance in *Psychology Today* about the work of Professor Reuven Feuerstein of the Hadassah-Wizo-Canada Research Institute in Jerusalem.

Dr. Feuerstein's work was a revelation. He designed the Learning Potential Assessment Device (LPAD) to test his theory that people learn most effectively through the intentional and explicit intervention of other people. He called the process "mediation." A mediator facilitates a student's learning by introducing him or her to new ways of perceiving information, determining goals, and distinguishing relevant from irrelevant details. The student learns to think strategically. Professor Feuerstein introduced me to the concept of brain plasticity—the notion that our cognitive abilities are not fixed but can be expanded. Better yet, he had developed a program—Instrumental Enrichment—that was designed to maximize an individual's potential. I went through training to become a certified instructor of Feuerstein's Instrumental Enrichment for children and saw remarkable, positive changes in their performance.

Shortly thereafter, I met Feuerstein and his colleagues and told them about the results I had achieved. I explained to Feuerstein that I envisioned a broader application of his concepts to help a wide range of adults think more effectively. I suggested that they might be particularly applicable to the corporate world. He was intrigued by my ideas, and for the next eight years we collaborated on a number of projects. Feuerstein's success with adolescents whom traditional educators had written off as unteachable greatly influenced my conviction that nothing was unlearnable under the right set of circumstances. When I returned to the United States and began working with children with severe learning disabilities, I discovered that some of their parents had similar, though not as blatant, mental rigidities. The parents had learned to "work around" their limitations but at tremendous physical and emotional costs.

Although I do work with children who have been labeled learning disabled and with individuals who have suffered traumatic brain injuries, most of my work has been devoted to high-functioning adults. Using Feuerstein's Mediated Learning Experience (MLE) as a template, I developed my own intelligence-building puzzles for adults.

I love my job. It allows me to make real changes in people's lives—a change for the better. Since 1981 I've been involved in a process that has the unfortunate sci-fi name of *cognitive restructuring*, I prefer to describe it as unveiling potential and enhancing mental agility.

CONTRARY TO COMMON BELIEF, INTELLIGENCE ISN'T FIXED

Neuroscience and Dr. Marian Diamond, particularly within the last 20 years, have provided substantial evidence for questioning the old fixed intelligence theory. The discoveries that brain cells can and do reproduce and that learning alters brain structure have given us a number of teachable intelligence gurus, including Howard Gardner, Robert Sternberg, Edward DeBono, and David Perkins. I am not going to offer a course in Brain Science 101 here, but you should understand that though our brains are hardwired in certain ways, they are also capable of change. The puzzles I've developed stimulate the brain and open neural pathways: the more pathways we have, the more options we possess to find solutions or pursue opportunities. By exercising different parts of your brain, you can strengthen neural pathways and create new behavioral options.

In other words, you can open your mind as well as the minds of others both literally and figuratively. Using the puzzles in this book, you can strengthen cognitive weaknesses. If you reflect on people in your group, you can probably name each person's flaws. John may overlook important details, whereas Mary fails to grasp the big picture. As a result, they are less effective than they could be. The puzzles will help everyone learn to process information in different ways, enabling them to develop skills in an area that has always been an Achilles' heel.

The theory that intelligence is teachable has its critics. Some eminent psychologists hold the century-old assumption that intelligence is genetically fixed and learning in one context cannot be transferred or applied to another discipline or activity. They have strenuously objected to any attempt at "teaching intelligence." This objection is reinforced by the underlying theory of standardized IQ tests, which suggest that you are what you score, and there's nothing you can do about it. Feuerstein, however, has argued that, at best, IQ tests present a snapshot of what an individual has already accomplished intellectually. What these tests cannot do is predict someone's potential to acquire new learning.

Over the years, I have helped people capitalize on their potential for new learning. The puzzles have enabled thousands of people to strengthen critical thinking skills. I'll share some of their stories with you throughout the book, but for now I ask that you give this theory the benefit of the doubt. By the end of the book, you'll be able to see for yourself how these puzzles have an impact on your own mental agility.

During the past 20 plus years, I've mediated the lessons—presented here as puzzles—to doctors, lawyers, entrepreneurs, corporate clients, and government agencies. Included among my clients are NASA, Los Alamos National Labora-tory, McDonald's Corp., Ameritech, Quaker Oats, Coopers & Lybrand (PwC), Opus Corp., the University of Chicago Hospitals, and the U.S. federal judiciary system circuit court.

My work has taught me that however intelligent people may be, however accomplished, however competent, they are probably missing something. In many cases intelligence, accomplishments, and competencies are the reasons they miss opportunities, fail to appreciate a problem, or just can't understand _____ (fill in the blank: quantum theory, economics, automobile mechanics, how to program a VCR, etc.).

Most people have a sense of what they're good at and where they're likely to fail. Consequently, they put a great deal of effort into avoiding failure by neglect-ing those things that make them feel uncomfortable. They set limits on themselves and on the results they expect to achieve.

To a large extent, the fear of failure comes from an educational system that emphasized efficiency over effectiveness. We were taught that getting the right answer was far more important than knowing *why* it was right. If we don't know why an answer is right, we cannot use the knowledge effectively. We cannot use it to get the results we want.

Many smart people can operate at such a high level of efficiency that they sometimes lose track of what they really want to accomplish. They don't get the results they want because they don't know how to be effective.

In a complex world, whether an answer is right or wrong is frequently a mat-ter of perspective. I use the word *perspective* to mean the intuitive way someone organizes information. People with different perspectives have difficulty com-municating with each other, even when they speak the same language and belong to the same culture. They just don't see "eye-to-eye."

Understanding how you personally perceive things is the first step in learn-ing how to function effectively in a multinational, multicultural, multidisciplinary ever-changing world. I designed the puzzles in this book to give you the oppor-tunity to watch yourself organize information, make decisions, and deal with ambiguities.

People in organizations need this book, especially successful people, because it will help keep their edge, reawaken their enthusiasm, and restore their hunger for risk and challenge. To do this, we need to first shake up things. As people become better at what they do, the process becomes increasingly automatic. They like the feeling of efficiency. Their decisions come rapidly. Their choices seem obvious. Their rationale is self-evident. But as good as this comfort zone feels, it may hold you back from your real potential.

This book is going to challenge your comfort zones. As the reader, you're the guinea pig in this experiment. To help your organization change, you need to experience the puzzles and see the process in action. It'll make you doubt your own judgment. It'll frustrate and confuse you. It'll bring you back, as is said in Zen, to the "beginner's mind"—where nothing is certain and no conviction is sacred. It will accomplish this with an ancient method: the puzzle.

My puzzles provide two crucial elements for improving mental agility: novelty and rehearsal. They require you to describe the steps that lead to a solution and identify various perspectives. Incrementally, they become more challenging. This method controls the amount of confusion that is necessary to elicit change and the degree of frustration that new challenges sometimes generate.

The puzzles will retrain your brain to be more effective by derailing it from the fast track of efficiency. My puzzles won't just make you stop and think. They'll make you think about how you ordinarily think. They'll also teach you new ways of thinking.

I've arranged the chapters in the same order I train corporate clients. You may be tempted to skip some chapters because the puzzles look too hard or too easy. PLEASE, DO NOT GIVE IN TO THIS TEMPTATION!

I designed the puzzles to give you a peek into how you think through different kinds of problems. Even if you know how to solve a puzzle, seeing what's going on inside your head is worth the visit. Many of my clients find the easy puzzles the most fascinating.

More important, the puzzles are made to exercise your mental muscles. They cross-train your brain. Just as with physical exercise, if you neglect some of the puzzles, your mental agility will pay for it in the end.

The book will start out with Peter Drucker's distinction between efficiency and effectiveness and explain how the puzzles facilitate the latter. It will also allow you to get your feet wet with some relatively easy puzzles as well as identify your specific thinking type. Before getting to the meat of the book, you'll also have the chance to practice your self-mediation skills—tools and techniques that help you when you become stuck or frustrated—that you can use with others.

The core of the book involves chapters that revolve around the following types of puzzles:

- Analogies
- Progressions
- Part-whole relationships
- Mistakes
- Verbal
- Connecting the dots
- Categories
- Decoding a system

As you'll discover, each type of puzzle is different, yet the process I'll help you master to work on them is remarkably similar.

HOW ALL THIS WILL HELP YOU AND YOUR ORGANIZATION

People who work with me know how much I enjoy doing what I do. I trust that my enthusiasm for these visual puzzles will come through in these pages. This enthusiasm is important when I work with clients, because it helps communicate my commitment to this process and my fervent belief that it will transform their work life. I am a bit of an evangelist for these puzzles, in part because some people are skeptical of the puzzles' ability to "change minds" when they first encounter them. Understandably, it's sometimes difficult to make the connection between visual puzzles and organizational skills. For this reason, let me give you an enthusiastic summary of why all of this will work for your company.

As I noted earlier, the puzzles give people the chance to think about how they think. To do the puzzles effectively, you have to slow down before you speed up. This slowing-down process provides people an opportunity to watch themselves organize information, make decisions, and deal with ambiguities. It also makes high-functioning, highly educated individuals aware of their "learning disabilities" and how these disabilities impact them and their organizations. These disabilities manifest themselves in inflexibility, the need to always be right, the use of a limited set of options, an aversion to risk taking, and a limited ability to communicate outside a specific domain. If this describes people you know and work with, join the club.

The exercises are meant to be fun. Play affords unlimited possibilities for trying new ideas and for elaborating and reworking old ones. THIS IS NOT A MENSA TEST! I hope that you and all the people with whom you share these exercises respond to them as my clients do. They become so wrapped up in the quest for solutions that they lose track of time. They become enmeshed in the process of comparing and contrasting geometric shapes and searching for visual clues that lead to answers. As they become comfortable with the "language" of visual puzzles, they start treating them like a challenging intellectual game rather than a formidable task.

Let your own reactions guide you. You can anticipate how others will react to these exercises by seeing how you react to them. If you're like most people, you'll be excited to discover how you habitually organize information. You'll find it fascinating to discover how other people do the puzzles and what that says about their ways of organizing information. You'll also enjoy the control these puzzles give you. When you're aware of how you think, you can respond thoughtfully to situations rather than react reflexively to them. When you develop different cognitive strengths, you give yourself options for responding—you're not limited to your traditional reaction.

If you want to make a real difference in your performance, your team's effectiveness, and your organization's success, this book provides the tools and techniques to achieve these goals. So get ready to get smarter! Get ready to retrain your brain!

● ● ●

When you see these three dots, stop reading and begin working on the puzzle that follows. Once you have completed the puzzle, continue reading—there is more ahead.

WORKING SMARTER, NOT HARDER

**"They always say time changes
things, but you actually have
to change them yourself."**

—*Andy Warhol*

Time is the only limit that all of us share. Some people have greater intelligence, some less. Some have more money, connections, energy, opportunities, and willpower. However, nobody has more time. In a 24-hour day, we all have 24 hours.

How we use those hours, and the minutes that make them up, can be measured in terms of efficiency and effectiveness. If we're running around like crazy getting a lot done, we may be very efficient but not particularly effective. In *The Effective Executive*, Peter Drucker defined *efficiency* as "getting things done right" and *effectiveness* as "getting the right things done." Because time is limited, it makes more sense to do the "right things" than to simply do "things right."

Effectiveness requires the mental agility to:

- Assess the present situation in terms of a defined goal.
- Acquire the resources needed to achieve that goal.
- Shift gears or even change course when setbacks occur.
- Redefine the goal if the initial one proves unattainable.

Many of us lose the ability to be effective as we become educated. Most of our education trains us to be efficient. This is not without reason. In order to read, write, and do arithmetic, we have to learn routines. Standardized spelling makes for more efficient communication. In fact, without standardized spelling, computer technology would be impossible. Similarly, learning the rules of grammar and math enable people of diverse cultures to interact more efficiently. One measure of a person's intelligence is how well she can apply standardized rules.

> **"Creative minds have always been known to survive any kind of bad training."**
> —Anna Freud

The purpose of this book is to help you and other key people in your organization make more effective use of the limited time you have. Research has shown that experts ration their time differently than do novices or even experienced nonexperts. Experts get the results they want because they know how to make better use of their time. They intuitively know how to:

- Identify problems.
- Prioritize efforts.
- Communicate goals.
- Handle setbacks.
- Adapt to changing conditions.
- Think on the fly.

To acquire this collective intuitive expertise, you'll have to retrain your brain and even the brains of other people in your organization. As daunting as that task may sound, it's a realistic goal with this book's assistance. You'll find that it will help you regain the mental agility you possessed before you were educated to be efficient and that you can pass this agility on to others. Paradoxically, in addition to making you more effective, retraining your brain is also likely to make you even more efficient in your daily routines. In short, it will help you work smarter, not harder.

> **"The brain is a monstrous, beautiful mess."**
> —William F. Allman

USING PUZZLES TO INCREASE MENTAL AGILITY

Brain-building exercises aren't new. You've probably encountered various forms of them in IQ tests or in high school math classes. However, there is a significant difference between those puzzles and the ones you'll find here. One of the most obvious differences is that this book is comprised almost entirely of visual or graphic puzzles. Another difference is that instead of a wide variety, many of the puzzles look similar. Be assured there are significant (though sometimes subtle) differences between them related to the differences between analogies, categories, and our other cognitive groups.

Why the lowly puzzle if one wants to improve mental agility? Precisely because it is innocuous. Puzzles give pleasure in much the same way that jokes do. They create suspense and a mild anxiety, and surprise us with counterintuitive answers. In effect, they prepare us for the somewhat odious, though important, task of questioning our own assumptions.

Puzzles can also produce scientific and mathematical breakthroughs. In *The Puzzle Instinct: The Meaning of Puzzles in Human Life* (Indiana University Press, 2002), Marcel Danesi relates that "Zeno's paradoxes led to the invention of calculus; Alcuin's River-Crossing Puzzle prefigured modern-day critical path theory; Euler's Königsberg's Bridges Puzzle led to the development of network theory and topology." Many initial discoveries are made "accidentally" by a prepared mind. Puzzles stimulate the imagination in ways that logical reasoning cannot.

Which is not to say that logic plays no role in puzzle solving. But to get started on the right road to the solution, you need insight. Insight is a mental projection composed of the observation of recurring patterns and the reordering of elements within those patterns. In his book *A Sense of the Future: Essays in Natural Philosophy* (MIT Press, 1977), science historian Jacob Bronowski said that reasoning requires the ability "to make images and to move them about inside one's head in new arrangements [because] unless connections between things are seen in the mind, there is nothing to reason about." As you'll discover, this ability to move images around in your head is what will help you and your organization outthink the competition.

> **"The important thing is not to stop questioning."**
>
> —Albert Einstein

IT'S NOT AS PUZZLING AS YOU THINK

All aspects of business have one essential element in common—they are all based on building relationships. As the puzzles demonstrate, not all relationships are the same. Someone who has excellent rapport with customers may not be a good team player. Many entrepreneurs lose fortunes time and again because they lack, and don't appreciate, managerial skills. Employee-management stress is due largely to conflicts involving short-term goals.

"People tend to think collaboration is about people working together. They are mistaken. The issue is not just collaboration in creative individuals, but creative relationships."

—Michael Schrage

Most people have a sense of what they're good at and where they're likely to fail. Consequently, they put a great deal of effort into avoiding failure by neglecting those things that make them feel uncomfortable. Initially, my puzzles help people give a name to the things they do well: "I'm good at making comparisons"; "I can see how the parts contribute to the whole"; "I'm good at planning sequences." Aptitude tests can tell us the same thing. My puzzles go beyond this by giving you the opportunity to experience and practice other ways of organizing information and creating relationships.

Solve any or all of these puzzles. Then in the space that follows, write a descriptive word that captures what's going on in your mind as you work on them.

Rather than merely listing the answers, allow me to mediate so that you can learn how to reorganize information to generate rules that can be applied to solve problems. Play the game. You will derive greater benefits if you don't cheat. Try to revisit the problem after each clue and see if you can solve the problem before the answer is revealed. I encourage you to document your work. Making notations can help you organize information, keep track of many details, and recognize patterns. Please note that there are numerous ways to solve each problem. The mediation is intended to guide you through the process of asking questions regarding the relationships between the images to find your answer. You may find other ways to tackle these problems. Remember: The purpose of these exercises is to rehearse identifying interrelationships and thinking in new ways. Finding the correct answer is secondary. Try working the following puzzle.

● ● ●

Hint 1. At first glance, the problem seems uncomfortable because of the variation in size and shape of the black and white patterns. It seems difficult to discern when you search for a pattern; you will notice that the image in the upper left corner is repeated in the upper right corner and lower middle row with different patterns of black and white. What else do you see? Notice that the middle image in the top row is repeated twice in the second row. Again, the black and white patterns are different. Last, the image in the lower row.

A
B
C
D
E

left is repeated in the center with the same pattern. In sum, two images are presented three times and one image is presented only twice.

So we now know that we will be looking for the circular-like image. Therefore, we can eliminate choices B and D. We are left with choices A, C, and E.

Hint II. We recognize that we are trying to identify a rule that creates a set of three different shapes. We have to find the relationship between the three images. We ask ourselves, How were the shapes created? Let's first look at frames 1 and 2 in the top row. The second frame appears to duplicate the image in frame 1, except the size changes and one image becomes a mirror image. Hmmm.

Try to identify the relationship between these two images and the circular-like image. If you look closely, you will notice that the oval-shaped petals that form a flower-like design represent negative (or empty) space. If those petals are empty space, they will always be white. Therefore, answer E can be eliminated. We are left with choices A and C.

Hint III. What is the difference between answers A and C? Identify the pattern of black and white in each frame. For example, in the top row, frame 1 is black-white-black-white. Frame 2 is black-white-black-white. Frame 3 is white-black-white-black. Once you find the pattern for each frame, you will notice that each family of patterns has one image of each shape. Do you understand why the correct answer is A?

Someone else may come to the same answer in a totally different way. He may read the top row across and recognize a repeat of two outside patterns and apply that rule to the row as a check. It works, so he looks for a circular design that is different from the first drawing in the bottom row. The same external image with a shift in the internal color (black or white in this case)—the answer is A.

Remember there are many different ways to solve this problem. The following puzzle is only one suggestion.

● ● ●

Hint I. Divide the matrix into three vertical columns.

Hint II. Look at the three vertical frames on the left. Let's look at the gray areas. We notice that the gray shapes appear in the same place in the top and middle images but not in the bottom image.

Objective: Select the answer that best completes the matrix.

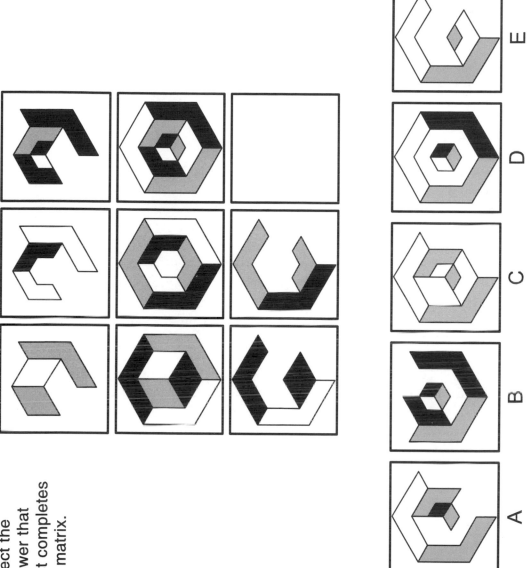

Hint III. Now let's look at the black areas in the same column. Black appears only in the middle and bottom squares. We can hypothesize that a shape can only have the same color two times. Let's test our theory.

Hint IV. Now let's look at the black shading in the three frames in the middle column. Black appears in each image. However, look closely at the specific sections. The black shading appears only in the same section two times throughout the series in the middle column. Our theory that a shape can appear only twice with the same color is correct so far.

Hint V. Let's test our theory developed in Hint IV. Look at the gray area in the middle column or the white sections. Does our theory hold true?

Hint VI. Based on what we've learned, it seems that the same color can appear in the same position only twice in each column. Let's apply this to the column at the right. If we look at the lower right portion of the image, we see that it is black in the first and second frame. Because each color can appear in the same position only twice, we know that black cannot be in the lower right portion of the image for frame 3. This helps us to eliminate choices B and D as answers. We are now left with choices A, C, and E.

Hint VII. Let's continue to look at the black pieces of the image for clues. Focus on the small black diamond in the center of the image. Again, this color is repeated in frames 1 and 2 and must therefore be a different color in frame 3. From this, we can eliminate choice A and are left with answers C and E.

What is the primary difference between answers C and E?

Hint VIII. The primary difference is that C has a gray shape in the central right corner of the image and E does not. Let's look again at the problem, and we notice that the same gray shape appears in the same spot in frames 1 and 2. The rule dictates that the same color can appear in the same position only twice in each column. Therefore, C must be eliminated. E is our answer.

And some people may simply look at the external shape of the horizontal figures and determine that E is the only option.

What word captured your thoughts as you worked on these exercises?

Perhaps your descriptive words include *frustrating, difficult,* or other more colorful expressions. Some people have said that these puzzles make their minds ache. Exactly! They are designed to exercise weak or little-used areas of your mind. Just as with physical exercise involving neglected muscles, a certain amount of discomfort and unease is to be expected. Your discomfort shows that this is an area where you're not as flexible or agile as you can be with the proper training.

Not all people will react the same way to each puzzle. The marketing executive has mental strengths different from those of the engineering manager. You may find some puzzles are more difficult for you than others because of your education and life experiences. I selected the puzzles in this book to give every reader's mind a full workout, regardless of what his or her present strengths or weaknesses might be.

My puzzles enhance mental agility and develop new insights because they facilitate "moving things about in your head." They allow you to view a familiar problem in a fresh way and to use unfamiliar approaches when solving them. Without these puzzles, people tend to automatically lapse into the approach that they know best, even if it doesn't get them the results that they want. This is because in school they were encouraged to avoid their weaknesses, specialize in their strengths, and organize their thought processes around those strengths.

Puzzles can help us see things differently. As you may well know, many people view things from relatively narrow perspectives. You can almost predict how Mary in Human Resources will respond to a problem or how John in Sales will pursue an opportunity. Each has a definite modus operandi, a set way of doing things, because each views the world in a particular, somewhat stagnant, way. For instance, Larry is a salesman highly skilled in interpersonal communications. He's good at small talk, can feel the pulse of a room, and knows when to close a sale. However, he frequently neglects to fill out order forms. He's poor with details and may forget specific follow-up requests or delivery information as he quickly moves on to the next customer. As terrific as Larry is verbally and at thinking on his feet, he's practically hopeless when it comes to putting things in writing or following through on complex tasks. Consequently, he may be losing more customers than he gains. But nobody keeps track of the losses, so Larry is promoted to management.

When superstar salespeople reach the managerial level, they often fail despite their people skills, because they haven't been trained to think in terms of cause and effect, progressions, priorities, and part-whole relationships. They lack the mental agility to deal effectively with conflicts between direct reports or to map out a workable strategy for their team. It's not a question of intelligence. It's just that sales skills are very different from managerial skills.

REGAINING MENTAL AGILITY

Take five minutes to complete the puzzle on page 11. When the time has elapsed, reflect on what the experience was like.

● ● ●

Please remember this is only one solution to this problem.

Hint I. Row 1 shows the same image from different perspectives. The image repeated in each frame is made up of nine rectangular blocks.

Hint II. Similar to Row 1, Row 2 illustrates different perspectives of an image composed of nine pieces. At first you might not see the correlation between Rows 1 and 2. With a closer look, however, notice that Row 2 also comprises the same image viewed from different perspectives.

Hint III. Let's start with Row 1. Look at each frame separately and divide the shape in each frame into three sections (3 bars at the top, 3 bars at the left, 3 bars at the right). Next, look at Row 2. Look at each frame separately and divide the bottom graphic into three sections vertically (3 left, 3 middle, 3 right).

Hint IV. Our goal is to identify which images best complete the progressions in Rows 1 and 2. To do this we should compare the relationship between the first and second images in Row 1 and apply the rules that govern that relationship to the first and second images in Row 2. Try this now. In Row 1, notice that the pieces of the image on the left and right do not change; only the central image changes. From this information, we assume that the same thing will happen in Row 2, frame 2—the images on the left and right will stay the same and only the central images will change. This helps us to eliminate choices D and E. Therefore, the best options are now A, B, or C because the left and right columns did not change.

Hint V. The solution to this problem is based on two separate issues, so we must consider another problem. To complete the fourth frame in Row 1, we look to Row 2 for guidance. In Row 2, we compare frame 4 to frame 5. What happened? Again, we must decide the rules that govern the relationship between frames 4 and 5 in Row 2 and apply these rules to Row 1. Try this.

Row 1

  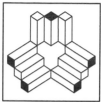 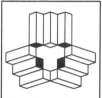

Row 2

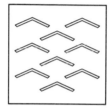   

Objective: Select the answer that best completes the progressions in Rows 1 and 2.

A

B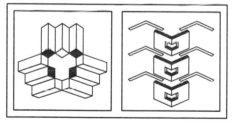

C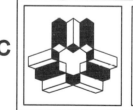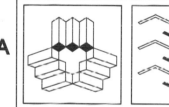

D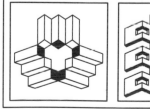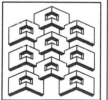

E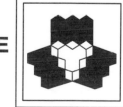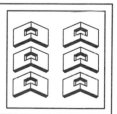

Here, the exterior portions of the image remain the same and only the middle portion of the image has changed. At first it appears that we have a choice of A or B. We cannot consider D because it won't satisfy Row 2 (and if we look carefully, there is a color change in the outside rectangles). There is a subtle color change in A as well. Based on this information, the only suitable answer is B. As we saw in Hint IV, B also helps to complete the progression for Row 2. B is our final answer. It's time to try another puzzle.

● ● ●

Remember this represents one approach to solving the problem.

Hint I. When you first look at the images in Row 1, it is difficult to figure out what is happening. Note the little hats. Is there any relationship between the number of hats in Row 1? 4 hats, 1 hat, 3 hats, 2 hats, __.

Hint II. What is the relationship between the images in Row 2? __, 4 cones, 5 cones, 1 cone, 6 cones.

Hint III. 4 hats – 1 hat = 3 hats; 3 hats + 2 hats = ___ hats
Let's apply the same symbols to the cones in Row 2.
___ cones – 4 cones = 5 cones; 5 cones + 1 cone = 6 cones
From this information, we mathematically identified that the final frame in Row 1 must have 5 hats and the first frame in Row 2 must have 9 cones.

Hint IV. Look for 5 hats or 9 cones. We find 5 hats in answers A (the black hats in the center) and D (the stretched hats in a circular formation). In addition, we find 9 cones (or circles) in answers A and C.

Hint V. A is the only answer that satisfies both progressions.
Other than mirroring the relationship from one progression to the other, can you find a rule that clearly dictates when to add and when to subtract? Hint—look at the shaded areas.
Make a check mark in the box next to the comments that capture what went on in your mind.

☐ It was pretty easy. I got the hang of it right away.

Row 1

Row 2

 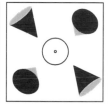 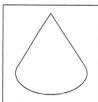  

Objective: Select the answer that best completes the progressions in Rows 1 and 2.

A

B

C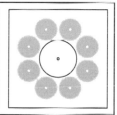

D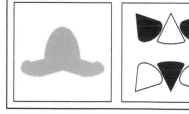

E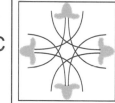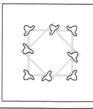

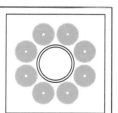 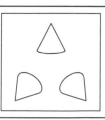

☐ The puzzle was challenging. It took a while but I applied myself. I think I got it right.

☐ It was frustrating. I felt the way I used to when I was in school and had to take a test on a subject that was difficult for me when I was not prepared. I'm not sure how well I did.

☐ This puzzle is impossible. No one could do it, except maybe a rocket scientist. I gave it my best shot, but I decided I didn't need to solve the stupid thing.

Most people think this is a very difficult puzzle. They usually check the last two observations rather than the first two. As you put pencil to paper and experimented with solutions, you may have felt frustrated, anxious, or a little upset. You might have experienced a physical reaction, such as the beginnings of a headache or "butterflies" in your stomach. If so, the puzzle "threw you." It made you feel off balance. Many people feel similarly off balance when they're given work assignments that force them out of their comfort zone. For example, the salesperson promoted to manager or the accountant invited to a brainstorming session may experience what cognitive scientists, who study mind-body interactions, term *disequilibrium.* It means we feel lost or find it difficult to think clearly. We may even feel a sense of panic because we can't unravel the problem in a calm, analytical manner. It's like beating our heads against the wall to secure a change. Nothing in our experience seems to work. The old tried-and-true approach we've always relied on isn't working. We don't know what else to do because our brains are wired to efficiently follow routines.

> **"Many of life's failures are people who did not realize how close they were to success when they gave up."**
>
> —*Thomas A. Edison*

In this case we lack the mental agility we need to regain our equilibrium, reorganize the information, and see the problem from a new perspective. If we had it, we could calm down and analyze the problem with a clear head. With mental agility we realize we don't have to latch on to the first idea that comes along or lapse into a familiar mode of problem solving. Instead, we can leave ourselves open to new ideas and to exploring different options.

After working through the gamut of puzzles, you may be surprised by the greater amount of external stress and disequilibrium you can tolerate. You'll observe the same reaction in people throughout your organization with whom you share these mental agility exercises. At a neural level, these puzzles simulate the difficulty and pressures that exist in a typical work environment. If you can learn to keep your cool during crunch times rather than give way to panic and simplistic thinking, you'll greatly increase your chance of effectively solving the problem.

"Success is the ability to go from one failure to another with no loss of enthusiasm."

—Winston Churchill

My puzzles serve as rehearsals. They give you the opportunity to struggle, and perhaps fail, without personal risk. With adequate rehearsal, you'll begin to feel more comfortable with your initial disequilibrium and find yourself solving even the more difficult problems. Imagine yourself in the business world armed with the ability to face uncertainty because of your increased mental agility. Or better yet, imagine how your stressed-out, overworked team or staff might perform if they didn't panic at difficult assignments or lapse into standard operating procedure when innovation is required.

The scientific "why" behind this is still open to debate. One theory is that doing puzzles strengthens neuropathways, thereby connecting more areas of our brain and consequently increasing behavioral options. Over the last 30 years, neural scientists have discovered that our brains are far more adaptable (they use the term *plastic*) than behaviorists imagined when they formulated their theories on intelligence almost 100 years ago.

Education, particularly higher education, greatly influences the way our brains are structured to think. Physicists and lawyers are trained to think in terms of cause and effect and progressive sequences. Engineers and economists look for part-whole relationships. Biologists and psychologists start problem solving by establishing categories. You'll find my puzzles require all of these different ways of organizing information and give explicit instruction and rehearsal for habituating to new patterns of thought.

"Change has a considerable psychological impact on the human mind. To the fearful it is threatening because it means that things may get worse. To the hopeful it is encouraging because things may get better. To the confident it is inspiring because the challenge exists to make things better."

—King Whitney, Jr.

Whatever your preferred method, with practice you can learn how to reorganize information, see different possibilities, and come up with solutions to problems that had previously baffled you. To put it another way, my puzzles will jar you out of your usual routines and give you additional options for effectively solving a wider range of problems.

You're probably ready to see some evidence of how my puzzles help people in work situations. Let's look at three examples.

PUTTING THEIR MINDS TO WORK:
How Some Individuals Increased Their Mental Agility for Fun and Profit

Having the flexibility to try another approach, to think "outside the box," to rebound from failure, and to stretch your mind to see what was hidden are all by-products of mental agility. The following examples will give you a sense of how my puzzles work for people in three different professions: law, aviation, and accounting. As you'll see, all the people involved had distinct mental strengths and weaknesses.

Tom is a brilliant lawyer. He analyzes legal problems with speed and insight, an attribute that helped him become a partner in a large legal firm. Over time, though, he found he was growing tired of his firm's politics and bureaucracy, so he decided to strike out on his own. Tom counted on his reputation as a great real estate attorney to help him build a strong group of clients quickly. At first, he was right; then he started losing clients almost as quickly. In the big law firm, he was often insulated from direct client contact. The firm's managing partners realized that Tom could be prickly, impatient, and even arrogant, sometimes rubbing people the wrong way. They usually teamed him with someone who was a better "communicator." When he struck out on his own, Tom lost that buffer.

An important side note: Tom was pretty "hopeless" when it came to fixing things around the house or doing any kind of hands-on work. If something broke, it stayed broken until he hired someone to repair it, or he replaced it with a new one. He couldn't program his VCR or even set the clock. In a rental car he could waste 10 or 15 minutes just trying to turn on the headlights.

When I began working with Tom, he was angry about how much business he was losing. Despite his intelligence, he couldn't figure out how things could go so wrong so quickly. At first, Tom dutifully did the puzzles, but nothing seemed to change. I gave him my high-level deductive reasoning puzzles. He'd solve them perfectly. Spatial puzzles, however, totally stumped him. Tom's excellent legal training was evident in his efficient use of deductive reasoning. When it came to spatial relationships, though, he thought like a little kid. In *The Unschooled Mind: How Children Think and How Schools Should Teach* (Basic Books, 1993), Howard Gardner referred to this condition as the "five-year-old" in all of us—the part of our mind that our education hasn't reached. So I took it slow. I led Tom step-by-step through the whole process of spatial reasoning from the beginning to the end.

After four months, Tom came to our appointment and announced that he had put a fan together. It was a simple home fan, but he was enormously excited about his accomplishment. The next week he came in and told me that he had put a bookshelf together. The real payoff came a few weeks later when he described a conversation he had had with a developer. The developer told Tom why he was hiring him: "You're not like other lawyers who just tell their clients what to do. You seem to hear what I'm telling you about our business goals."

This was the first time anyone had told Tom he was a good listener. In the past, clients thought Tom was simply arrogant and stubborn, although he wasn't aware of their perceptions. His inability to communicate effectively was directly related to his poor spatial reasoning. Tom had lacked the ability to intentionally make images move about inside his head. Consequently, he didn't understand how he thought about relationships. That's why he had difficulty solving spatial puzzles, completing do-it-yourself projects, and communicating with others.

To put a fan or a bookshelf together, Tom needed to look at a diagram and see the drawings as three-dimensional. He had to rotate the parts in his mind. Similarly, to have a good working relationship with a client, he needed to "rotate" his point of view so that he could see the problem from the client's perspective. Through my puzzles, Tom learned how to maintain his professional perspective and integrate it with the developer's point of view.

Unlike Tom, who had problems communicating, Dennis communicated well and could establish good working relationships. As a top pilot for a major airline, he was the likely choice to fly the new type of plane the company wanted to add to its fleet. But he first had to pass a paper-and-pencil test about the plane. Surprisingly, he failed. He was not accustomed to failure, nor was he about to let anyone else fly the new plane first, so he sought help from a neuropsychologist. Her evaluation indicated he possessed an exceptionally good visual memory and a high IQ but provided no explanation as to why he had failed the test.

The neuropsychologist referred Dennis to me. As I worked with him, his inability to "see the big picture" emerged. In particular, he had difficulty with the part-whole puzzles that required him to construct a larger picture from different geometric shapes. With his efficient near photographic memory, he could take in and hold innumerable details. What he couldn't do was reverse the process and work backward from the whole picture to the smaller parts, which indicated to me that he had a problem establishing priorities.

Dennis had an efficient way of learning. He could read and easily memorize any passage. The new plane test required him to read, question, and analyze; to pass the test, he needed a more effective way of learning. He had to prioritize new information. To solve the part-whole puzzles, he would have to develop the mental agility to hold an image of the big picture in his mind and shuffle around the smaller pieces until they fit together in a specific pattern. He also had to practice asking himself questions about how each piece related to the whole. Armed with this new mental agility, he passed the new plane test.

In addition to private clients like Tom and Dennis, I also work with groups. In one training program I worked with many talented but underperforming actuaries from a midsized accounting firm. As might be expected, each member of the group demonstrated different levels of cognitive strengths and weaknesses. However, most of them were highly gifted in mathematics and had found college and graduate classes relatively easy. They were successful and had their own way of doing things. They had no patience for the creative process and would quickly interrupt people who expressed opinions they didn't agree with. Their managing partner warned me that actuaries could easily get wrapped up in long-winded, esoteric explanations about numbers. Their clients frequently left meetings with glassy eyes and a dazed look on their faces. Not particularly good for business.

After a number of weeks, I noticed a significant and welcomed change. At our first meeting, the actuaries had greeted me with vocal skepticism or stony silence. By our last meeting, they were talkative and enthusiastic. Much to my relief, my puzzles had managed to make them more open-minded about entertaining new ideas. They had encountered new ways of presenting and processing information, which encouraged them to risk sharing their thoughts and expressing their expectations.

A bit later, this accounting firm held an international conference to which many actuaries from all of the national and international offices were invited to attend. When my group returned from the conference, I was informed that each member had been chosen as a leader when the managers split up the attendees into teams.

> "Aim for success, not perfection. Never give up your right to be wrong, because then you will lose the ability to learn new things and move forward with your life."
>
> —David M. Burns

Though I was pleased by this news, I wasn't surprised. My actuaries were among the few who deviated from the traditional, mind-numbing actuarial mode. The puzzles had made them mentally agile and more adaptable. When I was working with them, they were delighted to discover that my puzzles could be solved in more than one way. If at first they didn't succeed, or even if they did, they had the option of trying another approach to solve the same problem. They learned to take risks, to dare to fail, and to pick themselves up and try again. This kind of daring and mental agility set them apart as natural leaders. Even the more traditional actuaries could appreciate my group's willingness to listen to differing opinions and to present well-reasoned, open-ended ideas.

SPECIFIC WORK SKILLS VERSUS GENERAL THINKING SKILLS

A lot has been said and written about the new economy in the 21st century. You'll find dozens of books offering advice on how to prepare for the brave new world that is already upon us. Among the favorite topics are:

- Creativity
- Decision making
- Team building
- Strategic planning
- Conflict management
- Global management
- Business communication

> **"The significant problems we face cannot be solved at the same level of thinking we were at when we created them."**
>
> —*Albert Einstein*

Most of the books offer theory. Some give practical advice along with check lists to make sure you're doing things right. But how do you know if you're doing the right thing? I can't tell you either. What is right for one person isn't necessarily right for another. What is right under certain conditions can turn tragically wrong when those conditions change. This is one reason why people need mental agility. Another reason is that many highly talented people fail to achieve the kind of satisfaction they desire from their work because of mental rigidity. Mental rigidity can appear in many different forms, including these:

- Avoiding risks
- Taking foolish risks
- Alienating other people
- Refusing to work within established processes or systems
- Inability to manage a diverse team or function effectively within one

- Inability to think outside the box
- Poor adaptability to change
- Inability to prioritize time and/or resources

My puzzles were designed to retrain your brain in ways that traditional training programs and coaching cannot. They are intended to make you and the people in your organization more effective in a complex world, not merely more efficient. They do this in the following ways.

Providing the opportunity for failure. Of course, nobody likes to fail, but learning how to rebound from failure can foster creativity. Success can breed rigidity. We come to expect it and to fear it. Before you went to school, you didn't know what it meant to fail. You were more daring, more willing to take risks because you learned naturally through play. You can't fail at play.

Individuals who come up with great new ideas have learned to think of failure as an opportunity to try something different. My puzzles help you recognize that failure is an important part of the learning process. It is where learning actually begins to develop.

Creating disequilibrium. You may be an excellent communicator or superb decision maker when time is on your side. Are you as good under pressure or when a deadline is looming? It's easy to succumb to routines even when we know they're inadequate, when we feel we're running out of time. With hindsight, we find ourselves second-guessing what we should have done, could have done, might have done, if only . . .

My puzzles simulate that same kind of pressurized, confusing environment without the personal risk. They prepare you mentally and emotionally to deal with the stress and chaos that have become an ubiquitous part of every work environment.

Offering alternatives. Sometimes we just don't know that there are other ways of doing something until somebody comes along and shows us. When you learn the alternative ways of organizing information, you'll begin to see possibilities springing up everywhere.

My puzzles give you the mental agility to generate alternative actions, think in shades of gray, and dare to set precedents.

Strengthening cognitive weaknesses. Let's face it, nobody's perfect. If we were honest with ourselves, we'd have to admit there are things we'd like to be able to do better. A lot of people take self-help courses and buy self-help books and tapes looking for that magic bullet. I've looked too. I can tell you from experience that it doesn't exist.

What does work is practice—and lots of it. That's why you'll find a lot of puzzles in this book. They're designed to retrain your brain on a neural level, to establish new neuroconnections so that thinking effectively becomes second nature to you.

Diagnosing Thinking Types

To work smarter, we need to understand *how we think*. Most people, however, are unaware of how they organize or take in new information. Although we may have a vague idea about our thinking processes, we usually are unaware of our cognitive styles. Of course, most of us know what we're "smart at" and "dumb at." School may have taught us that we're good at math and bad at writing essays, for instance. Work may have taught us that we're skilled at giving presentations but have trouble meeting deadlines.

This awareness, though, doesn't really get at how we think. If we want to use our minds more effectively in work situations, we need to be aware of the way we take in information. Some people look at details and never see the big picture, whereas others look at the big picture and miss all of the details. When we know the specific way we take in information, then we recognize our cognitive style; more significant, we also recognize our cognitive weaknesses. Recognizing our cognitive style allows us to choose tasks and projects that capitalize on our natural way of thinking, whereas recognizing our cognitive weaknesses enables us to strengthen all areas of the mind so we have more options available to solve problems, capitalize on opportunities, and prevent errors.

In addition, when we're familiar with the various thinking modes, we can work more effectively with others. Managers, for instance, can communicate better with their direct reports. When they know how people take in information, they can use that knowledge to get their points across faster and more clearly. If John is a linear thinker, then his manager can present points to him using logic and detail. If Mary has a more creative way for dealing with information, her manager might tell a story that gets the point across with greater impact.

> **"The great leaders are like the best conductors—they reach beyond the notes to reach the magic in the players."**
>
> —*Blaine Lee*

In short, knowing how we think is like gaining an incredibly valuable piece of information about ourselves. It's analogous to a coach spotting a hitch in a baseball player's swing. When that player becomes conscious of the hitch and works to correct it, he becomes a much better hitter. Self-knowledge gives us the awareness we need to act in a highly conscious manner. When we know how we think, we can be aware of our intellectual strengths and weaknesses and act accordingly.

The diagnostic tool in this chapter gives you a sense of where you are now; I provide labels for simple reference. This tool isn't designed to define all your capabilities or to categorize all people. Think of it as a snapshot, a photo of you standing in front of the Grand Canyon or some other vacation landmark. It's where you are at this point. Nothing says you have to stay here, and, ideally, the puzzles help move you to a different cognitive place.

Though I'll occasionally refer to the reference labels later in the book, they're not really necessary for working on the exercises. They do, however, put you in the right frame of mind for working on them. Thinking about how you think—as well as how others think—is important for increasing mental agility. In fact, after diagnosing how you take in information, you'll be able to use this same tool to stretch your mental muscles; it's a good warm-up for the exercises to come.

THE DIAGNOSTIC EXERCISE

Copy the figure on page 25 onto another piece of paper using colored pencils. Use the pencils in the following order:

1. *Red*
2. *Green*
3. *Blue*

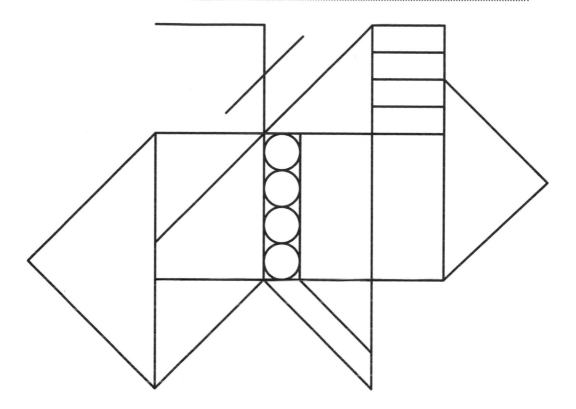

4. *Brown*
5. *Black*
6. *Yellow*
7. *Purple*
8. *Pink*

Start with the red pencil and switch to the next color every 20 seconds. If you can, have someone else monitor the time so you can concentrate on your drawing. It doesn't matter if you finish before you use all the colors. If you run out of time, just complete your drawing with the pink pencil.

Although you can take this "test" by yourself, making it into a game with one person monitoring the time and everyone else drawing the same figure, you'll discover that people can look at the same thing and see it differently. This reinforces the value of the exercise. All of the figures will look roughly the same (allowing for different levels of artistic talent), but different people will draw the triangles, trapezoids, rectangles, circles, and lines in different orders. You can tell by the colors. Tony started with the triangle on the left. Susan did the circles first. Bob zeroed in on the big rectangle.

This color chronology provides insight into how people organize information. It is a *reflective tool*—a snapshot that reflects how one's mind works—but it is not a mirror image. This tool provides general insights into different cognitive styles, not highly specific descriptions of personalities, capabilities, or intelligence. Two people whose drawings would categorize them as having similar ways of thinking can possess vastly different levels of skill and insight.

Use this tool to teach yourself and others that the same information can be organized in many different ways.

I. Left-to-Righter

As illustrated on page I-1, this individual starts with the triangle on the left side of the page, does the two trapezoids next, then draws the rectangle, and completes the drawing with the triangle at the far right. The left-to-righter is a classic linear thinker, moving through the assignment with great logic and diligence. He has a system for getting things done and rigidly sticks to this system.

The left-to-righter is often the first to arrive at work and the last to leave. You can almost see the motto "A place for everything and everything in its place" hanging over his desk. He's highly organized, and his desk is neat as a pin. If you are crystal clear about the assignment, he'll handle it efficiently and meet reasonable deadlines. Just don't count on him for creative solutions. He won't suggest a better way of achieving a goal or propose a daring new initiative. He also prefers specific directions and needs them to successfully complete an assignment.

2. Direction Changer

When you look at direction changer's drawing on page I-1, you see that this person started with the left triangle and may even have done one or two more shapes like the left-to-righter but then followed a different sequence. She may have drawn the far right rectangle or triangle in green (second pencil) or blue (third pencil). Based on her recognition of the drawing's complexity, she altered her linear approach. She saw a relationship between disparate pieces of information. At some point (you can tell by the colors), she decided she wasn't looking at a simple left-to-right project. She was able to shift her thinking process midstream, thus demonstrating mental agility.

The direction changer takes more risks than the left-to-righter. She is more comfortable with change, although this may not be evident at the start of a project or when she first joins the team. She likes to get her bearings, to get the lay of the land. Her creativity can confuse people because her logic isn't always self-evident. She may suddenly abandon a project if she's decided it was going nowhere. On the other hand, she can quickly organize what other people see as absolute chaos, detecting patterns and relationships just as they are beginning to emerge.

3. Central Shapers

Architects, engineers and physicists are apt to be central shapers (see page I-1). They tend to focus on the central image first. Notice that here the rectangle in the center was drawn in red (first pencil), although your central shaper might have started with the triangle above it or the partial triangle inside it. A part-whole thinker, he'll begin with a central image (or theme) and relate all the remaining parts to that central image.

A central shaper is an excellent problem solver. He goes straight to the heart of the matter and isn't distracted by tangential issues. Very goal oriented, he enjoys constructing programs, putting together presentations, and creating things from scratch.

Sometimes a central shaper has difficulty working with people who don't think the way he does. For instance, a hard-core engineer may communicate well with other engineers but poorly with nonengineers. He has trouble altering his frame of reference, that is, putting himself in someone else's place. He may quickly become impatient when people express different opinions. Empathy is not usually his strong suit.

4. Outliners

This individual draws the outermost figures first, almost like someone laying down the edges of a jigsaw puzzle (see page I-1). She started with the triangle on the left, went to the upside-down V at the bottom, and then proceeded to the triangle on the far right. Notice that there are pieces missing from her drawing. She ignored the circles in the center and some of the interior lines. As a big-picture thinker, she is attracted to large geometric figures. She may be an entrepreneur or a visionary, but she needs to know her boundaries. Although an entrepreneur-visionary may relish breaking the rules or ignoring boundaries, she has to identify the limits before she can push past them.

The outliner is often the founder of a company or enterprise. Even if she's not the boss, she'll get involved in positions where risk taking and strategic planning are important. Aggressive, state-of-the-art companies value her gift for seeing the big picture, presenting fresh perspectives, and proposing daring ideas. However, she is hard to pin down on specific details. Her decisions can lead to serious, expensive mistakes because she overlooks small, but crucial, matters. In many instances, she lacks the patience to follow through on a project and the perseverance to implement a complex plan successfully. She comes up with great ideas, but she needs someone else to implement them.

5. Creators

As you might expect, the creator's drawing on page I-2 is only one of a number of ways that creators might approach this exercise. This individual chose to start with all the diagonal lines, proceed to the circles, and then draw the outside triangle. Don't bother looking for a logical progression. There is none. This is characteristic of how creators organize information. Notice, too, how he has deviated from some of the geometric forms—one section of the puzzle looks like a butterfly wing. Creators frequently take flights of fancy.

You'll generally find this type in marketing positions within companies or in other areas where creativity is prized, such as product or package design, graphic arts, Web site design, and so on. Unlike the outliner, the creator really isn't interested in knowing the boundaries. He craves the freedom to innovate; if you want a new idea, ask the creator. Just don't expect him to function in a buttoned-down culture or work well under a left-to-righter boss. Because the creator's impulsive, he'll quickly get bored with routine tasks, even if they're crucial. Expect him to possibly disrupt team meetings or to even quit his job because he doesn't enjoy his work.

6. Disconnectors

In this drawing by a disconnector on page I-2, the order is not as important as the gaps between the figures. As you can see, the triangle is not connected to the rectangle. Although a disconnected figure sometimes indicates a visual problem, it usually means this person doesn't see the interrelationships between the images—the connection between cause and effect. Instead, she reacts to the moment. The adult disconnector does not usually perceive every part as separate from the whole. There is usually a direct relationship between the number of images disconnected and the intensity of the behavior described. If a company's stock goes down, she'll immediately jump to the conclusion that the company is headed for bankruptcy. Or if the boss criticizes her, she'll assume she's about to be fired. This inability to put things in context—to relate what happened in the past to what's happening now—is evident in the disconnector's drawing. Without a sense of context, she cannot interpret events realistically. She is at the mercy of her emotions.

A disconnector works well at jobs that require "crystal" intelligence (assuming that their job requires them to handle data). Physicians who pride themselves on their expertise in a specific specialty but find it unimportant to habitually integrate a holistic medical approach to their treatment are an example of high-level disconnectors. Disconnectors may appear to be an expert in their field, demonstrating a tremendous quantity of information, but they cannot make imaginative leaps or adjust to new situations. Because they can't readily adapt to the unfamiliar or unexpected, they feel greatly overwhelmed by minor setbacks.

7. Random Connectors

As with the creator's and disconnector's drawings, this complex figure on page I-2 by a random connector lacks any easily discernible pattern. Unlike the creator, however, the random connector reproduced the geometric figures exactly as pictured without any butterfly wings or similar embellishments. Though this diagnostic doesn't measure the speed with which the drawing was done, the odds are that this person completed it at warp speed.

A random connector is a high-energy individual. He often makes a very good sales representative or party planner. He knows how to work a room, and he likes the action. He's a great team player and can get people revved up and moving on the "iffiest" of projects. However, he loses focus easily and doesn't know how to implement transitions. He has so much energy and ambition that he manages to get by without any kind of system. Consequently, he can drive subordinates crazy.

8. Bottom-Liners

Sometimes someone will start the drawing either with the middle vertical line (as illustrated) or with the four circles. Like the central shaper, she—the bottom liner (see page I-2)—gets right to the point, but the point is always the bottom line. You have "25 words or less" to tell her what it all means, and she'd prefer you used "less." If you can convey your message quickly to the bottom liner, she'll give you more time to fill in the details. Just don't expect her to participate in the discussion; she's already absorbed all she wants to know.

A bottom liner goes through life as if she were looking through the crosshairs of a gun sight. She can be phenomenally successful but extremely lonely at the top. A bottom liner tends to become oblivious to everything but her target. Her mind can calculate costs and benefits faster than a supercomputer. If you're on her team, you'll reap the rewards, but she'll push you unrelentlessly to achieve them.

DO'S AND DON'TS:
How to Get the Most from This Diagnostic Tool

As with any inventory, this one may tempt you to label yourself or others. Please, don't be seduced into thinking that my quickie profiles are definitive. You may recognize yourself in one of these "snapshots" and may like most of what you read. Maybe you even recognize your boss, a direct report, or a colleague. I hope I've given you some insight into how behavior and perceptions may interact. I want to emphasize, though, that each thinking type has advantages and disadvantages. Having the mental agility to alter your perceptions and your behavior greatly enhances your chance of getting the results you really want without the downside.

If you're a manager or even a member of a team, you'll find that having insight into how other people organize information vastly improves your ability to communicate with them. As you become more aware of what goes on in your mind

"I not only use all the brains that I have, but all that I can borrow."

—Woodrow Wilson

and theirs, you'll be able to make better use of their skills faster. So much misunderstanding and conflict occur in organizations because we don't recognize how someone else takes in information. If we give an outliner a highly detailed, 100-page document, we're setting her up for failure. Do it time and again, and resentment will build. She'll feel unappreciated for the things she does well.

Ideally, every business should have a healthy sprinkling of all thinking types. A small business needs to have all the types embodied in one person or a handful of people; larger businesses can be less demanding. This doesn't guarantee that the right person is doing the right job. As Peter Drucker pointed out in *The Effective Executive* (HarperBusiness, 2002), too often the applicant who gets the job is not the best qualified but the "least misfit." This occurs because emphasis is placed on what the job entails rather than on the reason for the job in the first place. In other words, what is the purpose of the job? What results do we want? What thinking type can produce those results?

ALTERNATIVE WAYS OF USING THE DIAGNOSTIC TOOL

Now that you're getting in the habit of thinking about the way people think, let's do some warm-up exercises for the puzzles ahead. These exercises use the diagnostic tool that you're now familiar with. As you'll discover, they will help you and your people to:

Improve memory and concentration. Study the complex figure on page 25 for a minute, put it aside for half an hour, and then draw what you remember—you don't have to use the colored pencils or time yourself. Unless you have what is referred to as a photographic memory, you'll probably have forgotten some details. Compare what you drew to the original figure. Make a mental note about what you missed. In a few days, draw the figure again from memory. Compare this new drawing with the original figure and your previous drawing. Have you added anything? Have you forgotten anything?

This memory exercise involves rehearsal. You're rehearsing attention to detail, noticing mistakes, and rebounding from failure—all valuable skills in a complex world. Everybody, no matter how smart or how accomplished, forgets things or overlooks important details. With practice we can reduce the number of times it happens to us. This exercise helps you improve your focus and your visual memory.

Notice subtleties and nuances. Use your nondominant hand (left for right-handers, right for left-handers) to draw the complex figure. If you're not ambidextrous, you'll probably find you draw more slowly and may feel uncomfortable and less efficient. High-functioning people tend to race through all types of job-related tasks. In routine situations, efficiency matters, but when circumstances change, efficiency can produce costly mistakes. By switching to your nondominant hand, you've created an unfamiliar circumstance. Now you can test your degree of effectiveness.

This exercise was inspired by a client who loved racquetball, although by his own admission he was only an average player. One day he broke his dominant hand. When he came to see me, he was more upset about the hiatus he'd have to take from his regular game than about doing my puzzles. I suggested he try playing with his nondominant hand until he recovered, and he played that way until his hand healed. He was astonished to discover that his game improved dramatically, a direct result of using his nondominant hand. Circumstance had forced him to slow down. Not being able to play efficiently, he had to focus on effectiveness—that is, on getting the result he wanted. His technique improved, and he noticed subtleties in his opponents' styles that he could use to his advantage.

Drawing the complex figure with your nondominant hand has the same effect. You concentrate more on the figure's various shapes, on the discrete elements that make up each geometric figure, on the relationships between line and circle, and on the white spaces between the figure's elements. If you pride yourself on speed, you may discover that altering your speed—slowing down or speeding up as circumstance demands—can make you more effective. If you use the colored pencils and the timer, you may also find your nondominant side perceives the world differently when compared with the way your dominant side perceives it.

Look at things from a fresh perspective. Turn the complex figure upside down and then draw it. Or if you're really up for a challenge, leave the figure right side up, but draw it upside down. Visualizing a familiar image in an unfamiliar way leads to insight and innovation and is an especially valuable skill to have in a complex world when you want to come up with a new strategy or business. We can't do what we can't visualize. By imagining things differently, we open our minds to new possibilities.

Use my complex figure to diagnose thinking types and stretch your mental muscles. You don't have to be an expert in psychology or even a human resources person to implement this tool in the ways I've discussed.

Benchmark improvements in mental agility. This last one is for use after you've completed the book and all the puzzles in it. Return to this chapter and draw the complex figure again. You'll probably find you're doing it differently. Maybe you've developed a whole new thinking style, one not mentioned here. If so, that's great! Take a little time and compare it with your initial drawing. The differences might be minor or they might be major. Either way, you've enhanced your mental agility. If there are no significant changes, it may be that the work you've been doing lately requires the same thinking type you were using when you first drew the complex figure. In that case, draw the figure a third time but intentionally draw it differently without using the examples as a reference. This indicates that you've flexed your mental muscles. People who have never done the puzzles will have difficulty altering their perceptions enough to make significant changes in their drawing.

You're almost ready to tackle the eight puzzle types. This chapter has helped prepare you for consistent reflective thinking, but there's one more preliminary step. You need to acquire self-mediation skills. By using them on yourself first, you'll be in a great position to help others later.

Mediation: Learning to Teach and Teaching to Learn

The puzzles in this book reveal their secrets only when you attempt to solve them; you can't just read about how they work and expect to transfer the lessons. Therefore, to become an effective teacher, you must first become an effective learner. This means first mastering the art of self-mediation.

Though I'll define mediation in the next section, for now think about it as a way to facilitate learning. It's what good teachers, bosses, and coaches do. Here, mediation is focused on helping you use various techniques and tools to master the process of working on the puzzles. You'll notice that I didn't write "solve" the puzzles. Though it's great if mediation helps you come up with the right answers, the more important goal is to become comfortable with the process. The techniques and tools of mediation will help you navigate around mental roadblocks that invariably pop up as you do the puzzles.

> "Leadership and learning are indispensable to each other."
>
> —John F. Kennedy

WHAT IS MEDIATION?

Mediation is not so much about teaching facts as it is about leading someone through the process of reasoning by questioning assumptions, demanding explanations, and offering alternative suggestions.

Mediation engages the participant in learning. The mediator creates a warm, nurturing relationship with the participant. Most skilled mediators are multifaceted individuals with "attitude" and a terrific sense of humor. The mediator encourages risk taking, supports exploration, and reorganizes information to enhance performance and develop the disposition for learning: truth seeking, risk taking, learning from failure, analyzing, and habituating discovery.

> "Imagination is more important than knowledge."
>
> —*Albert Einstein*

The mediator recognizes that stress, in various degrees, accompanies all learning. Without the tools to control it, high levels of stress can interfere with or even immobilize learning. The mediator teaches tools to control stress, which help the participant engage in the learning process.

Mediation is a process by which people learn to filter out external and internal noise and focus their attention on results and the steps relevant to achieving those results. Most people are familiar with a form of mediation called *mentoring*. Good mentors do more than just "teach you the ropes." They help shape your perspective and acclimate you to the culture that shares that perspective.

Good mentors know what they're doing, but they usually don't know how they do it. In this case, the mentor's knowledge is *implicit*—that is, hidden from the conscious mind. Mediation itself is an *explicit* process, a conscious and intentional examination of the various ways information can be organized.

The first step in mediation is discovery: How does a particular person usually organize information? You experienced this first step in the previous chapter when you drew my complex figure and interpreted it. Like handwriting analysis, the complex figure is a diagnostic tool that reveals the way someone organizes information.

The mediator is gently and subtly influencing our perception. As we practice applying the hints, we can consciously organize bits and pieces of information and recognize relationships that help to make sense out of what appeared to be chaos. The choice allows us to respond intentionally, not just react impulsively.

Mediation makes us aware of our current behavior and helps us create new behaviors. Through self-awareness we achieve self-control. Behavioral options give us more ways to achieve the results we want.

ADDRESSING COMMON CONCERNS ABOUT THE PUZZLES

Invariably, people want to know about the cognitive magic behind these puzzles. What is it about them that turns average performers into highly productive professionals? Why are these puzzles better than any others—why aren't there crossword puzzles in this book? I'm often asked these and similar questions. Part of the mediation process is to help people understand the rationale behind the puzzles. Though I've provided that rationale in the book's introduction and the first chapter, I think you'll find the following explanations useful, both in terms of self-mediation as well as mediation with others.

Graphic puzzles allow us to "see" ourselves thinking. They slow down the process, like watching a superslow motion video of an Olympic figure skater. At regular speed everything is a blur. With "superslow mo," you can detect the flaws even if you know practically nothing about figure skating.

Just as coaches use videos to improve their athletes' physical agility, I use graphic puzzles to improve my clients' mental agility.

In *The Act of Creation* (Macmillan, 1964), Arthur Koestler wrote:

Thinking in pictures dominates the manifestations of the unconscious, the dream, the hypnogogic half dream, the psychotic's hallucinations, the artist's vision. (The visionary prophet seems to have been a visualizer, not a verbalizer; the highest compliment we pay to those who trade in verbal currency is to call them "visionary thinkers.")

My puzzles give you practice in becoming a "visionary thinker." You'll develop the mental agility necessary to successfully achieve results in a complex world. This will allow you to:

- Make new connections.
- Generate new ideas.
- Think faster.
- Organize information in new ways.
- Achieve higher levels of creativity and innovation.

> "Conquering any difficulty always gives one a secret joy, for it means pushing back a boundary line and adding to one's liberty."
>
> —Henri Frédéric Amiel

When you begin working with my puzzles, you may find that some of them make you mentally tired. That's because you're using your mind in unfamiliar ways. The process of retraining your brain is similar to training your body. Just as learning to play a new sport makes new demands on your muscles, learning new visual imagery skills makes greater demands on your mind. With practice, you'll become more mentally agile. You'll experience more energy, more effectiveness, and more enjoyment.

GETTING TO "AH-HA":
How to Self-Mediate

Solving a puzzle is tremendously satisfying. It brings closure to the problem. We can stop thinking about it.

One of the frustrations some people experience with these puzzles is that the primary goal is not to solve them; the primary goal is change. The puzzles were designed to change your mind as well as to enhance your perceptual abilities.

You'll know your perception has changed when you experience what I call "ah-ha"—as in "Ah-ha! Now I get it." An ah-ha occurs when you suddenly see a similarity between two very different things or understand the logic of a progression. It occurs when disparate pieces come together, and you suddenly grasp the whole idea. It also occurs when you recognize a common element shared by diverse objects.

The ah-ha doesn't only bring closure to a puzzle—it retrains your brain. You will never look at that puzzle again without knowing how to solve it.

I use the following techniques to help my clients arrive at the ah-ha. Though I'll specify how to apply them to various puzzles in the following chapters, it's a good idea to familiarize yourself with the types of techniques available. If my explanations seem abstract here, they'll make more sense once you start working on the puzzles.

Coloring. The use of colors helps people see patterns and/or shapes they previously missed. Colors draw our attention to specific details. They help separate the distinct parts of a complex and confusing image. For example, coloring all the parallel lines in a puzzle blue may help you recognize similarities and differences in a progressive series.

Numbering. Counting or lettering elements in a puzzle may help you keep a series of similar objects straight. Noting how many lines make up an image and writing the number next to it helps you retain the image in your mind's eye.

Covering. Use an index card or another piece of paper to cover part of the puzzle. This helps you isolate your attention. It's difficult to concentrate when complex stimuli make you feel overwhelmed and confused. Limiting your visual field lessens the feeling of disequilibrium a highly detailed puzzle may cause.

Let's next look at a puzzle that provides you the opportunity to apply some of these mediation techniques.

Clock Puzzles

In real life we seldom get the opportunity to work on a project from its inception. Even when the assignment is new, implicit workplace traditions set limits on what we can do. When we're brought in to solve a problem, we have to wade through even more history.

The clock puzzles in the following pages are designed specifically to give you the experience of "being thrown into the middle of things." There is an overall pattern to the clock, such as a sequential change in color, size, direction, and so on. This overall pattern can be thought of as an established office routine—as in "That's the way we've always done it." The overall pattern (like the routine) has to be discounted before the real work in solving the problem can begin.

As with many real-world problems, the beginning and the end aren't always clear. You have to determine where the progression should start in order to eliminate the images that don't fit the pattern. This is similar to how we go about cutting the waste and redundancies that tend to get embedded in work routines. To solve such problems, we have to think both forward and backward (hence the symbolic clock shape of the puzzle).

Once you think you've solved the puzzle on page 40, go back and verify that your logic is sound. If you can explain the rule, you're thinking like an expert.

Notice that there are 12 images on page 41 arranged in a circle—like the numbers on a clock. If the image at the very top represents the number 12—as it would on a clock—the image to its right would be the number 1.

Visualizing the puzzle as the face of a clock helps fix the images in your mind's eye. It takes the unfamiliar and turns it into something familiar. It also gives you a way of verbalizing what you see: "Images 6 and 11 on the clock are the only ones with blunted corners on the outside."

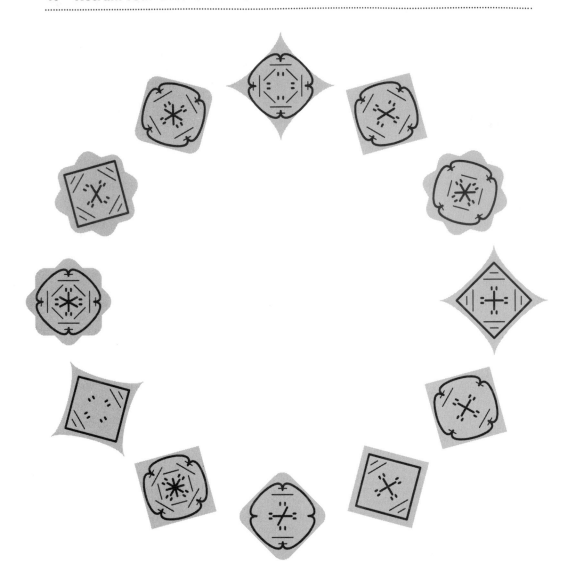

Concealed within the clock formation is a logical progression.

Objective: Reveal the progression by crossing out the images that do not follow the established logic.

Hints: The progression consists of six images.
Two variables are used.

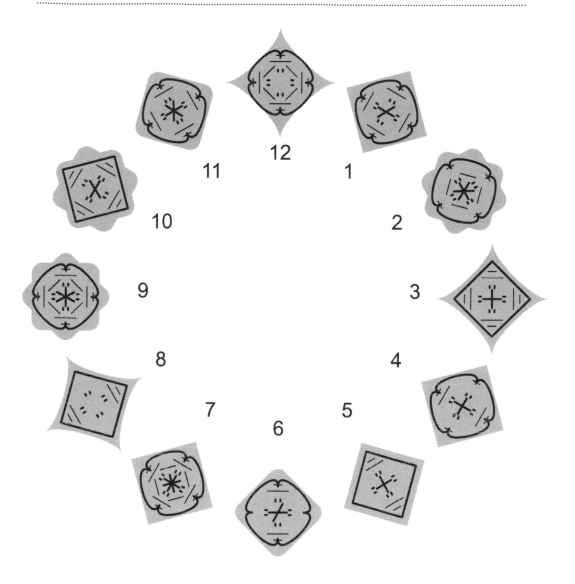

Write the numbers 1 through 12 next to the images just as if you were numbering a clock face.

With a colored marker or pencil, outline the outer border of each image. Use the same color for all the images. Remember that color helps us isolate a distinct detail—in this case the overall shape of the images.

Notice that there are five different shapes among the 12 images. Choose five different colored markers or pencils. Select one color for each specific shape.

Outline the same shapes with the same color. You've just created new information. You've distinguished the images and you've grouped them according to shape. See the puzzles on page I-3.

This is a progression puzzle. Therefore, you're looking for systematic changes from image to image. This means you can ignore any feature that is shared by all the images.

Notice the four pairs of marks in the center of each image that look something like quotation marks. Because they look the same in all the images, you can eliminate them from consideration.

I drew the marks to create a distraction. You can physically remove them by scribbling over them, x-ing them out, or covering them with "white-out" as shown on page 43.

Mediation techniques help you physically and mentally reorganize information. The object of mediation is to get an ah-ha from you. Remember the ah-ha indicates that your perception has changed.

KNOWING WHAT TO SAY AND WHEN TO SAY IT:
How to Mediate Other People

Many of my clients report that their family members, friends, or colleagues like to help them work on the puzzles. Sometimes my clients feel guilty about not solving the puzzles themselves. Remember, getting the "right" answer isn't the goal. Learning how you perceive the problem is the goal. Comparing your perception to someone else's is a valuable experience—it enables both of you to be more aware of how you perceive things and how you learn. This skill is the key to learning how to learn for lifelong adaptability and growth.

In some cases, you may be called upon to mediate because you're in human resources or a management position and are responsible for helping others learn. You may be an organizational leader who wants to help implement these puzzles throughout the company. Or you may simply want to help your colleagues or direct reports do the puzzles more effectively. Whatever your motivation, these mediation techniques will help you help them.

As people work on the puzzles, watch their body language. How do they sit? Hunched over? Leaning back in the chair? How do they concentrate? Furrowed brow? Rapidly tapping a pencil? How do you know when they're ready to give up? Sudden shift in posture? Deep sigh?

Concealed within the clock formation is a logical progression.

Objective: Reveal the progression by crossing out the images that do not follow the established logic.

Hints: The progression consists of six images.
Two variables are used.

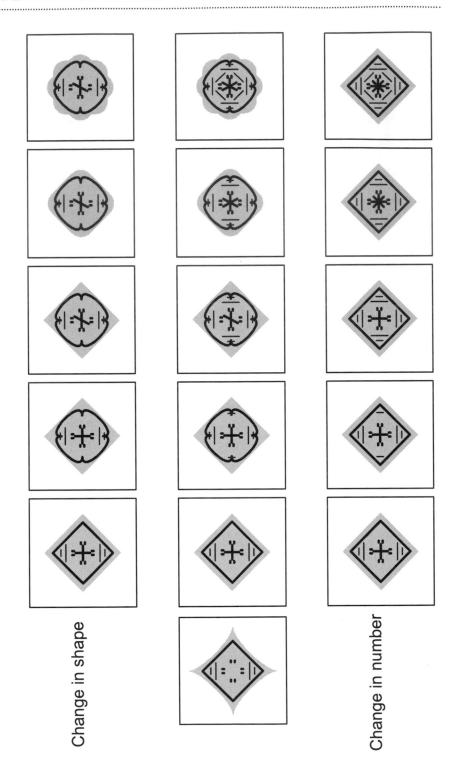

Progressions distinguished by shape and by number.

Change in shape

Change in number

To mediate effectively, you have to get inside the other person's head. Try to recognize when someone needs help even before he's aware of feeling frustrated. Frustration makes him want to give up. Individual frustration levels vary. My students report their frustration thresholds increase dramatically with experience doing my puzzles. But timing mediation before someone reaches his peak frustration threshold is critical to maintaining engagement and continuing the learning process.

Some people will never admit to feeling frustrated. They'll just quit. It's as if they can't say, "I don't know."

The simple fact is that we can't learn anything we already know. Learning requires awareness that we've reached the limits of our knowledge about something. **When we can admit we don't know something, we're ready to learn.**

The art and magic of good mediation is recognizing when someone is ready to learn.

Here are some tips to help you help others learn:

Tell people the puzzles weren't meant to be easy. Frustration can make us feel stupid. Some people even say, "I'm such an idiot." Sometimes they mean it; sometimes they don't. If they mean it, letting them quit isn't going to help. Tell them that the puzzles were meant to be challenging and demanding but also solvable when correctly perceived. Working through the puzzles changes our perceptions, which in turn helps us "see" the right answers.

Use other people's frames of reference. I referred to the puzzle in this chapter as a "clock," but some people won't see it that way. They'll see it as a bracelet or the outline of a faceless head; other people just see a series of design elements. Find out how others relate to the images.

Accept others' interpretations of the puzzle. Ask them what it reminds them of and use their words to refer to it. It'll help you get inside their head and see things from their perspective.

Think Socrates. The Greek philosopher Socrates was the first mediator. When he was asked why he was considered the wisest man in the world, he replied, "It's because I know I know nothing."

Socrates never told anybody how to think. He asked questions. Through a series of questions, he nudged people to the ah-ha.

Remember there is no single right way to solve the puzzles. *Instead of telling people what to look for, ask them what they see. You'll learn new ways of organizing information.*

Be open-minded. Some people solve the puzzles differently than you or I would, which is one of the things I enjoy about my work. I'm amazed at how often people see possibilities that I missed. In this way we learn from each other.

Relate the puzzles to real-life situations. Sometimes the perceptual process you used to solve a puzzle will remind you of a real-life experience, because both required the same thinking process. Make a mental note to yourself to remember the experience. It'll help you in two ways:

1. If a similar situation arises in the future, you've already got a process for understanding it.
2. You'll have a concrete way of explaining an abstract process to someone else. Stories help us envision concepts that are difficult to grasp.

Give them a hint if they get stuck. Sometimes you just have to forget about Socrates. Sometimes people get so lost and confused that you just have to tell them what to do next. It's an act of mercy, but just don't overdo it. The goal is to keep individuals engaged and have them go at their own pace through the process of self-discovery and learning how to learn.

Remember that getting the "right" answer isn't the goal—getting to the ah-ha is. You can give people a nudge in the right direction without having to carry them to the top of the hill.

INDIVIDUALS VERSUS TEAMS

Mediating a group of people is different from working one-on-one. Even though you use the same techniques, you'll experience a different interaction. When I present my puzzles in a group setting, people get to "look inside" their colleagues' minds and can watch the wheels turning. They learn to appreciate other people's strengths and forgive their weaknesses. They leave my presentation with a clearer understanding of perceptual differences.

I'm often called in to mediate with corporate teams that are having difficulty functioning effectively. The puzzles give team members the opportunity to explore their perceptual and problem-solving processes without high financial or professional risk.

When I mediate in corporate settings, I always point out how one team member processes information and solves problems differently than does another member. This encourages people to talk about how they thought through the puzzle and what prompted them to do what they did. A by-product of this experience is that team members begin to bond. They begin to trust each other faster than they would under ordinary conditions. Once they've gotten into each other's heads, they express a greater tolerance of differing opinions and problem-solving approaches.

As you probably suspect, in a group everybody becomes a mediator. People want to help each other when someone gets stuck. They also enjoy "showing off" their own unique approach to the puzzle. As if by osmosis, people intuitively pick up mediating techniques. I smile to myself when I hear someone suggest: "Why don't you try numbering all the straight lines" or "Maybe coloring the shape will make it stand out for you."

People are often more willing to accept advice from a fellow team member than from an "official" mediator. When this happens, rest assured you've done your job well. They are developing a shared perspective and a common bond.

At the start of the training session, team members want your feedback and mediation. I've experienced this same dependency with children, corporate executives, and NASA scientists. They want to feel that they're doing things right.

As their brains are retrained to think about doing the right thing, they gradually let go of my apron strings. They get excited about exploring new possibilities and learning from each other. They become better communicators inside and outside the team setting.

Because puzzles are fun things, people enjoy sharing them with family, friends, and colleagues. At first they try to stump each other. Soon they're sharing ideas and discovering new things together. Mediation is about getting the results *you* want by helping others get the results *they* want. Mediation is about bringing out the best in everyone all of the time.

C H A P T E R

Analogies

In the movie *Forrest Gump,* the oft-quoted line "Life is like a box of chocolates" is an analogy. Gump made a comparison between life and a box of chocolates, and he went on to explain that they were similar because both can surprise us. Just as we don't know what will happen tomorrow, we can't tell what's hidden under the chocolate coating.

We create an analogy when we perceive a similarity between two different things, which lets us treat them as if they were the same. When Benjamin Franklin observed that electrical sparks looked, sounded, and smelled like lightning, he decided to find out if lightning was electrical. Having proved it was by flying a kite with a key tied to a string during a thunderstorm, he further reasoned that lightning should flow through metal the same way other forms of electricity did. Thus, Franklin invented the lightning rod.

The telephone is another example of an analogy put to good use. Its inventor, Alexander Graham Bell, taught people who were deaf. He noticed that electricity traveling through wires produced audible clicks in a telegraph machine much like sound waves traveling through the air reach our eardrums. He reasoned that electricity could be controlled to produce other sounds as well, maybe

"Computers are good at swift, accurate computation and at storing great masses of information. The brain, on the other hand, is not as efficient a number cruncher and its memory is often highly fallible; a basic inexactness is built into its design. The brain's strong point is its flexibility. It is unsurpassed at making shrewd guesses and at grasping the total meaning of information presented to it."

—Jeremy Campbell

even sounds that the deaf could hear. His efforts led to the invention of the telephone.

Both Franklin and Bell perceived problems that other people ignored. They saw opportunities to make life better. The 19th century psychologist William James wrote, "The faculty for perceiving analogies is the best indication of genius." Analogies are the spawning ground for brilliant strategies and innovation. People who create truly original products, services, policies, and processes are skilled in analogical thinking.

Analogies also help us understand and communicate abstract concepts. Describing the Internet as a web is an analogy, allowing people who aren't technosavvy to quickly envision how computers around the world are interconnected.

Strategic thinking, innovation, and *communication* are obviously skills that organizations value. The traditional way to help people acquire these skills is through case history analysis, benchmarking, brainstorming techniques, role playing, and other training tools. There's nothing wrong with these approaches; they can provide incremental benefits in all three skills. The analogy exercises in this book, however, can offer more than incremental benefits. Rather than attack the surface of the problem, they get to the core. They directly impact our brains and help us strengthen the parts of the mind that control strategic thinking, innovation, and communication.

THE DEVIL IS IN THE DETAILS:
Learning from Our Mistakes

Just as athletes stretch to warm up their muscles before they compete, you need to warm up before tackling the analogy exercises. I don't want you to be overwhelmed by the analogies. As the first of the eight puzzle types, they may seem overly difficult because you're being asked to do something unfamiliar. That's why I'd suggest you start with the following "mistake" puzzles. I use mistake puzzles because many people find it easier to spot someone else's error than to correct their own work. Correcting another person's work requires us to figure out what the other person

"Much of the success of life depends upon keeping one's mind open to opportunity and seizing it when it comes."

—Alice Foote MacDougall

was thinking. When we try to get into someone else's head, we intuitively slow down our own thinking process.

I've included an entire chapter of mistake puzzles for later practice, but the following ones provide you with a useful introduction to the mental "stretches" you need to work effectively on analogies. As you do the mistake puzzles, look for specific details when comparing and contrasting the images. Pay attention to changes in size, place, shape, and orientation. Take as much time as you need.

> **"The test of a first-rate intelligence is the ability to hold two opposed ideas in the mind at the same time, and still retain the ability to function."**
>
> —*F. Scott Fitzgerald*

Following each puzzle, I've provided you with self-mediation techniques. Complete as much of a puzzle as you can on your own before you read the mediation. Similarly, if you're using a puzzle with other people, hold back on your mediation intervention until you see they are struggling or are asking you for help. Begin to work on the following puzzle.

Above each picture on page 52, notice the labels indicating what might have changed in each of the four pairs of figures. For instance, in letter A the label suggests that the differences between the first and second figures are in size and place. Do you think that the label is correct? If yes, leave it the way it is. If no, cross out the mistake and write in the correct answer. Before you go on, find all the mistakes on the page and correct them.

Some people have difficulty identifying the mistakes. Let's review a few of the techniques I discussed in the previous chapter:

- Number or color each corresponding shape so that what you're comparing and what you're contrasting clearly stand out.
- Trace over each corresponding shape with a pencil, pen, or marker to help you identify subtle changes you might otherwise miss.
- Look at a pair of figures. Then go through the list step-by-step and ask yourself if you see a change in:
  1. Size
  2. Place
  3. Shape
  4. Orientation

At least one set on the page has been mislabeled. Find and correct the mistake(s).

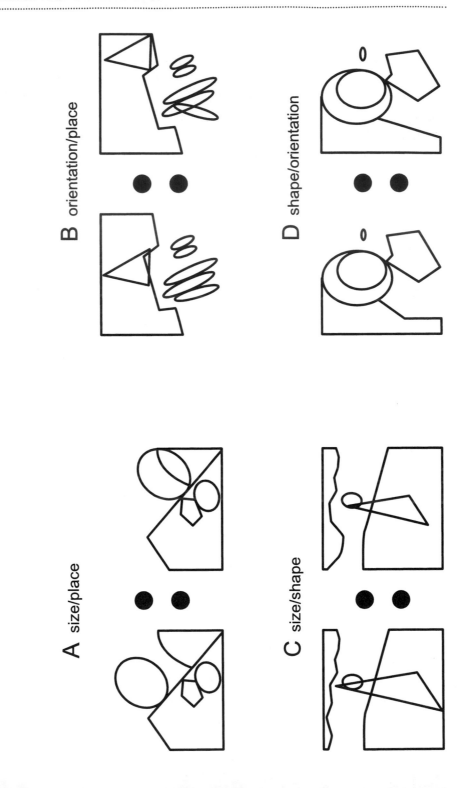

A size/place

B orientation/place

C size/shape

D shape/orientation

Remember that some comparisons and contrasts are more subtle than others. For instance, figure D has a slight, but still observable, shape change. Sometimes I'll suggest that my client imagine all the ovals in the figures are diamonds. The oval-diamond on the right would be considerably more valuable than the one on the left. Of course, you can imagine that the ovals are anything you want so long as it helps you to see the difference.

As you can see, figures B and C are mistake free. Sometimes figure D confuses people, as it is the only pair in which the mistake involves a category that wasn't listed. You had to recognize the mistake, name the type of error, and then take the initiative to record it.

Solve these additional puzzles. However, be warned! The mistakes become increasingly difficult to detect with each successive puzzle. Remember, my puzzles were designed to retrain your brain and make you more effective. Efficiency can get you only so far. Some discomfort is to be expected when you do things you've never done before because you have to pay close attention.

Our brains quickly establish routines through mindless repetition, which is why habits are so hard to break. I train brains to be agile and mindful—to pay attention to the goal and the details. With practice, you'll find it's just as easy to be effective as it is to be efficient. It's more fun too.

● ● ●

FINDING THE RULE:
The Object of Analogies

In the analogy puzzle on page 58, which shape in the bottom row best completes the analogy ("A is to A Prime as B is to B Prime") in the top row? What do you think the second best, third best, and fourth best answers are? A few people understand this puzzle right away, but most people don't. They'll stare at it for a while and wonder where to begin. If you're feeling confused, think back to the mistake puzzles you just completed. Remember that you were looking for changes in number, shape, size, orientation, place, and the like.

Go easy on yourself. Instead of trying to absorb all the information on the page at once, look for specific details that you can name in A and A Prime. In other words, what happened from the first picture to the second picture? Can you identify a rule for the change that occurred? How is A Prime different from A?

At least one set on the page has been mislabeled. Find and correct the mistake(s).

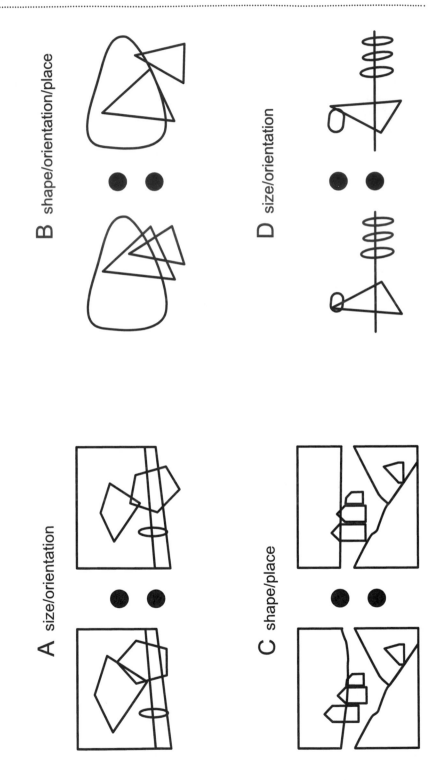

A size/orientation

B shape/orientation/place

C shape/place

D size/orientation

At least one set on the page has been mislabeled. Find and correct the mistake(s).

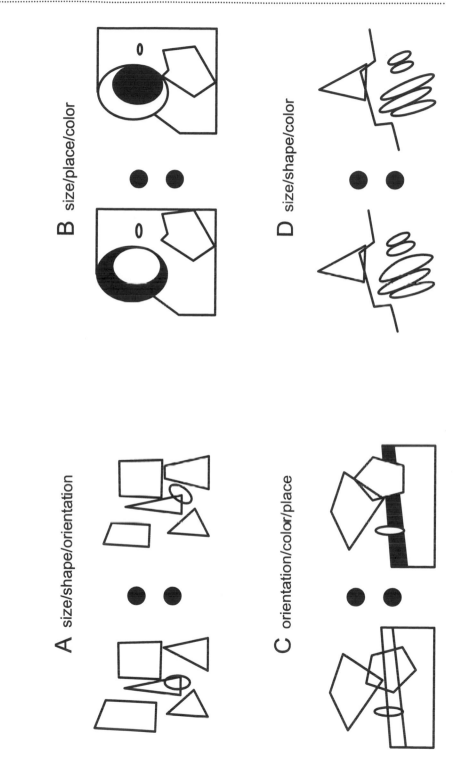

A size/shape/orientation

B size/place/color

C orientation/color/place

D size/shape/color

At least one set on the page has been mislabeled. Find and correct the mistake(s).

A orientation/number

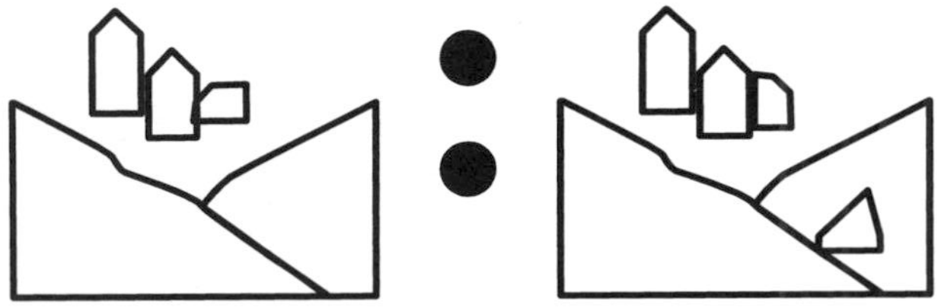

B size/orientation/place

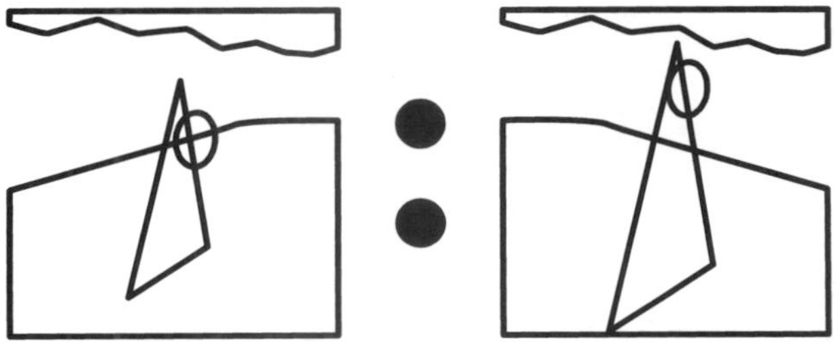

C size/place

D place/number

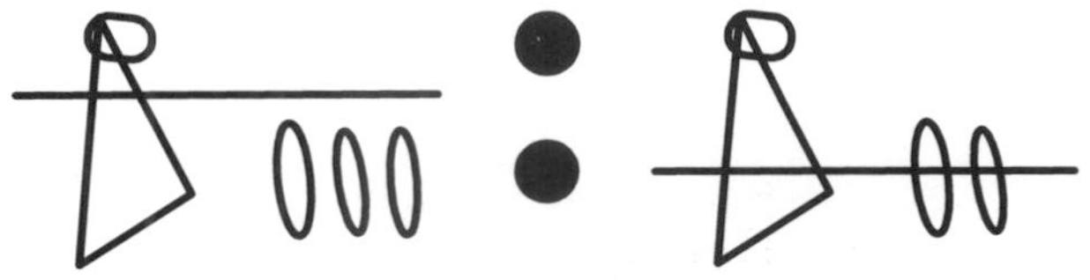

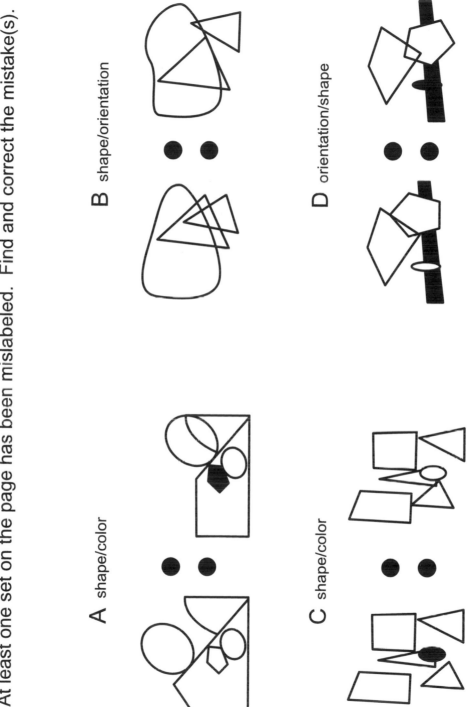

At least one set on the page has been mislabeled. Find and correct the mistake(s).

A shape/color

B shape/orientation

C shape/color

D orientation/shape

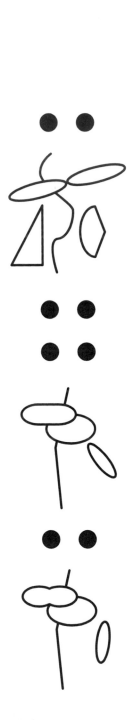

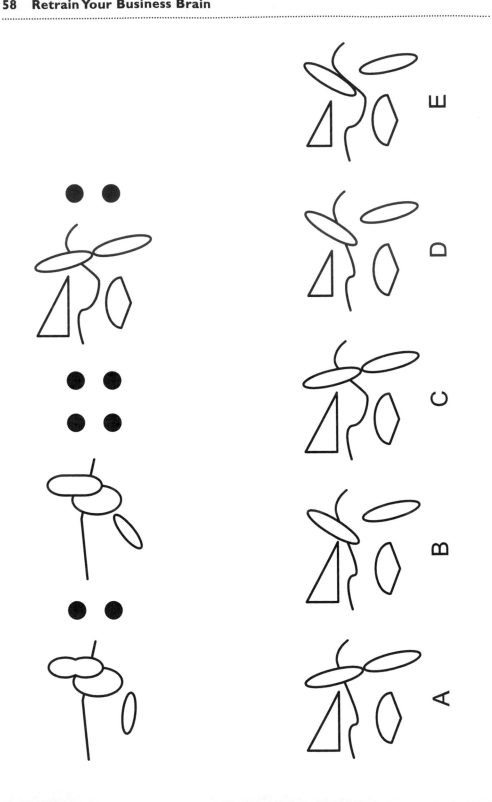

The first difference many people notice is the orientation of the oval at the bottom. It looks as if it's been rotated from tipping slightly downward to tipping upward at a sharper angle. A second, more subtle difference is that the larger oval with the indented middle becomes rounder or more inflated in A Prime. So we can say there was a change in shape.

Now write down the specific differences: "Orientation and Shape." Having named the differences between A and A Prime, you know what changes you're looking for between B and whatever B Prime is. You have identified the rule that dictated the change.

Look at your choices in the bottom row. Look at each option one at a time. Sometimes it helps to isolate each choice by covering the others with your hand, an index card, or paper.

Look for something that has changed shape when you compare B with one of the options given in the bottom row. Sometimes tracing over matching shapes with colored pencils or markers helps people remember what they've already compared.

As you compare each choice with B, name the difference you find and write it above the choice. One option will have a difference in both shape and orientation. Label that as your "Best." The second best choice isn't as perfect a match, but it's closer than the others. Label that one as "Second Best." Continue locating and labeling the remaining options as they become less and less perfect.

Write out the rule you've discovered. For example, there is a change in shape and orientation. I have included answer puzzles with detailed notations to help guide and slow down your thinking.

In school we're trained to look for the right answer. Mensa workbooks and lateral-thinking puzzles also reinforce the expectation that there is only one perfect answer to any problem. In a complex world, no solution is perfect for long. As you've probably learned from experience, it's difficult to come up with the perfect solution to a work problem. Today's great new software becomes outdated faster than anyone could have imagined. The strategy to enter an emerging market needs to be modified repeatedly. You and your people need to be adept at generating alternatives, because the more viable options you can give yourself, the better your chances of being effective. I designed the puzzle you just completed to help people face the fact that sometimes we have to settle for second or third best. We can't always get the results we want, but we

> **"When I was young . . . there never was any question about right and wrong. We knew our catechism, and that was enough."**
>
> —*George Eliot*

should know what we're willing to accept and why to help us make better decisions, communicate our choices, and reduce stress.

Sometimes we can't distinguish between a right and wrong course of action. We can't get all the information we need when we need it. Pilots call this condition "flying by the seat of your pants"—when all the sophisticated technology in the cockpit can't tell you much of anything and you have to depend on your own instincts.

The people we consider experts pull off miracles time and again, and they seem to possess extraordinary instincts or luck. In fact, they are highly skilled analogical thinkers. They habitually make comparisons between how things are and how they want them to be, weighing and measuring the value of each choice as it presents itself. They know that the world is less than perfect, and they also know what they'll accept.

TRANSLATING ANALOGIES INTO WORKPLACE SKILLS

As you become more proficient by working with my analogy puzzles, you'll discover that you're developing new skills and using them instinctively. These skills facilitate strategic planning, innovation, and communication, and they include boundary spanning, recognition of false assumptions, and seeing things in new ways.

Boundary Spanning

The saying that "nothing succeeds like success" explains why there are so many spin-offs and copycats. Success is so elusive that once we find something that works, we want to do it over and over again.

The sad truth is that most spin-offs and copycats fail because people don't understand the "rule" that allowed the original product, service, or process to succeed. My analogy puzzles train your brain to instinctively look for rules.

Think about how you created a rule to explain the difference between the first set of figures and the second in the puzzle on page 58. The rule then helped you understand and solve the puzzle. You examined what took place in one situation and applied that information to a seemingly dissimilar situation. Discovering the analogy led you to recognize that the situations weren't so different after all.

In business, this ability is called *boundary spanning*. You extrapolate a rule from one type of business and apply it to another. For example, the first products with interchangeable parts were guns made for the Civil War; when Henry Ford perceived that other products could be made following the same rule, he applied it to building automobiles with interchangeable parts. Through boundary spanning, Ford invented the assembly line and changed how products are manufactured.

Recognition of False Assumptions

Behavior controls our perceptions, but rules control our behavior. Most people aren't aware of the rules that govern their decisions. They're called *assumptions* and are products of our efficient brains. They allow us to clump together things that may have only superficial similarities. As a result, we are lulled into feeling efficient at the price of effectiveness.

For instance, imagine you're interviewing candidates for a job. One applicant's résumé indicates that he went to Harvard Business School. The other candidate has more experience and a good track record, but he attended Podunk State College. Subconsciously, you apply a rule that says someone who attended Harvard is a cut above the rest. You select this applicant on the assumption that he will perform better than the other candidate.

Now imagine that a colleague objects to your choice of candidates on the grounds that he doesn't have the experience the job requires. You may find yourself vigorously, perhaps even emotionally, arguing that the applicant is still the best qualified. Are you defending him because he's really the best candidate or because he went to Harvard?

Recall that analogies allow us to treat two dissimilar things as if they were the same. But not all analogies are equal. If you recognize that you're basing your assumption about the candidate on one factor only—Harvard Business School— you can reevaluate your assessment of his qualifications in a more objective and less emotional way. Is an academically based, test-taking intelligence sufficient proof that your candidate can perform the job? Does he have the right people skills? Can he keep his cool under pressure? Is he a team player? Does he have a sense of responsibility? The more factors that you match, the more confidence you can have in your decision to recommend him as the best candidate for the job.

By recognizing that past experiences influence our present decisions, we gain control over seemingly minute, yet crucial factors that determine whether we'll get the result we want in the future.

Seeing Things in New Ways

Necessity is not the only mother of invention. In a highly competitive global market, we can't always wait for needs to arise; sometimes we have to go out and create them. None of the corporate wise men at IBM expected the average person to be the least bit interested in owning a computer, so they turned down the opportunity to invest in Apple computers. Likewise, the technology to send faxes has been around since the 1940s, but many naysayers laughed at the idea of people wanting a quick, easy way to send written messages. Thus, faxes have only been common since the late 1980s.

Solving the analogy puzzles will retrain your brain to process information more effectively. You'll be able to utilize more of your knowledge and experiences to discover and appreciate new ways of solving problems that other people can't recognize—or simply ignore.

You'll also discover a new resiliency when faced with setbacks and a new agility when confronting failure. Sometimes things don't work out the way we want or expect. Being able to recoup our loses, regroup, and adapt to constant change is a vital skill for surviving and flourishing in a complex world.

ANALOGY #2:
Rehearsing Finding and Applying the Rule

Now that you've completed one analogy exercise, let's see what you can do with the next puzzles. Remember that you can make it easy for yourself by doing any or all of the following:

- Make liberal use of colored pencils or markers to help identify identical shapes. This technique focuses your attention on the simpler parts and away from the complexity of the whole.
- Look for two or more differences. But look for them one at a time.
- Name the differences and write down the names. This establishes the rule you'll apply to the second set of figures.
- Eliminate distracting information by isolating the choice you're considering in the bottom row, covering the other answers with your hand, an index card, or paper.
- Write down the name of each difference you find in the options in the bottom row. Be sure to label each choice correctly. You'll use this information when you apply the rule and choose the best answer.

● ● ●

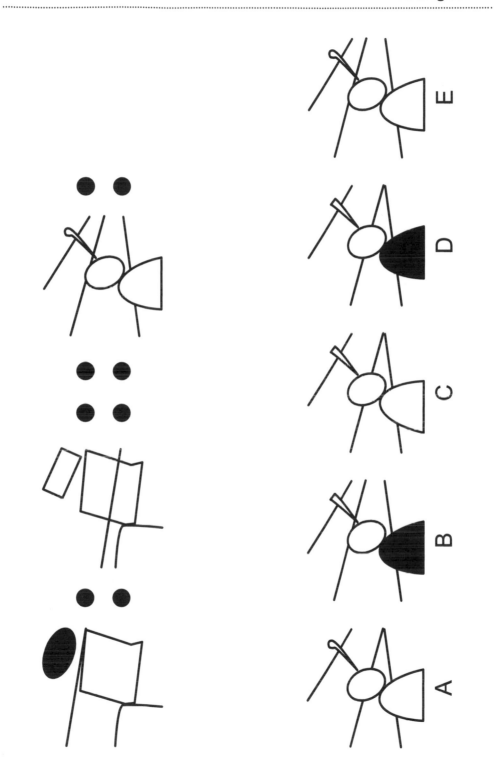
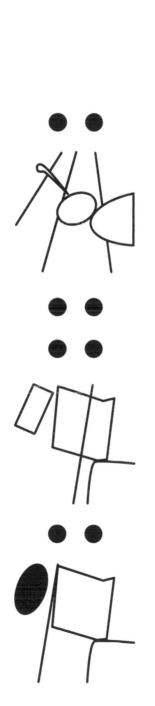

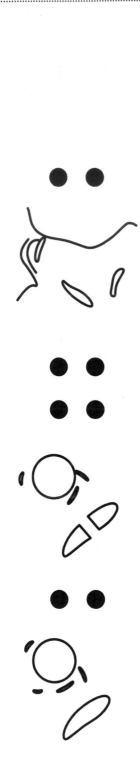

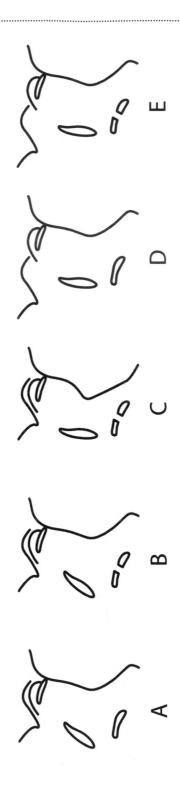

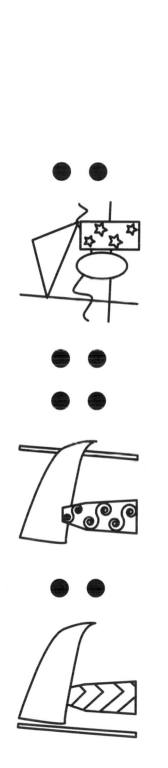

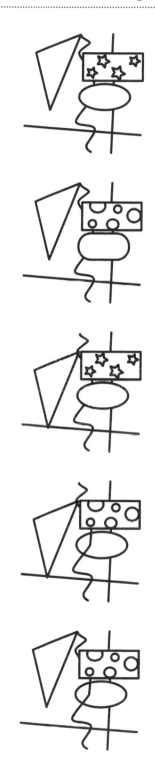

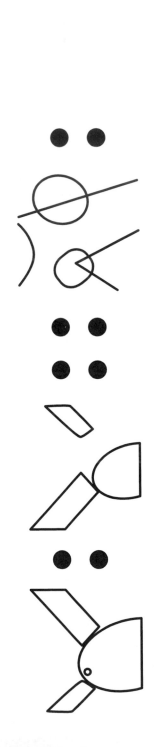

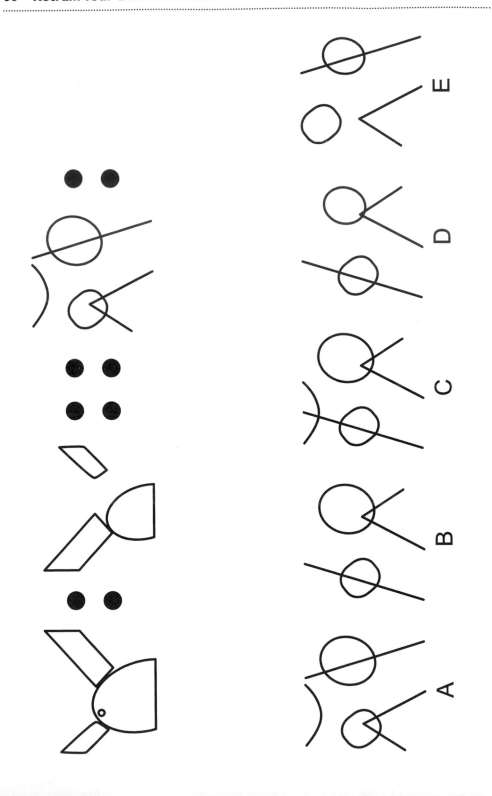

In the set of figures on the top left of the color exercise on page I-4, the squiggly line is duplicated. The oval and circle at the top of the figure change places. The rule is: Switch and add. Sometimes people think that the little snowman-like figure changed places. The change of place is an illusion created by the addition of the second squiggly line.

At the bottom of the answer sheet, I've listed which answer is best, second best, and so on and why. We established a rule that said we would have one switch and one addition. We apply that rule to determine the result we want to see. You may disagree with my assessment of which choice is third or fourth best. That's all right as long as you feel you can present a reason for your opinion.

Practice will accustom you to the analogical thinking I've discussed here. I encourage you to practice as much as possible.

Just as you want to push yourself to develop physical strength and agility, you'll find your mental agility improves faster with greater effort. Look for ways to make my puzzles harder for yourself or for people you work with. You may find that a puzzle that was difficult for you is relatively easy for someone else. In this instance, instruct her not to use colored pencils or markers to trace shapes or ask her not to cover the other choices in the bottom row. In other words, adding more "distractions" and allowing her to use fewer tools will help her mental agility.

BEST OF ALL, IT MAKES WORK FUN

There's an adage that proclaims: "Happy workers are productive workers." Although this adage may have originated in a less enlightened time, it's relevant to the situation many people find themselves in today. People work "stupid" when they're bored; they make mistakes through inattention and apathy. Analogies don't transform bored, unhappy employees into interested, happy ones, but they do have the potential to make work more interesting because they allow people to see their work in fresh ways, to apply new rules to old problems.

In a very real sense, analogies allow workers to reinvent tasks they've done a hundred times before. A corporate executive I worked with claimed he "hated" his job. In truth, what he hated was the overwhelming amount of work he had and the difficult challenges he faced daily. After working on my analogies (as well as other types of visual exercises) over a period of time, this executive began color coding his projects. Colors represented degrees of urgency and importance, and he found categorizing projects according to color was, in his words, "a lot of fun." It was fun in part because he was able to approach his work in a new way, and his brain appreciated the novelty. And it was also fun because his system of prioritizing projects made the work more manageable.

When I talk about how analogies can help make work fun, audiences sometimes react skeptically. A certain leap of faith is required, I suppose; all of the visual exercises, in fact, require this leap. It would be much easier to believe in the power of analogy exercises to create smarter, more productive employees if their benefits were transparent—if, for instance, by doing the exercises, you could make analogies at work that would increase your effectiveness. Unfortunately, many of the benefits take place on a subconscious level. You're incorporating the processes of comparing, contrasting, and rule making that accompany analogies more than the conscious skill of drawing analogies (though this conscious skill is also a benefit).

All I can ask people to do is practice using these analogies and see how it impacts their work. Invariably, they report leaps in productivity, effectiveness, and enjoyment. Of course, they're not relying on analogies alone.

When we get too efficient, we get bored. Sometimes we use the word *bored* when we really mean we're confused and disengaged. Our brains get tired of doing the same old thing. When we're bored, we make stupid mistakes through inattention and apathy. An analogy instinct makes us look for problems and answers to them, keeping us interested and engaged in our complex world.

ANSWERS FOR ANALOGY MISTAKE PUZZLES

Page 54:
  a: Correct
  b: Orientation and place change only
  c: Correct
  d: Correct
Page 55:
  a: Correct
  b: Correct
  c: Orientation and color change only
  d: Size and shape change only
Page 56:
  a: Correct
  b: Correct
  c: Size change only
  d: Correct
Page 57:
  a: Shape, place, and color change
  b: Shape, orientation, and place change
  c: Place and color change
  d: Orientation and color change

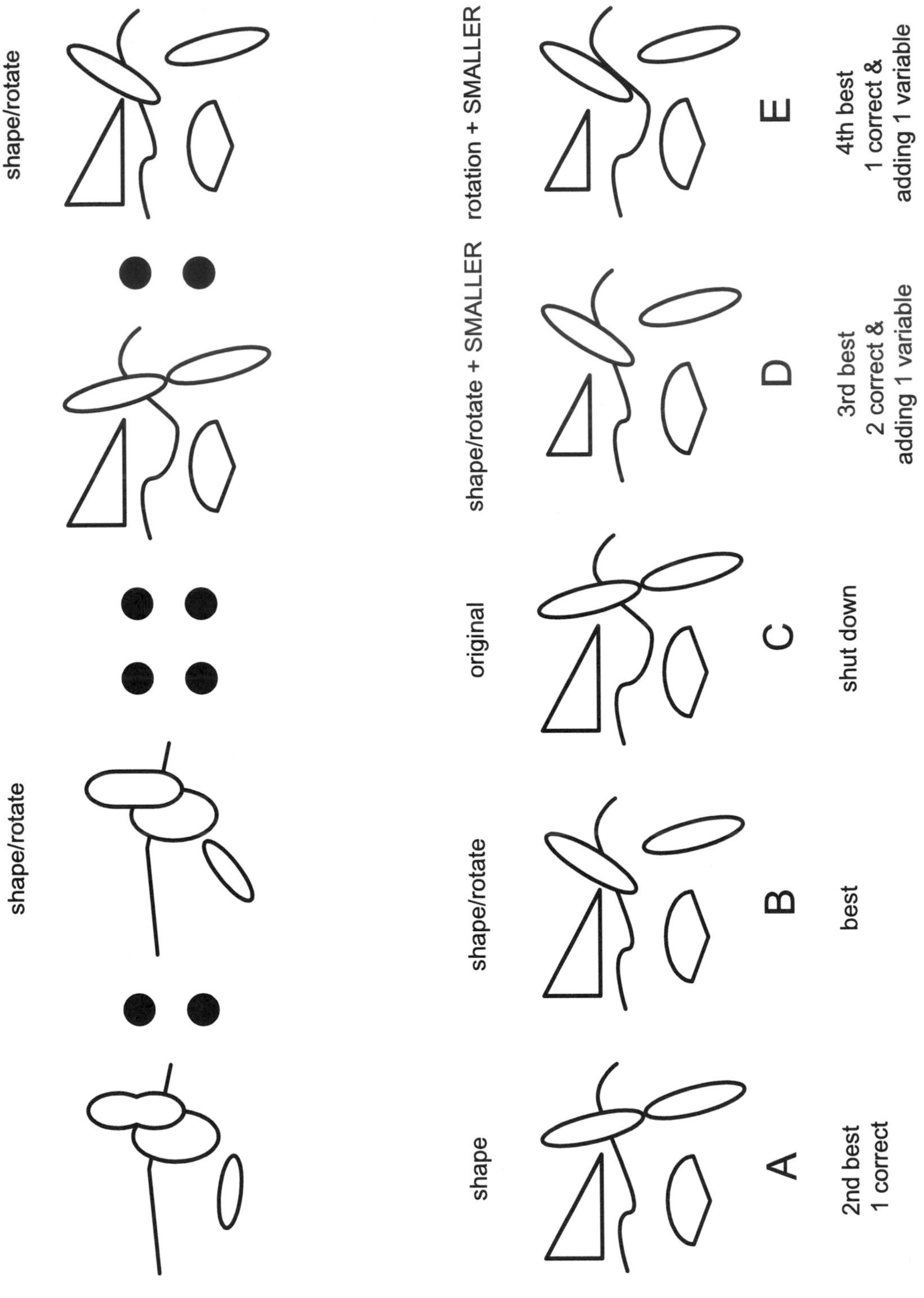

shape/rotate

shape/rotate

shape/rotate

shape/rotate + SMALLER   rotation + SMALLER

original

shape

E

4th best
1 correct &
adding 1 variable

D

3rd best
2 correct &
adding 1 variable

C

shut down

B

best

A

2nd best
1 correct

shape/down/color

shape/down/color

original

shape/down/color

shape/down
+ HORIZONTAL FLIP

shape/color

down

E

shut down

D

best

C

4th best
2 correct &
adding 1 variable

B

2nd best
2 correct

A

3rd best
1 correct

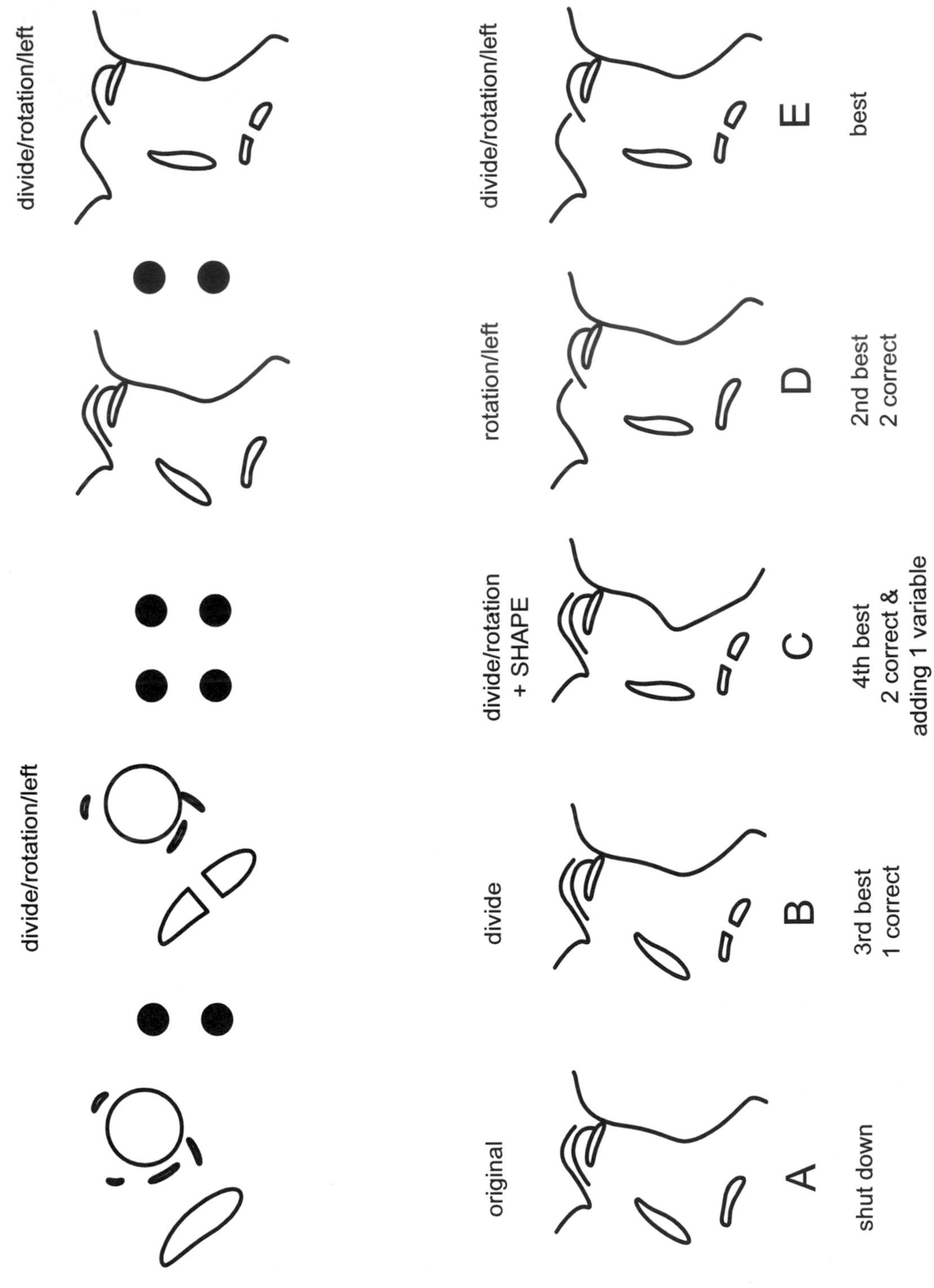

divide/rotation/left

divide/rotation/left

divide/rotation/left

divide/rotation/left

rotation/left

divide/rotation + SHAPE

divide

original

E
best

D
2nd best
2 correct

C
4th best
2 correct &
adding 1 variable

B
3rd best
1 correct

A
shut down

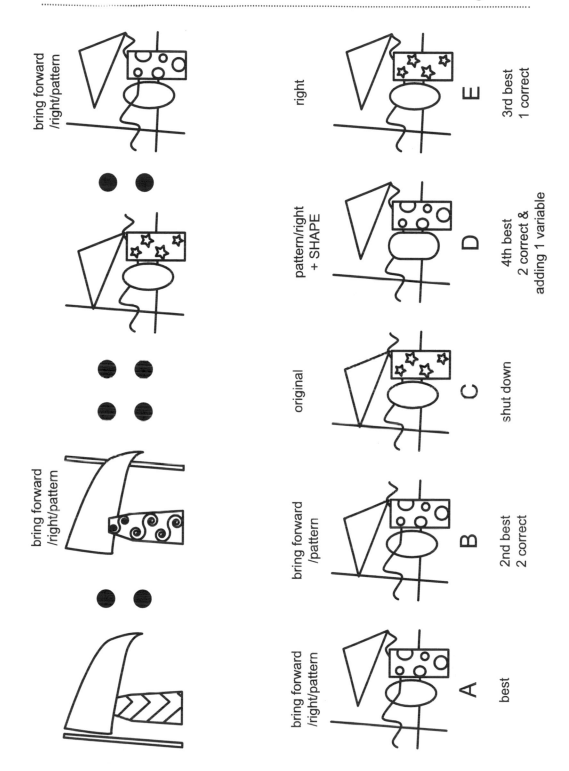

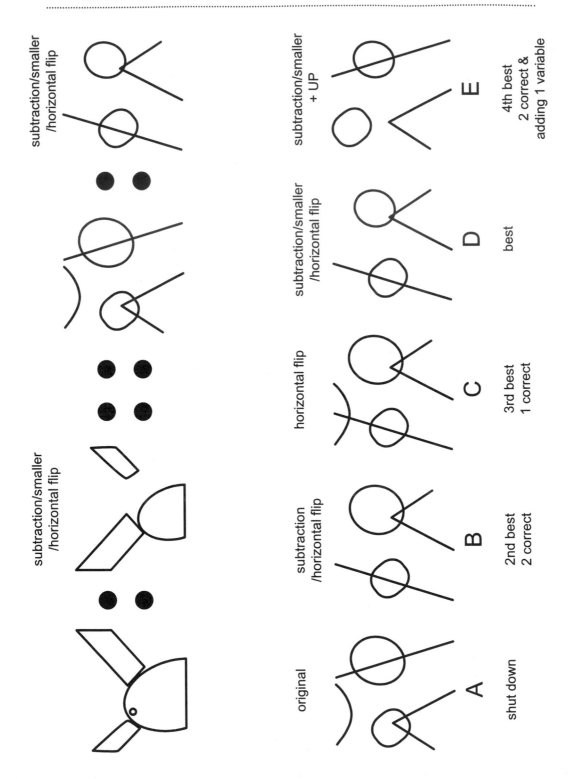

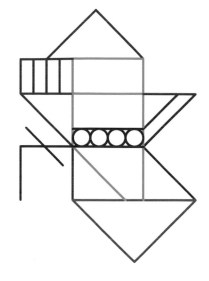

Direction Changer

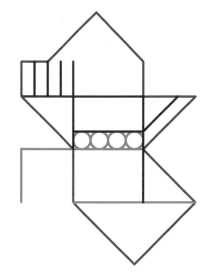

Outliner

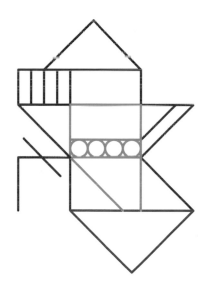

Left-to-Righter

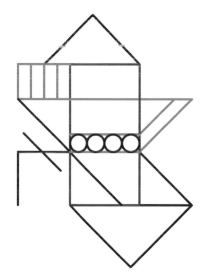

Central Shaper

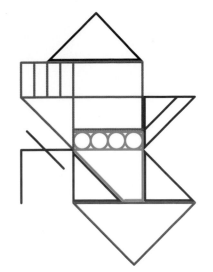

Creator

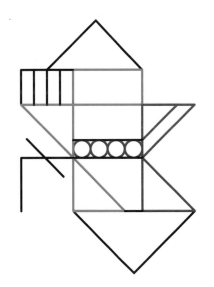

Disconnector

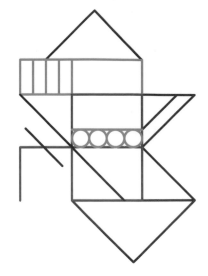

Bottom-Liner

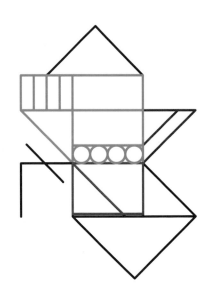

Random Connector

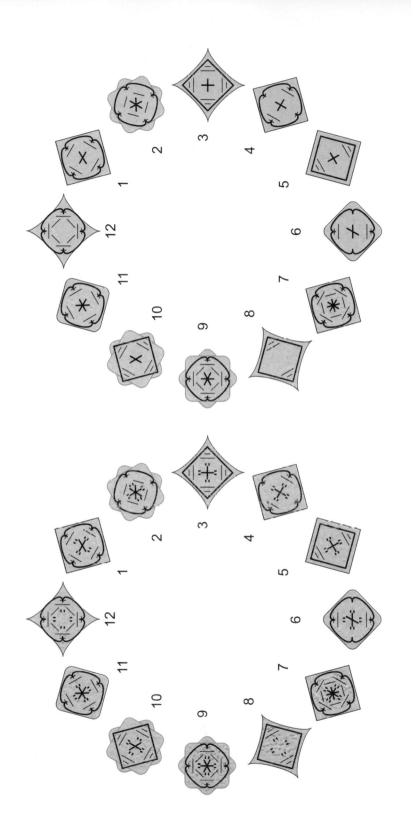

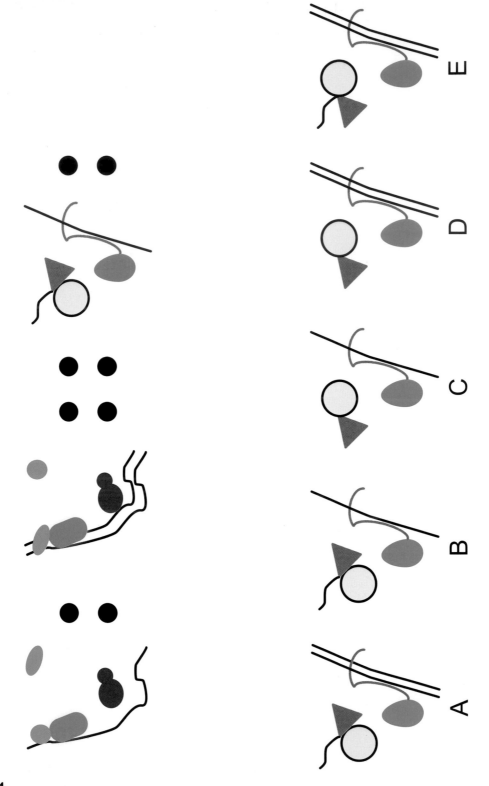

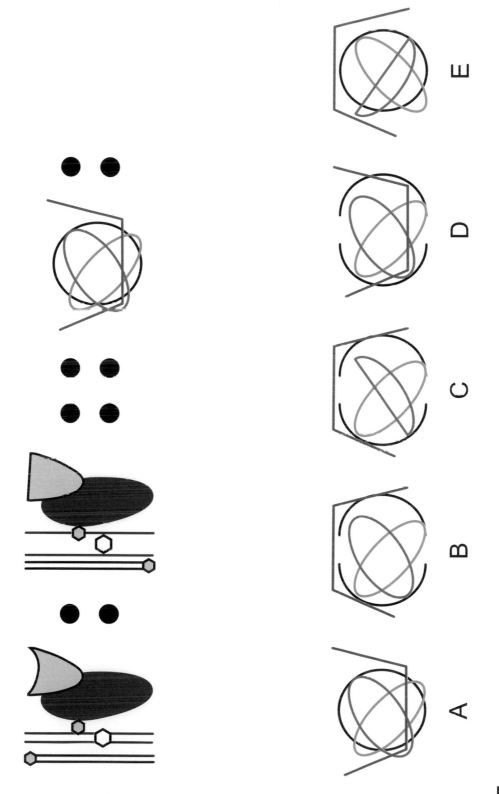

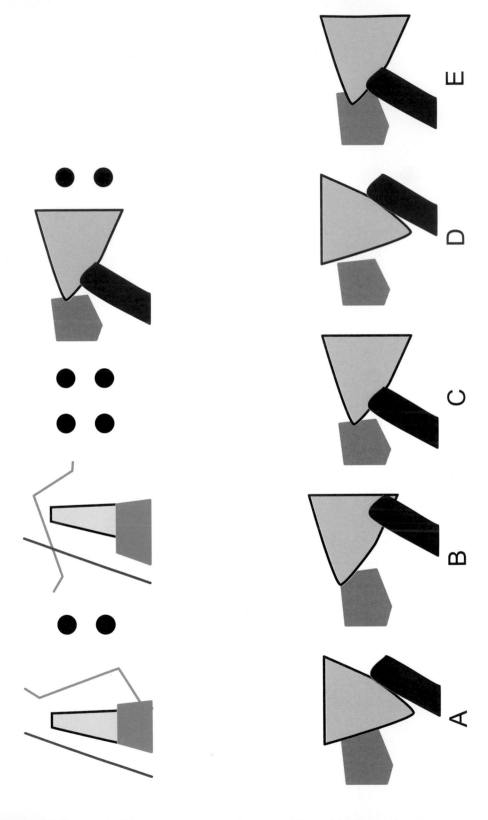

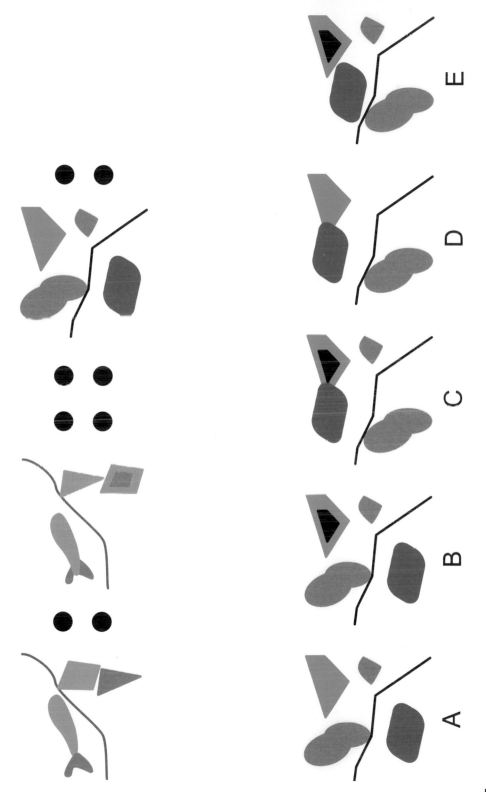

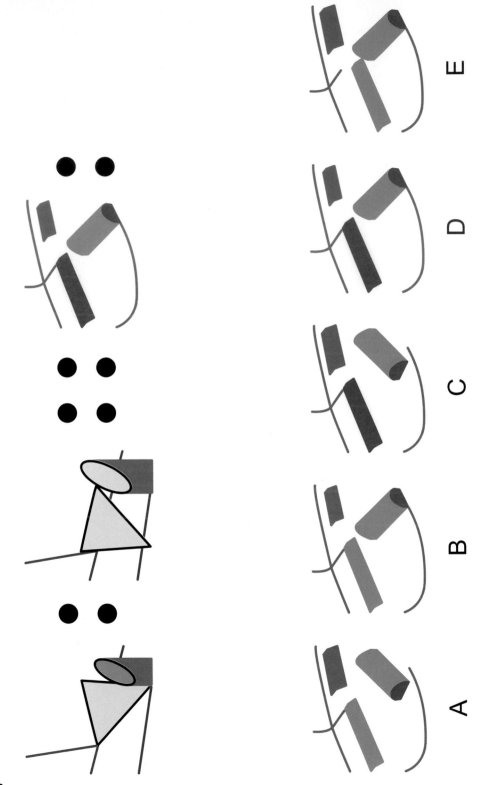

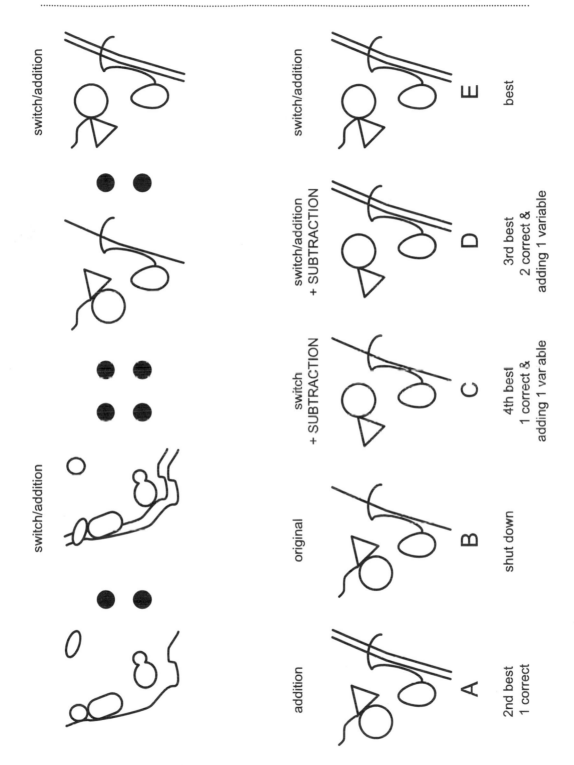

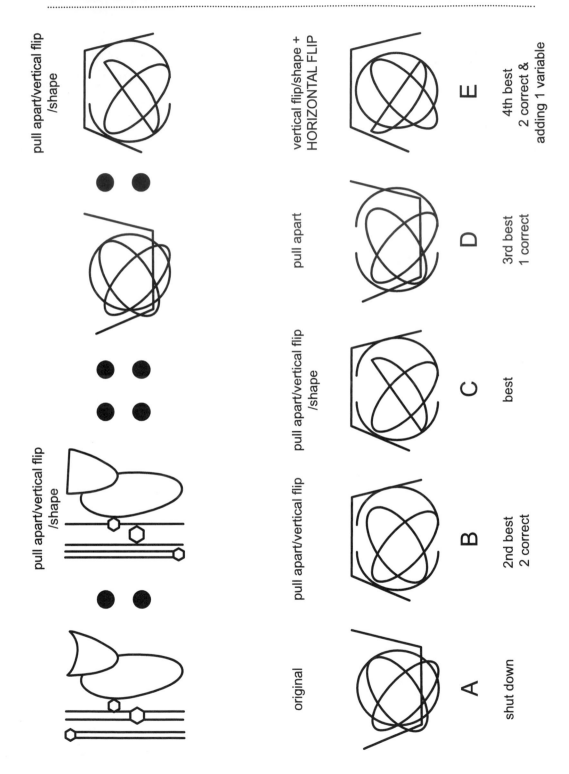

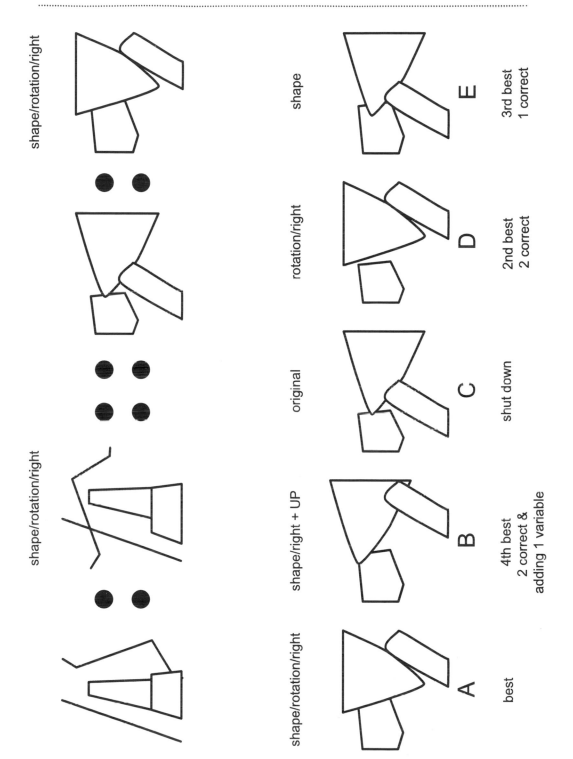

shape/rotation/right

shape/rotation/right

shape/rotation/right

shape

original

rotation/right

shape/right + UP

shape/rotation/right

A
best

B
4th best
2 correct &
adding 1 variable

C
shut down

D
2nd best
2 correct

E
3rd best
1 correct

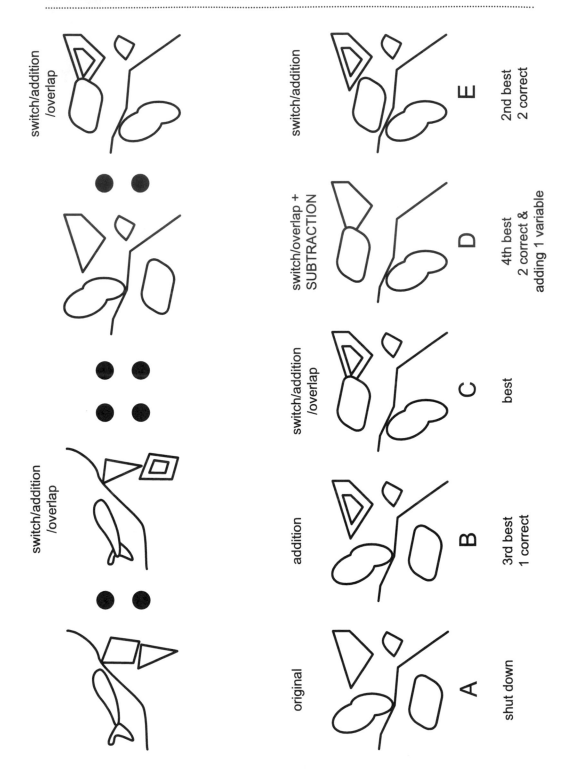

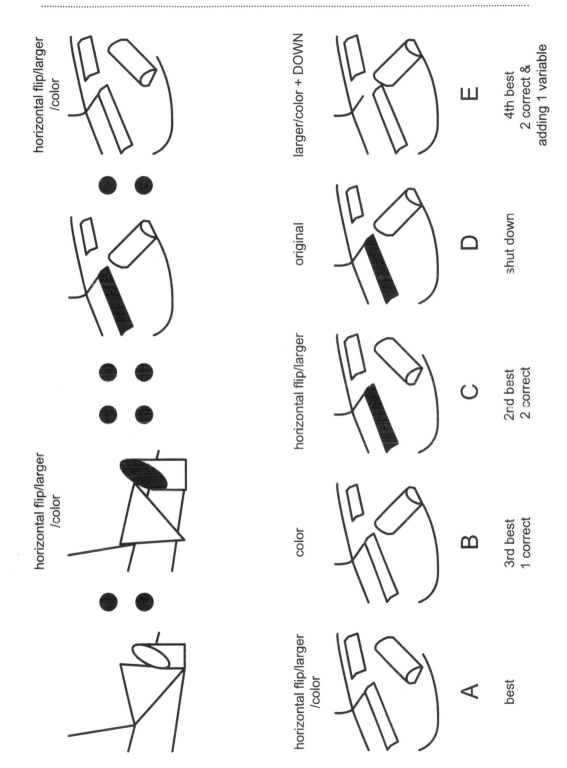

horizontal flip/larger /color

horizontal flip/larger /color

larger/color + DOWN

E

4th best
2 correct &
adding 1 variable

original

D

shut down

horizontal flip/larger

C

2nd best
2 correct

color

B

3rd best
1 correct

horizontal flip/larger /color

A

best

Progressions

What would you give to have a crystal ball that could predict the "next big thing"? Certainly it would be worth more than its weight in platinum. Some people have a knack for identifying trends just before they take off. They seem to know instinctively when to sign up and when to sign off.

How do they do it? Are they more intelligent, more astute, or just luckier than most of us? They may be all or none of the above. What they have is a highly refined ability to detect patterns. The good news is that with practice you and the people in your organization can develop this skill.

Trends have a natural life cycle. They start small, grow big, and then taper off. They follow an identifiable progression. The trick is to recognize where within the cycle any specific trend is when you first learn of it. Invest too early and you could end up with a portfolio of wanna-bes that never really pay off. Invest too late and you have has-beens that you can't unload. In between, everybody invests and no one receives much of a return.

Pattern detection means perceiving where things were in the past, where they are now, and where they will be in the future. Athletes like basketball player Michael Jordan have this ability. Amid the constant turmoil of moving bodies and bouncing balls, they perceive a logical progression based on the physical laws of nature.

Of course, athletes aren't consciously working out formulas in their heads while they play the game. Subconsciously, after endless hours of practice, they've learned what to expect in a complex and constantly changing environment. To command multi-million-dollar paychecks, they have to possess both the physical and mental agility that makes them effective on and off the court.

Second-team athletes practice mindlessly. They go through the motions, and their bodies develop muscle memory. They look as if they know what they're doing, but they really don't. They've learned to become efficient. They're good at routine plays, but they choke when the pressure is on.

Elite athletes of Jordan's caliber practice mindfully. They learn something new from every play, whether in practice or during a game, and they habitually look for progressive patterns. They've learned to perceive logic where others see only chaos. They are in a constant state of attention.

In this chapter, the goal is to solve puzzles by identifying the next logical figure in a pattern. These progressions contain several variables. To detect the pattern you'll need to analyze the differences between each image just as you did with the analogy puzzles in the previous chapter.

CONCRETE AND ABSTRACT PROGRESSIONS

● ● ●

Start by covering the bottom row of answers on page 83, and concentrate on the three squares in the top row. This helps focus your attention on the problem. Look at the progression. What do you see? There are four chairs in each square; one is big and three are small. Naming these facts helps us to remember them.

Next, compare and name (size, shape number, orientation, etc.) the difference between the far left square and the second square, just as you would with an analogy puzzle. Begin by identifying the big chair's change in place. Where was it at first? Where did it go? What happened after that in the third square? Where would you expect it to be in the fourth square?

Uncover the bottom row and look at the possible answers. Can you eliminate any of the answers? Remember that in the progression there are four chairs in each square. So we can expect the answer to have four chairs—a big one and three little ones. The second choice in the bottom row has only three chairs. The third choice has four small chairs. These answers don't match our expectations,

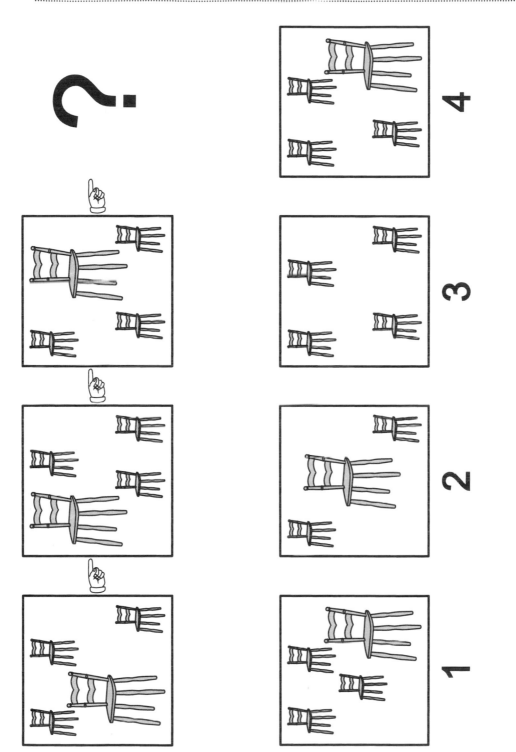

Circle the number of the picture that best completes the series.

so cross them out; you don't have to think about them anymore. This leaves us with two choices: answers 1 and 4.

Go back to the progression on the top of the page and look at the smaller chairs. Notice how they change places. Where *wouldn't* you expect to find a small chair? Probably in the middle. In answer 1 we find a small chair where it shouldn't be. Therefore, the only choice that fulfills the logic of our progression is answer 4. You solve this puzzle by making use of your expectations, which include a specific number of chairs, their size, and their place in each square.

Many people feel that expectations can lead only to disappointment. Of course, life is full of disappointments. We don't get the raise we want. We don't get the promotion we desire. We don't land the customer we've been pursuing. We don't have the success we hoped for with a new product introduction. Some people become so discouraged that they give up all hope. "What's the use?" they ask. They know the result they want, but they don't expect to get it.

Hopelessness is directly attributable to not knowing what we'll settle for and why. People who possess the resiliency to pick themselves up, brush themselves off, and start over again after all their hopes and dreams have crashed down on them always have a Plan B. Sometimes they also have Plans C, D, and E. They don't let their expectations blind their perceptions.

Expectations can help us detect possible problems before they develop into crises. They allow us to mentally superimpose what we expect to happen over what we really see happening. Experts use this technique to determine whether they should continue their chosen course of action or change it because it can't produce the results they want. Experts are highly effective because they have the mental agility to change their expectations. They are highly efficient because they don't invest any more resources than are necessary to achieve their goals.

"The Chinese use two brush strokes to write the word *crisis*. One brush stroke stands for danger; the other for opportunity. In a crisis, be aware of the danger—but recognize the opportunity."

—*Richard M. Nixon*

As you probably realize, the previous puzzle helps build *expectation flexibility*. Now let's look at another progression puzzle on page 85 and gain mental agility in another area.

Some people find this puzzle on page 85 more difficult than the previous one because they are more familiar with chairs. Things that we're familiar with are easier to visualize. However, to solve this puzzle we'll use the same step-by-step process:

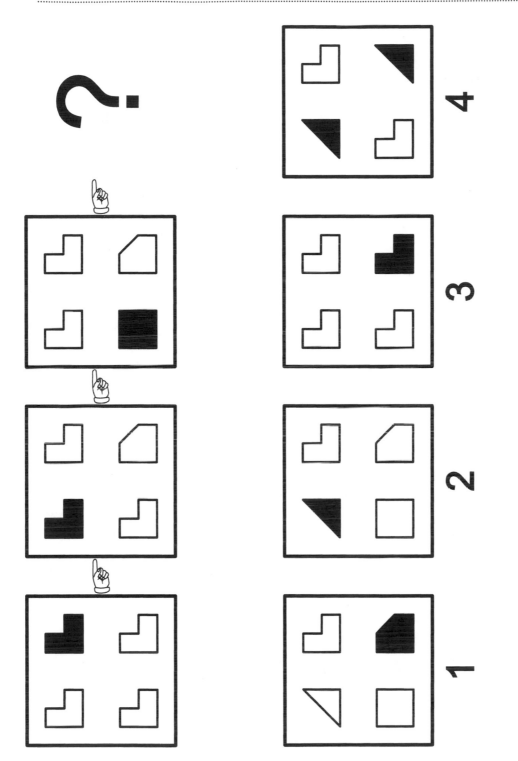

Circle the number of the picture that best completes the series.

1. Start by covering the bottom row of answers and concentrate on the three squares in the top row.
2. Look at the progression. What do you see?
3. Next, compare and name the difference between the far left square and the second square. What happened? What happened after that in the third square? What would you expect to happen in the fourth square?
4. Uncover the bottom row and look at the possible answers. Can you eliminate any of the answers? If you can, cross them out.
5. Go back to the progression on the top of the page. Let yourself get an instinctive feel for the pattern. What would you *not* expect to see?
6. Cross out the unexpected answer.
7. Before you quit, verify your answer. Does it follow the rule you formulated for the progression? If yes, congratulations. If no, backtrack and figure out what you missed. (By the way, the answer to the puzzle is number 1.) The shape change is clockwise; the color change is counterclockwise.

Because some people have difficulty rotating images in their mind, they find progressions like this one overstimulating. Overstimulation can make our brains freeze, leading us to stop thinking and go with a hunch. If you feel yourself losing focus, take a break: stretch, walk around, put the book aside for an hour or so. When you come back, look over the puzzle again. All the time you thought you were doing something else, your brain was busy processing the problem. You may be surprised by the new insight you've gained.

Knowing when to quit is just as important as knowing when to persevere. When we're faced with deadlines, when everybody wants something from us at the same time, when we're getting too much information too fast, it is very easy to fall into a mindless routine. It makes us feel efficient; we're getting things done. Unfortunately, a lot of these things we're getting done will probably have to be undone because we don't like the results.

Letting yourself mentally walk away from a problem for a couple of minutes can do wonders for your effectiveness. It gives your brain a chance to sort things out on its own. I'm always amazed by how well my subconscious mind can put things together once I've given it a break and supplied it with a goal and the relevant details. For additional practice, try these progression puzzles. Remember, if you become frustrated, use some of the mediation techniques you've learned and feel free to talk about the progressions with someone else.

●   ●   ●

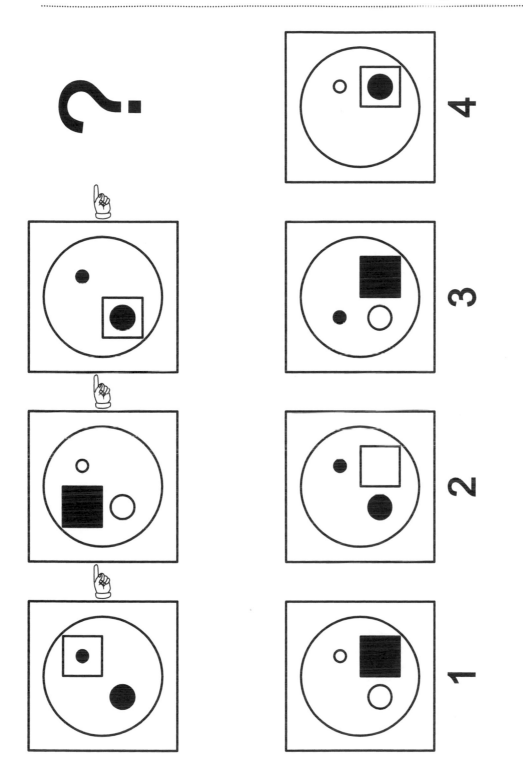

Circle the number of the picture that best completes the series.

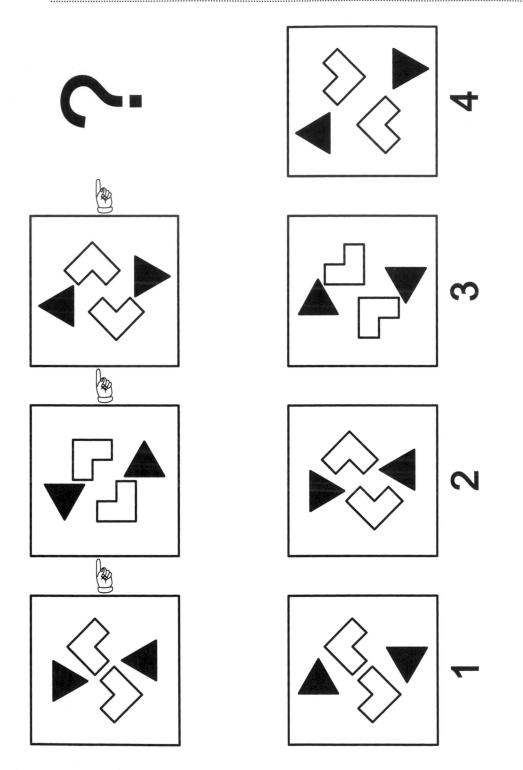

Circle the number of the picture that best completes the series.

LEARNING TO LOOK FOR PATTERNS

This next series of progressions is more complex. In the puzzles that follow, you will be asked to examine a progression and to explicitly identify the rules that govern the change from one frame to the next. Then, you will be given the first and last frame of a new problem. Your goal is to apply the established rules from the first progression to this new problem. Fill in the empty squares with the next logical figure in the progression from the eight choices. There may be some ambiguity—remember that some choices are not perfect, so we are often forced to choose the second best or the least objectional fit.

Many people find the puzzle on page 90 daunting, and you might be one of them. Start by looking at Column A on the left. Can you perceive a pattern? Compare the topmost image to the one directly beneath it. Compare the image in the second square with the image in the third. Do the comparisons make sense? Does it look as though the first image plus the second image equal the third image?

Look at the squares 3, 4, and 5. Does the third image minus the fourth image equal the fifth image?

Here's another way to approach the problem. Look again at Column A. Can you find two images that look somewhat similar? What about the first image and the fourth? If you subtracted the first image from the fourth image, would it look like the second image? Let's create a rule: 1st + 2nd = 4th. Apply this rule to Column B. Then fill in the blanks using the images provided. Continue looking for a pattern in Column A, creating a rule, and applying it to Column B. You might want to develop formulas for the rules in Column A and apply them to Column B.

As you have seen, this progression demands you use the necessary skills to complete analogies and apply these skills to a progression, a more complex problem. These are important skills, and I have included additional progressions for your rehearsal. Answers to these puzzles can be found at the end of the chapter.

● ● ●

HOW PROGRESSIVE THINKING HELPS DECISION MAKING

Life requires decision making, but not all decisions are made intentionally. Sometimes we don't know what we really want when we make a decision. We haven't thought about the results. We may feel pressured by deadlines or the fear of being left behind or the unreasonable demands of someone else—boss, subordinate, customer, and so on. We make a decision to relieve the pressure. It works. We get

Column A	Column B

Column A demonstrates a pictorial progression.

Objective: Determine which four of the eight pictures below can be used to show a similar progression in Column B. List them in sequential order in the spaces provided under Column B.

Column A	Column B	Column A demonstrates a pictorial progression.

Objective: Determine which four of the eight pictures below can be used to show a similar progression in Column B. List them in sequential order in the spaces provided under Column B.

Column A   Column B

Column A demonstrates a pictorial progression.

Objective: Determine which four of the eight pictures below can be used to show a similar progression in Column B. List them in sequential order in the spaces provided under Column B.

Column A	Column B	Column A demonstrates a pictorial progression.

Column A demonstrates a pictorial progression.

Objective: Determine which four of the eight pictures below can be used to show a similar progression in Column B. List them in sequential order in the spaces provided under Column B.

Column A	Column B

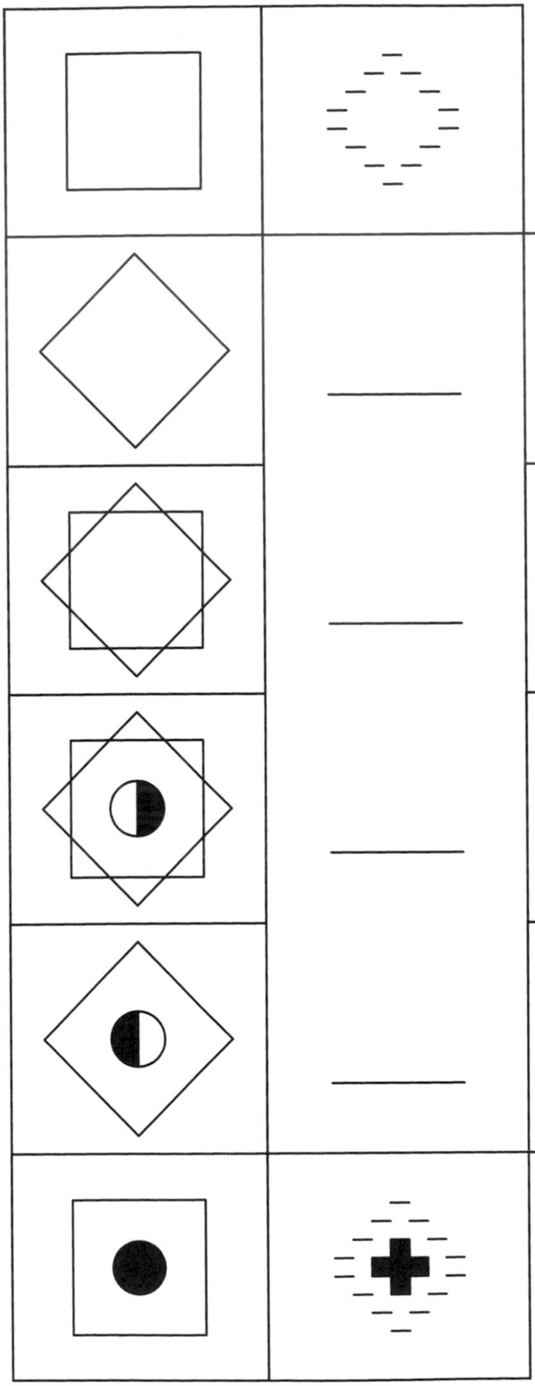

Column A demonstrates a pictorial progression.

Objective: Determine which four of the eight pictures below can be used to show a similar progression in Column B. List them in sequential order in the spaces provided under Column B.

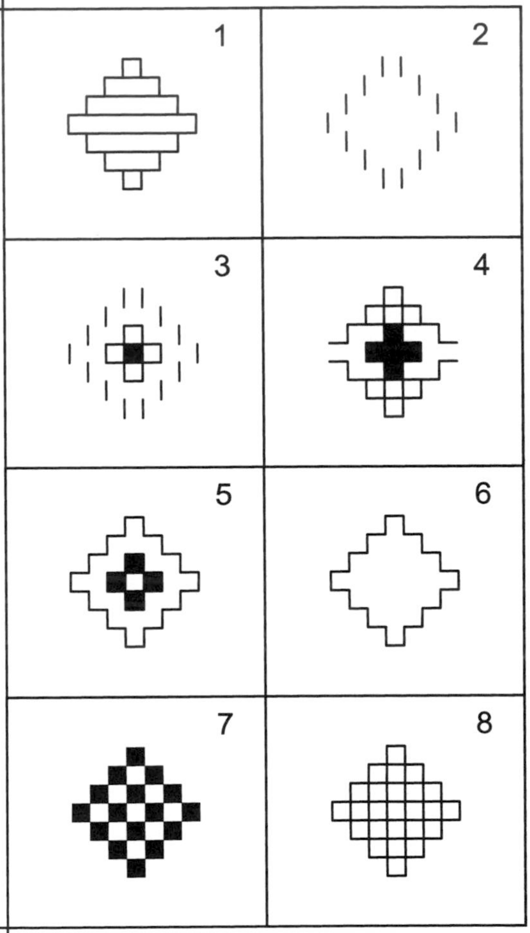

1

2

3

4

5

6

7

8

Column A	Column B

Column A demonstrates a pictorial progression.

Objective: Determine which four of the eight pictures below can be used to show a similar progression in Column B. List them in sequential order in the spaces provided under Column B.

Column A	Column B

Column A demonstrates a pictorial progression.

Objective: Determine which four of the eight pictures below can be used to show a similar progression in Column B. List them in sequential order in the spaces provided under Column B.

1	2
3	4
5	6
7	8

the immediate result we want, albeit temporarily. Unfortunately, decisions made this way almost invariably have undesirable repercussions. Consider a recent decision that you now regret, and then fill in the blank at the end of the following sentence: I would have made a better decision if only I had had more_____

- Time
- Money
- Information
- Help
- Resources
- Choices
- Energy

As I said in the previous chapter, we can't always get the results we want, but we should know what we're willing to accept and why. We also should know what to expect from the decisions we have to make and when we really have to make them.

Many executives fall into a decision-making pattern without realizing that they're in this pattern. They consistently make the same decisions about the same issues without being aware that they've made them before. Every time they have to submit a budget, they approach this task as if they must reinvent the wheel. They are always amazed and upset when subordinates with school-age children request vacation time in July or August. They're caught off guard when a direct report resigns, even though they have sufficient experience to realize that one of their direct reports is likely to resign each year. It's as if they just don't see these things coming. They don't know how to plan for them.

Cognitive psychologists call this type of behavior an "episodic grasp of reality." In his book *The Dynamic Assessment of Retarded Performers* (Scott Foresman, 1979), my mentor, Dr. Reuven Feuerstein, defined it as "a lack of orientation toward seeking and projecting relationships, grouping, organizing, and summing events." In other words, executives (or others) exhibiting this behavior lack the mental agility to look for patterns in everyday life and make sense of them.

An episodic grasp of reality causes a lot of executive burnout. People who cannot detect patterns micromanage because they can't decide which projects their subordinates can handle routinely and which ones require executive oversight. They fail to learn from their mistakes because they can't relate current conditions

> **"The only real mistake is the one from which we learn nothing."**
>
> —*John Powell*

to past decisions. They fail to detect trends because they don't understand that the past sets the parameters for the future. If, on the other hand, people can master the process involved in progression puzzles, they can become much more effective decision makers and lessen the likelihood of burnout.

RELATIONSHIPS ARE BUILT PROGRESSIVELY

Some people in your organization are brilliant at building and maintaining relationships. They just seem to have a knack for working well with direct reports, bosses, customers, and suppliers. Everyone wants them on his or her team, and they excel at creating alliances and working toward consensus. Though these relationship-building skills are often natural gifts, almost anyone can acquire these skills, and these progression exercises will help him achieve this goal.

Dan is a brilliant relationship builder. When you meet him, you feel special. His greeting is a series of small but significant progressions. When Dan is introduced to someone, the first thing he does is make eye contact, and he holds that contact. Then his face lights up, his eyes twinkling and his mouth smiling. He extends his hand and doesn't simply shake one's hand but makes another point of contact with his left hand, either grasping the other person's hand in both of his or using his left hand to touch the person's shoulder lightly but warmly. Then he speaks, and his words are thoughtful and sincere. He always seems to remember small details about the other person and recalls them orally when they meet.

All this has been learned behavior for Dan. He grew up in poverty without an adult who could be a model for this behavior. But he realized that if he were going to be successful in the business world, he needed to study how successful people formed relationships. What facilitated this study were my progression exercises. They helped Dan learn to compare and contrast variables and see how they created a pattern. As a result, he was able to examine a number of different relationship builders, identify the traits they had in common, and integrate them into his personality. The progression exercises helped Dan to develop a system for analysis and provided him with a system to hone these skills. He was able to reach a higher level of confidence, develop greater leadership skills, delegate responsibilities, and become an expert leader.

Bill, on the other hand, attended private schools, summer camps, music and sports programs, and the like. Everything was relatively easy for Bill, so he tended to view the world from his perspective—there seemed no need to see things any other way. Bill attended an elegant party held the week before Halloween. The hostess, Jane, was beautiful, and she appeared at the party with her red hair cut in a chic style and wearing a black cocktail pantsuit with a hot pink collar and pink bows on her black shoes. Bill, a business executive, went up to her and said, "Well, it looks like you're all ready for Halloween."

Bill did not intend to offend her, but that was the effect. He was simply making what he thought was a humorous, topical reference inspired by her striking outfit. He failed to see that Jane had spent a great deal of time to make sure that everything about the party—including her appearance—was perfect.

By his behavior, Bill revealed that he was not a member of the "club." In other words, he demonstrated a lack of the knowledge and skills necessary to establish a relationship that goes beyond the superficial. Even though Bill is a very smart man, Jane considered him a clod, seemingly clueless about acceptable social behavior.

In many work situations, managers are excluded from various groups because they just don't seem "to get it." A prospective customer rejects someone because he doesn't know how to talk the talk of the industry. People on a team exclude a new member because she just doesn't understand the team protocols. A new employee feels as though he doesn't fit in at a company because his previous employer's culture was very different from his new employer's.

It's natural to feel rejected and excluded at first when you're in new situations. People who are skilled at progressions usually adapt quickly because they can identify the implicit rules shared by the group and are ultimately invited to join the group.

RECOGNIZE THAT THINGS DON'T JUST HAPPEN:
Gain Control

Many highly intelligent and capable people struggle with the challenges they face in today's complex world. Any corporation, regardless of its location or area of expertise, can be quickly destabilized by advances in technology, increased competition, government regulations, global unrest, and so on. Uncertainty can lead to a kind of "shoot-from-the-hip" approach to decision making. It's easy to succumb to the feeling that nothing we do matters because it's out of our control anyway.

Mental *rigidity* makes us passively accept conditions as we currently perceive them. Mental *agility* allows us to actively generate desirable results. To succeed as an activist, you need to:

- Know the result you want.
- Know what you're willing to accept and why.
- Identify what is relevant to achieving the result.
- Establish a step-by-step plan of action.

I developed my progression puzzles to give you practice in activism.

ANSWERS FOR PROGRESSION PUZZLES

Page 83:
  4

Page 85:
  1

Page 87:
  1

Page 88:
  3

Page 90:
  6, 2, 5, 1

Page 91:
  6, 7, 1, 8

Page 92:
  7, 6, 1, 8

Page 93:
  3, 7, 5, 1

Page 94:
  2, 6, 5, 3

Page 95:
  8, 1, 3, 6

Page 96:
  7, 3, 2, 6

Part-Whole Relationships

White is the most popular color of a rental car. The social scientists who study things like this say it's because, when we're in unfamiliar territory, we want to blend in and be part of the group. A bland color helps us feel more secure.

Corporate changes can make us feel we're in unfamiliar territory, too. The experience of sudden or severe change may occur with:

- Growth
- Takeovers
- Downsizings
- Mergers
- Reorganizations
- Technological advancements

> **"Challenges are what make life interesting; overcoming them is what makes life meaningful."**
>
> —Joshua J. Marine

Some people thrive on change, quickly and easily embracing the challenge of the unknown. They perceive new opportunities for growth and advancement. They recognize that change may be a bit unnerving and cost them a sense of security for a time. However, in the long run they expect to gain more than they lose.

Other people expect nothing good to ever come from change. They retreat into their shells much like a turtle does when faced with a perceived threat. Any change, even one as small as a new restriction on an employee benefits program, may produce feelings of anxiety, anger, or disenfranchisement. When people feel that change has been forced on them, they lose their sense of "social" security. As a result, they gravitate toward the corporate equivalent of the white car. They start making decisions based on what's "safe" and "traditional" rather than on what's the right thing to do in a given situation. They feel the world has passed them by, and because they no longer believe they're integrated into the company's current direction, they become less effective.

Companies that are the least effective at incorporating new technologies and new directions ignore our very human need to feel we are part of something greater than ourselves. When we feel disconnected, when we can't see how we fit in anymore or where the new decision will lead us—no matter how positively the opportunity is presented—we resist. Because we evolved as social creatures, we need to perceive how we contribute to the whole to function most effectively. Even in the most tumultuous times, people with the mental agility to formulate part-whole relationships can keep their footing and flourish.

Perceiving how a particular assignment contributes to the larger goal of the team or how your job influences the company's profits is part-whole thinking. Realizing that a competitor's strategy or a downturn in the economy will impact your bottom line is also about part-whole relationships. Deciding how to allocate resources to three direct reports to achieve your team's objective while staying within the budget is also an example of part-whole thinking.

In today's corporate world, most projects require interdepartmental committees. In *The Fifth Discipline: The Art and Practice of the Learning Organization* (Doubleday, 1990), Peter Senge reported that, on average, it takes two years of interaction for us to recognize how, and appreciate what, people outside our field of expertise contribute to the team's objective. Without this recognition and appreciation, we may not be providing others with the information they need when they need it. We also might view them as spoilers when they express opinions or concerns that differ from ours.

> "It is the mark of an educated mind to be able to entertain a thought without accepting it."
>
> —Aristotle

Thus, we must do a better job of training people to become part-whole thinkers, and the following puzzles are a good starting point to achieve this goal.

HOW DO YOU MAKE A STAR?

Draw a star like the one below. Compare your drawing with mine. Does your star have eight points like Sample A on page 104? Did you draw it by overlapping two squares—Sample B? Can you see an octagon surrounded by eight triangles in yours—Sample C? Is your star the same size as mine? Does it have the same proportions? Did you draw yours with the same color ink?

Some people will make exact duplicates of my star. Others will make reasonably similar copies. People with an artistic eye may add some of their own flourishes to it, but most people will draw the kind of stars they learned to make in kindergarten.

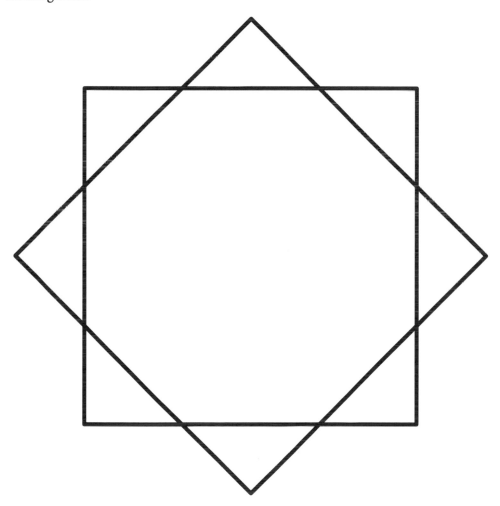

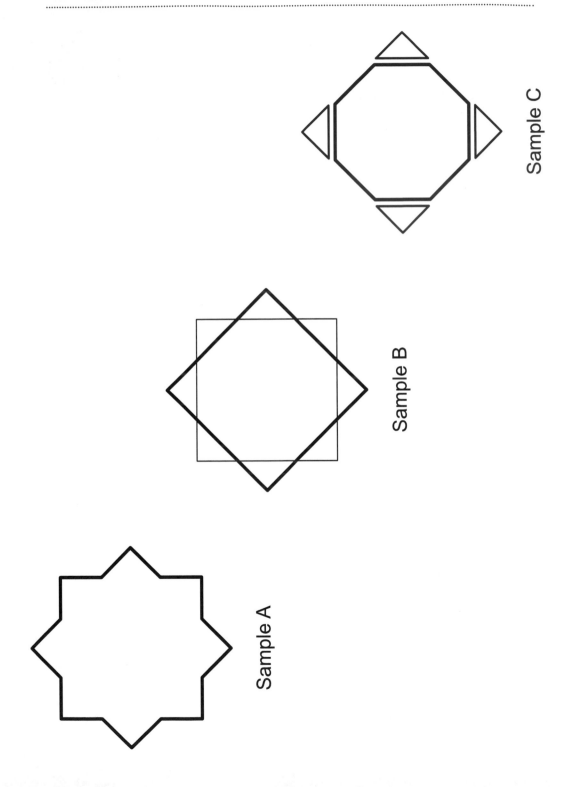

Sample C

Sample B

Sample A

How people draw the star indicates how they perceived my instruction. When most people hear the word *star,* their minds shift into automatic. Of course they know how to draw stars; they've been doing it for years and are very efficient at it. The *efficiency* shows up in their drawings. They always draw a star the same way because they draw it mindlessly.

At the other extreme are the people who can never draw the same star twice. They look at the example, and their minds race with all kinds of new ideas, each more creative than the one before. They don't realize it, but they're being efficient too. They have mindlessly shifted into their creative mode.

A few people will perceive my star as a whole comprised of parts. Some of these people will have trained as engineers or learned mechanical drawing; others just have a fondness for geometry. The point is they have learned to think *effectively.* They knew the result they wanted—to replicate my eight-pointed star—and produced it as well as their artistic skills and resources allowed.

The mental agility to perceive the parts and the whole has numerous organizational benefits, including worker satisfaction, getting it right the first time, working effectively in diverse cultures, managing conflict, and using effective people skills. Let's review these benefits.

Worker Satisfaction

Most organizations recognize that employees who enjoy what they do generally do it better; they bring commitment and passion to their work. It's difficult for them to enjoy their jobs, however, if they don't grasp how their specific duties relate to a larger purpose—team, group, or corporate goals. Becoming astute about part-whole relationships helps them grasp this connection. They see how what they do every day makes a real contribution to the company, a recognition that is tremendously satisfying for most people.

Getting It Right the First Time

At the earliest stage of the creative process, we have to define the relationship of the pieces to each other and to the desired result whether we're creating new software or a new flextime policy. Understanding how the pieces fit ensures we don't leave out anything that is essential. We may not have the opportunity, time, or resources to go back and correct it.

Working Effectively in Diverse Cultures

In an age when communication can take place instantaneously anywhere around the world, we need the mental agility to explain where, when, why, and how our efforts can produce the most effective results. Often, we not only face traditional communication challenges of working with others, as illustrated in Chapter 2, but cultural and linguistic challenges as well. We need to be able to separate beliefs, methods, and personalities from the overall objective. This requires that we carefully make the implied (or implicit) rules that guide our decisions explicit, minimizing our error for miscommunication. A strong understanding of part-whole perspectives allows us to understand how:

- Assignments integrate with team goals.
- Team goals assist unit objectives.
- Unit objectives contribute to division goals.
- Division goals produce corporate profits.

Conflict Management

When the American colonists were debating the merits of a revolution, Benjamin Franklin wrote: "We must all hang together or we will surely all hang separately." He clearly understood that the disagreements existing among the thirteen colonies were insignificant when compared to the dangers of war and the value of freedom.

Conflicts arise most often because the people involved are approaching the same problem from different perspectives. Whether we're protecting our own interests, our team's interests, our department's interest, or our corporate interest, without a part-whole perspective, we can quickly get bogged down into fighting a turf war over minor, insignificant issues. Without a part-whole perspective, we have a tendency to respond emotionally when individuals disagree with us, and we approach a disagreement as an all-or-nothing battle. Strong understanding of part-whole relationships allows us to not only view things from different perspectives but also break the whole into different parts and view each part from a different perspective. In this way, we have an opportunity to communicate more effectively with our peers and, it is hoped, negotiate a compromise, a win-win situation rather than an all-or-nothing battle.

Effective People Skills

For all the bad things that wars do, there is one thing they do extremely well. They unite people in a common cause. When we feel threatened by something far greater than ourselves, it is easy to set aside differences and recognize similarities. Unfortunately, after the danger is over, many people take up those differences again, rebuilding barriers of fear and prejudice.

An individual who truly understands and lives according to part-whole relationships appreciates that everyone (coworker, assistant, boss, client, etc.) has a life outside work. An individual is multifaceted like a diamond. If someone reacts negatively or responds inappropriately or out of context, you shouldn't immediately take it personally. Rather than react quickly, it is important to step back and reflect on your relationship with this individual—his past performance and behavior—and recognize that this is possibly out of character.

Today, more than ever, we must recognize that differences in age, gender, religious beliefs, skin color, and nationality are merely superficial. All people have the same basic needs and desires for themselves and their families. If we are to make the most effective use of Mother Earth's limited resources, we have to perceive ourselves as part of the whole human race.

SUPERIMPOSING THE PARTS ON THE WHOLE

A *whole* is an abstract concept even when we're assessing a seemingly concrete thing like a whole apple pie. Apples, spices, sugar, flour, and butter are not a pie. They have to be combined in specific quantities in a specific way and baked at a specific temperature for a specific amount of time. If all goes well, the end result is an apple pie that for some people represents a delicious dessert but for others means an extra inch or two on the waistline.

Because wholes often possess hidden, emotionally laden associations, we may have difficulty imagining them clearly. Try to imagine your whole family at once. How about your whole corporation? It's a mind-blowing exercise.

I developed the following puzzles beginning on page 108 to let you practice visualizing part-whole relationships. Let's work on the puzzles now.

● ● ●

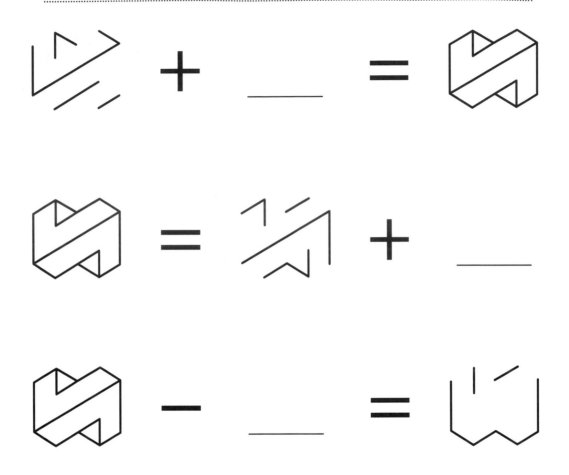

Fill in the blank. Complete the "equations" by selecting the best answers from the choices below.

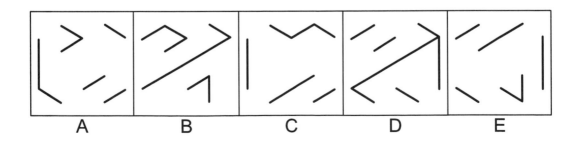

A   B   C   D   E

I confess I could have made the puzzle on page 108 easier by providing you with a flat-looking two-dimensional figure as the whole. Instead, I used an optical illusion—one that tricks your brain into perceiving a four-dimensional image. You are looking at something that would be physically impossible to construct—in other words, an abstraction.

To get a grip on an abstraction, we have to name it. If you rotate the puzzle a quarter turn to the left in your mind, the whole on the top left corner looks like the letter N or a Z on its side. For convenient reference, let's refer to this as the lazy Z. As you can see, my part-whole puzzle contains three equations that use these mathematical signs: +, −, and =. They don't include numbers, which are also abstractions. Nevertheless, treat the equation in the same way. The Z on the right is the sum of the two segmented images to the left of the equal sign.

Optical illusions are designed to confuse our brains, so I'm going to retrain your brain to handle confusion. Notice that the Z in the top row contains only two vertical lines. The segmented image on the left has only one vertical line on the left. So we know we have to find the missing line.

Go to the bottom of the page where you'll see five choices labeled A, B, C, D, and E. Only choices D and E have a vertical line on the right. Therefore, these are the only two answers we need to consider.

Look again at the segmented image in the top row. Notice it has a very long diagonal line. Because choice D has a diagonal line of the same length, we can eliminate it on the basis of redundancy. The process of elimination has led us to choice E. To quote Sherlock Holmes, "When you eliminate the impossible, all that remains, however improbable, has to be the answer."

Complete the next two equations on the page. They may look a little more daunting because they don't follow the standard a + b = c formula. Just remember you're looking for missing pieces.

In the second equation the vertical line on the left is missing. Therefore, we can eliminate choices B, D, and E as they don't have the left vertical line.

Look at any of the Zs on the page. If you start at the top of the left vertical line and trace down it, you'll come to a point where a long diagonal line branches up and a short diagonal line branches down. Look at the segmented image in the middle equation. Notice that it has a long diagonal line. Choices A and C are both missing the long diagonal line. We can't use that piece to solve the problem. However, only choice A has the short diagonal line branching down. The segmented image in the middle equation is missing that line. Therefore, the answer is A.

In the third equation, we can see that the segmented image on the left has both vertical lines. Looking at the choices on the bottom of the page, we notice that only choice B is missing both vertical lines. Therefore, the answer has to be B.

Of course, you don't have to use the pieces I selected to solve the equations. The examples I gave were easy to describe. Also, you might want to eliminate a choice once you've used it in an equation. For example, you could cross out choice E after you discovered it belonged to the first equation. Then you would only have to consider four choices for the second equation. Using choice A there leaves you with only three choices for the third equation. In this way you're looking at the three equations as a whole rather than as three distinct problems.

Remember that wholes are abstractions. How we define them determines what parts constitute them. Please turn to the next puzzle.

● ● ●

At first glance this puzzle on page 111 may appear more complex because the whole is composed of more lines that are closer together. Some people see the optical illusion as made up of three L shapes impossibly joined together. Other people notice that the whole consists of four vertical lines that decrease in size from left to right, four ascending diagonal lines, and four descending diagonal lines. You'll have to hunt further for clues because the segmented images share several of the same lines. You may find that using colored pencils or markers to trace the lines of the segmented images on top of the whole helps you isolate what is missing.

Approach the puzzle the same way you did the previous one. If at first you don't succeed, select another line and look again. Eliminate choices as soon as you can.

For your rehearsal, here are some additional puzzles.

● ● ●

If you found these puzzles frustrating, just remember that few of the courses you took in school taught you part-whole thinking. It is difficult to integrate information when we're being herded from class to class every 50 minutes. Many of the subjects we had to study seemed to hold little relevance to our young lives. We learned to efficiently recite facts but not to effectively think about results.

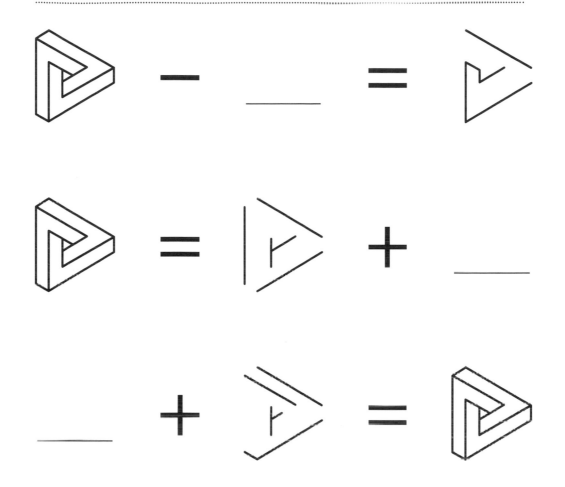

Fill in the blank. Complete the "equations" by selecting the best answers from the choices below.

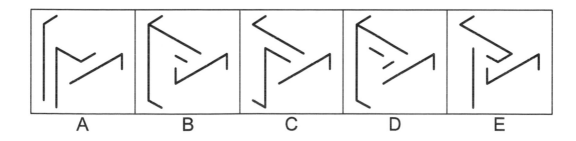

A   B   C   D   E

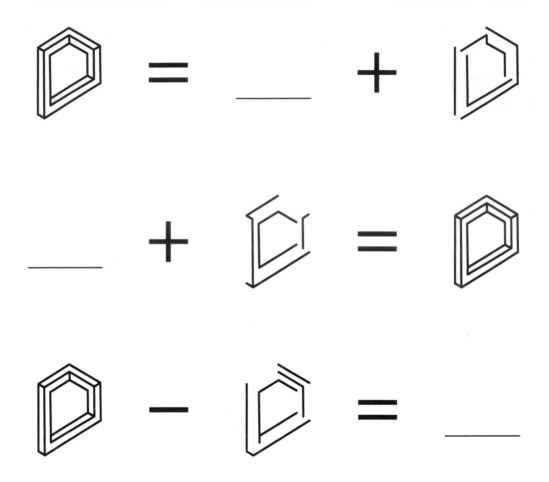

Fill in the blank. Complete the "equations" by selecting the best answers from the choices below.

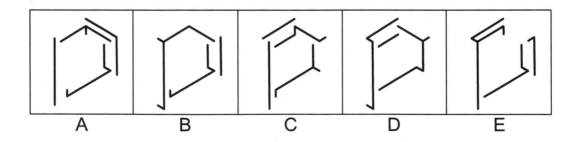

A   B   C   D   E

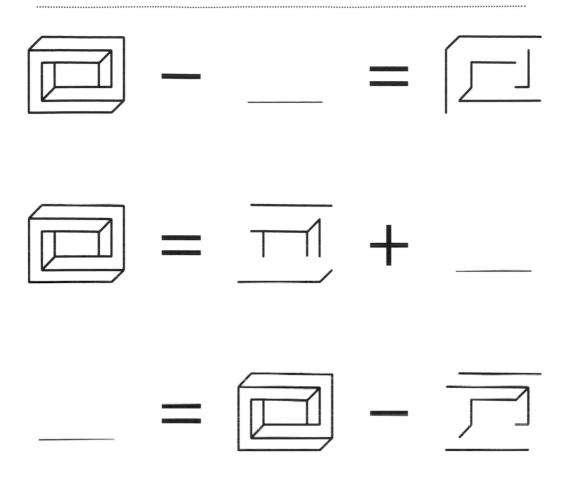

Fill in the blank. Complete the "equations" by selecting the best answers from the choices below.

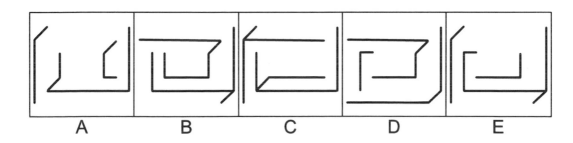

A   B   C   D   E

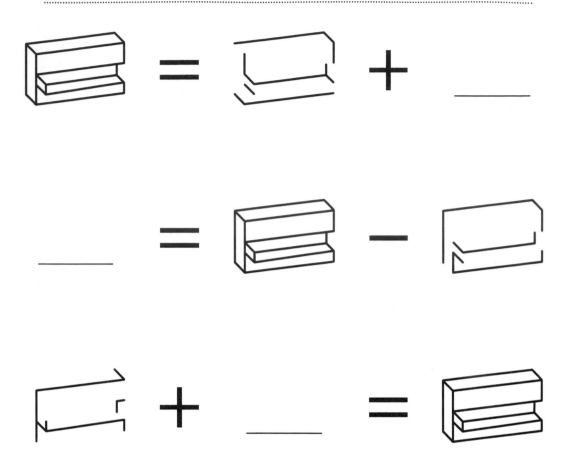

Fill in the blank. Complete the "equations" by selecting the best answers from the choices below.

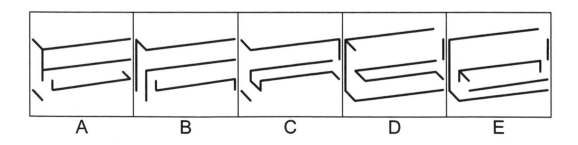

A   B   C   D   E

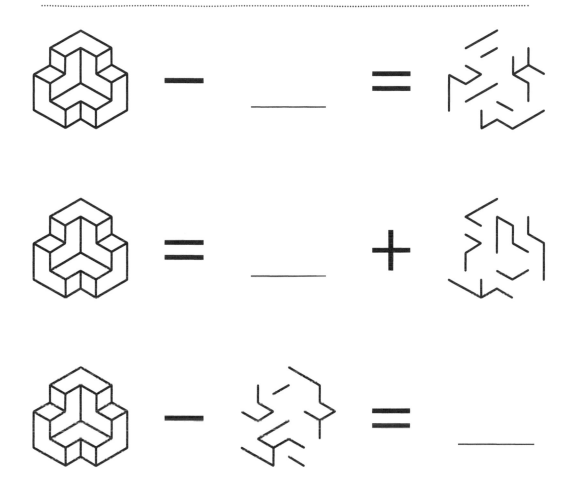

Fill in the blank. Complete the "equations" by selecting the best answers from the choices below.

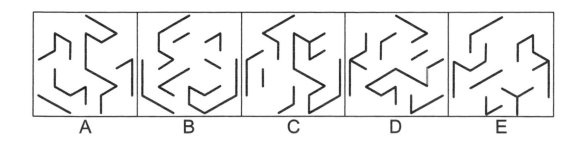

A   B   C   D   E

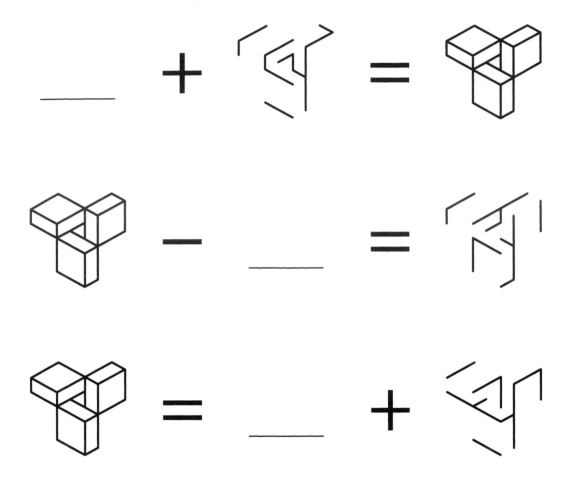

Fill in the blank. Complete the "equations" by selecting the best answers from the choices below.

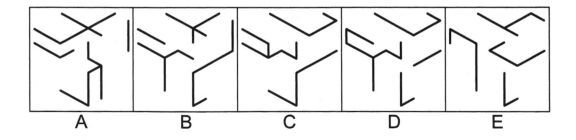

A   B   C   D   E

_____ = 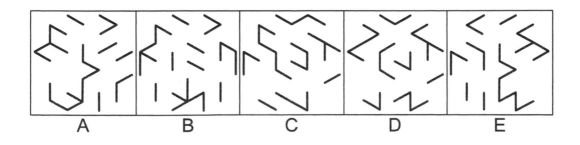 − [figure]

[figure] + _____ = [figure]

[figure] = [figure] + _____

Fill in the blank. Complete the "equations" by selecting the best answers from the choices below.

| A | B | C | D | E |

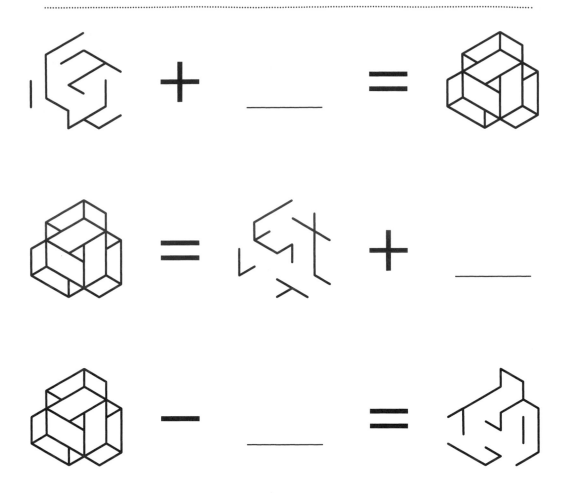

Fill in the blank. Complete the "equations" by selecting the best answers from the choices below.

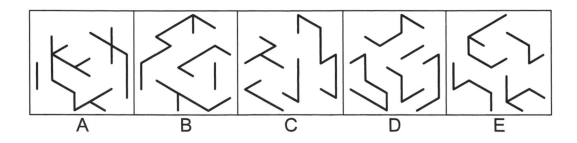

| A | B | C | D | E |

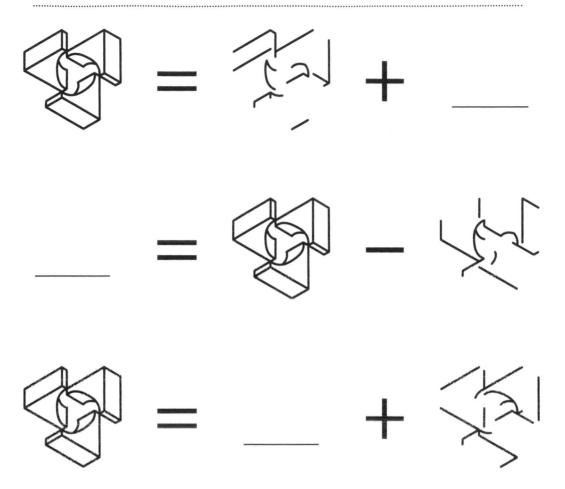

Fill in the blank. Complete the "equations" by selecting the best answers from the choices below.

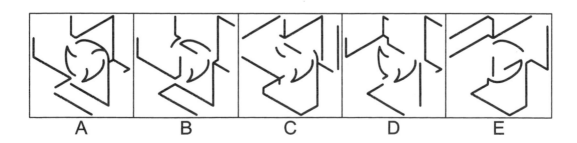

| A | B | C | D | E |

Business training programs that utilize case histories try to demonstrate how other people achieved results. Their perceptions of the situations, however, are never examined. We may be able to identify the results they wanted, but we remain uncertain about how they determined what was relevant to achieving those results. In other words, we don't know how the parts contributed to the whole.

THE SUM OF THE PARTS IS GREATER THAN THE WHOLE

Is your organization suffering from a lack of part-whole thinking? To answer the question, consider the following business-related symptoms of this malady:

- Recycling the same idea or project year after year
- Cross-functional teams that don't accomplish their goals because of internal bickering
- Difficulty with restructuring efforts
- Angry confrontations between direct reports and bosses
- Alliances with external firms that fall apart because of a lack of consensus about how to accomplish objectives
- Problems with creating effective, implementable plans
- Frequently hearing the refrain, "The left hand doesn't know what the right one is doing"
- Slow or inadequate responses to change; an inability to reorganize policies and procedures in response to new circumstances or events
- A rigid culture that has difficulty accommodating anything that's new or different

If your organization is beset by some of these symptoms, you should understand that it's not in the minority. Except for engineering circles, people aren't usually trained to be part-whole thinkers. Schools, especially, are guilty of this teaching sin. They give students one idea after the next on the assumption that the students will be able to put these ideas to use in other situations—a bad assumption. They are teaching students to be "part" thinkers and not teaching them how the parts relate to the whole. As a result, neophyte employees can't integrate their learning into "foreign" contexts. In business schools, students study numerous case histories, but it's very difficult for them to apply the lessons learned from these case histories when the environment shifts. People may study the mistake IBM made by overlooking the burgeoning personal computer market, but they can't translate that case history into their own company's strategy. They fail to build into their organization a strategic component designed to detect small, but quickly growing, markets.

The exercises in this chapter facilitate the type of thinking that allows people to integrate this overlooked market piece into a larger strategy. They demand that people identify relationships between parts and the whole and "play" with these relationships until they make it a regular part of their thinking process. Just as a strategy is composed of research, a mission statement, budgetary limits, competitive analysis, and so on, the exercises also have myriad elements, except that the elements are abstract rather than concrete. They prepare the mind for real-world problems by providing a risk-free forum to practice part-whole thinking.

ANSWERS FOR PART-WHOLE PUZZLES

Page 108:
    Top Equation - E
    Middle Equation - A
    Bottom Equation - B
Page 111:
    Top Equation - B
    Middle Equation - C
    Bottom Equation - A
Page 112:
    Top Equation - D
    Middle Equation - A
    Bottom Equation - E
Page 113:
    Top Equation - D
    Middle Equation - C
    Bottom Equation - E
Page 114:
    Top Equation - B
    Middle Equation - A
    Bottom Equation - D

Page 115:
    Top Equation - A
    Middle Equation - D
    Bottom Equation - C
Page 116:
    Top Equation - B
    Middle Equation - C
    Bottom Equation - E
Page 117:
    Top Equation - E
    Middle Equation - A
    Bottom Equation - C
Page 118:
    Top Equation - C
    Middle Equation - D
    Bottom Equation - E
Page 119:
    Top Equation - B
    Middle Equation - E
    Bottom Equation - D

Mistakes

More than one athletic coach has lamented after a loss, "Mistakes killed us," and more than one business leader, on hearing such a lament, has said, "Amen." If you're like most managers, you've seen more than your share of mistakes. Some may have been as minor as a misspelled word in a letter to a customer or as major as a poorly conceived strategy that cost the company millions. In trying to figure out how these mistakes happened, you've probably looked back and identified various causes: pressure, laziness, false assumptions, overwork, and so on. Based on these causes, you've tried to help people avoid mistakes by decreasing pressure, motivating them to work harder, challenging their assumptions, and encouraging them to delegate. In most instances, though, they still make mistakes.

The exercises in this chapter will help you and your coworkers reduce mistakes, but they won't do so in traditional ways. Think about what happens when you commit an error. You probably beat yourself up for it and say to yourself, "Next time I'm going to work harder and make sure I don't make that mistake." In reality, working harder is likely to result in more mistakes, not less. The harder we work, the more emotionally attached we become to our work. As a result, this emotional investment makes it difficult to examine our work objectively. Such reasoning helps to explain why we're generally better at catching mistakes in other people's work than in our own. Lacking an emotional investment, we look at the efforts of direct reports with a keener eye, identifying flaws that we might completely miss in our own work. We have the perspective to analyze intelligently.

> **"We had all simply wandered into a situation unthinkingly, trying to protect ourselves from what we saw as a political problem. Now, suddenly, it was like a Rorschach inkblot: others, looking at our actions, pointed out a pattern that we ourselves had not seen."**
>
> —*Richard M. Nixon*

The error exercises found in this chapter help you bring this perspective to your own work. It gives you practice in identifying and learning to anticipate errors, and with practice this will translate into an error-detection reflex. By comparing and contrasting images in every imaginable way as you search for mistakes, you will develop a system for error analysis. In a very real way, you'll train yourself to spot something that doesn't look quite right and to look for details that suggest something might be wrong. One of the exercises literally asks you, "What's wrong with this picture?" Becoming skilled in answering this question from a visual standpoint facilitates answering it from a content standpoint: "What's wrong with our new product introduction plan?" "What's wrong with our new software?" With greater mental agility, you'll have a much better chance of sidestepping the thought process that caused you to do something that with hindsight seems stupid.

THINKING CLEARLY IN COMPLEX TIMES

Over 200 years ago in *Poor Richard's Almanac*, Benjamin Franklin declared, "To err is Human, to forgive Divine, to persist Devilish." Even though he lived in a far simpler time than we do today, Franklin was a man of great insight. Persistence in the face of complexity causes more errors in human judgment than do ignorance, indifference, and indolence combined.

That stick-to-itiveness should bear such a dubious distinction seems counterintuitive. After all, many of us have been encouraged from childhood onward to apply ourselves in the face of adversity, to keep our noses to the grindstone and our shoulders to the wheel. In many cases, this kind of single-minded drive pays off. It gets us through college, and it gets us the promotions we want. It also can get us into a lot of trouble when we have to solve complex problems with unanticipated side effects and long-term repercussions.

Persistence works best when the solution to a problem has no significance beyond itself: finding the right pair of shoes, deciding what to have for dinner, surfing the Internet for the cheapest airfare, and the like. However, complicated problems are the result of interrelated elements and unpredictable consequences. Ignorance contributes but is rarely the real cause of these problems. Instead, persistence and the accumulation of minor mistakes—as happened with the near nuclear meltdown at Chernobyl or the financial debacle at Enron—generate the most devastating errors. Most investigations into major disasters and scandals rarely find a smoking gun because the people involved thought they were doing everything right and exactly the way they had been trained.

In his book *The Logic of Failure* (Perseus Publishing, 1996), Dietrich Dorner tells of German researchers who have been investigating the issue of judgment errors for several years. They concluded that our mistakes are due more often to bad habits than to flawed genes. Most people plan actions and gather information before they think about the results they want. When stark reality, in the form of unanticipated consequences, confronts them, they lack the mental agility to stop what they're doing and effectively change course.

These are the four main reasons for error-prone behavior:

1. Conscious thought is a slow, energy-consuming process compared to knee-jerk reactions. We economize on time and effort by limiting our search to one or two variables.
2. We like to feel competent and in control. To maintain this self-image, we limit our efforts to the things we already know how to do well.
3. Every second of our life we are exposed to far more sensory experiences than our brains can quickly process. We tend to limit our focus to things that have the strongest emotional impact or are the most familiar.
4. Much of our workday is spent dealing with real problems. We often feel we don't have enough time to consider potential problems that may never arise anyway.

Careful analysis of these reasons reveals that, as Shakespeare wrote, "The fault . . . lies not in our stars, but in ourselves."

Overall, our success in solving complex problems comes not from a higher intelligence, as measured by IQ tests, but from mental and emotional agility. We must realize that all problems cannot be solved the same way no matter how hard we try.

LEARNING TO CATCH MISTAKES

Learning from other people's mistakes saves a lot of wear and tear on our egos and our emotions. It also saves us money and effort. Most people don't know how to benefit from other people's mistakes, but top athletes do. All top-seeded tennis players, for example, have the same high level of skill and the same intense drive to be the best. The mental agility that distinguishes the trophy winners from the rest of the field is their ability to perceive and take advantage of their opponents' mistakes. They do this by "getting inside the other guy's head." This isn't the same thing as trash talking—it's much more subtle and elegant. Trophy winners perceive the world through someone else's eyes. To see the world from this foreign perspective, you'll need to develop some of the abilities previously mentioned—applying detailed analysis, quickly sizing up a situation, and so on.

Before getting into the mistake exercises, let's look at an example of a smart person who made a dumb mistake.

THE MIND OF THE MISTAKE MAKER

Carol is a consultant who also gives about 50 presentations annually to different business groups. Typically, audiences respond enthusiastically to her presentations because she adroitly combines conceptual information with practical ideas. A few months ago, Carol gave a talk to a group of business professors from around the world. Using her standard presentation on the assumption that the professors, like her other audiences, would like the combination of conceptual and practical, Carol was surprised, when she finished her talk, to be greeted with only lukewarm applause. Even worse, a number of the speaker evaluation forms noted that some of the professors found the conceptual material "thin" and could have done without the exercises and tools explained in the latter half of the talk.

How could Carol have made this mistake? Why didn't she anticipate that her standard talk was ill suited to this group of professors? Part of the problem involves the ego I alluded to previously. Just as entrepreneurs can't envision how their second ventures can fail, Carol couldn't see how the presentation might bomb. After all, she'd given the talk many times before, and it had always seemed to inform and inspire her audiences. In addition, Carol failed to differentiate her audiences. They were all businesspeople, and so she lumped them together and created a talk that met a general business audience's needs. The business professors seemed to fit into that group for a number of them were consultants like Carol or had worked for organizations in the past. What she failed to see was that this group—living and working at least part of the time in the rarefied air of academia—was much more concerned about concepts than were the other groups she had talked to. They would have relished hearing more about the research and theoretical constructs underlying Carol's work rather than listening to her talk about how her concepts could benefit organizations.

Carol could have easily prevented herself from making this mistake. All she would have had to do is ask her contact at the sponsoring group to have the participants select from a list of areas of interest. Invariably, her contact would have mentioned that the group really liked thought-provoking ideas and wasn't particularly fond of practical information. Or Carol could have asked for a list of the most successful presentations to the group over the past year, and she would have immediately realized she needed to adapt her talk to those specifications.

Like most people, though, Carol wasn't cognitively trained to spot her own mistakes. In fact, if you look at some of the classic business mistakes—the introduction of "New" Coke, IBM's slow response to the burgeoning personal computer market—you realize that very smart people made these mistakes. To err is human. High intelligence doesn't protect anyone from this all-too human failing. Though companies have all sorts of internal processes, systems, and policies in place to prevent and identify mistakes, such devices don't stand a chance against our innate mistake-making tendencies.

The following puzzles will help you develop the ability to identify and correct mistakes.

CREATING ERROR-SPOTTING RADAR

●　　●　　●

The figure in the upper left corner on page 128 is a sample of how the images should look. We'll call the images an L and a triangle. Each of the frames on the page should have an L and a triangle of the same proportions as the figure in the upper left. They do not, however, have the same spatial relationship to each other, since they may be rotated and consequently the shapes will overlap.

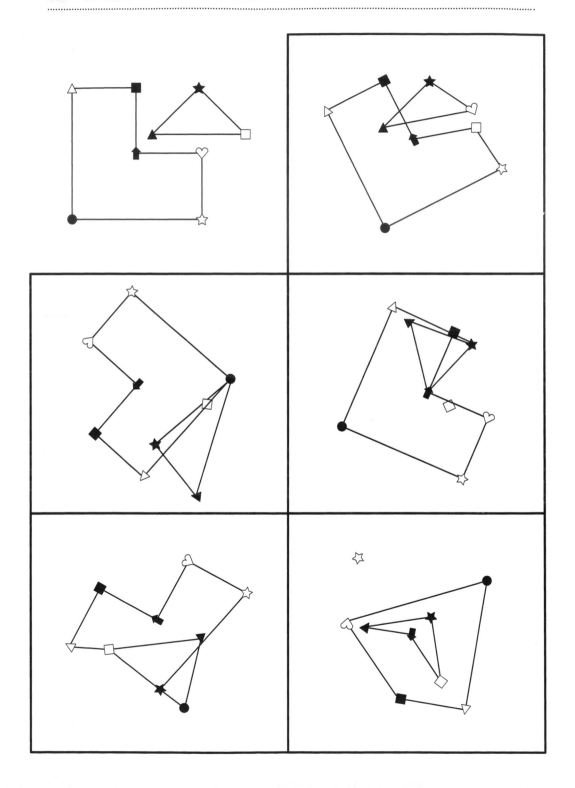

To solve the puzzle, reconnect the dots so that the figures in each frame resemble the L and the triangle in the upper left corner. I recommend using a pencil and keeping an eraser handy.

Some people initially have difficulty with my mistake puzzles because they don't know where to look first. They try to attend to all the details at the same time, which is a mistake that can be corrected easily. Take your time and look for something identifiable in the upper left corner. Let's say the triangle. Notice that the three connecting points are made by a square, a star, and a triangle.

Now go to the upper right frame and locate the square, star, and triangle. Draw a line between the connecting points with your pencil. Now you have a triangle of the same proportion as the sample. By the process of elimination, you also can redraw the L.

Repeat this process in the other frames—first connecting the square, star, and triangle. Then redraw the L. Remember that even though the orientation of the figures in each frame changes, the shapes and proportions stay the same.

Sometimes it helps to draw circles around each of the triangle connectors, which further isolates them and focuses attention on the shape created by the dots.

Another method is to use your pencil to trace the triangle in the upper left corner. Trace the same triangle again with a pen or marker. This process helps create a muscle memory between your eyes and your hand, so you'll get a more intuitive sense of the triangle's size and shape.

Here are some additional mistake puzzles with subtle differences. Before you start making corrections, look at all three pages. How are the puzzles the same? How do they differ?

In the first puzzle (page 128), you found the triangle's connectors were a white square, a black star, and a black triangle. In the second and third puzzles (pages 130 and 131), your only clues are the colors of the connectors (black and white). Circling each of them may make finding the triangle easier.

The fourth puzzle (page 132) fiendishly takes away your clues. All the connectors are the same color. Can you think of another way to locate the triangle? Notice that it is a right triangle that looks as if a square had been sliced diagonally, leaving us with our triangle.

Alternatively, notice that the L is composed of two sets of three parallel lines: two short lines and one long one in each set. The sets are at right angles to each other.

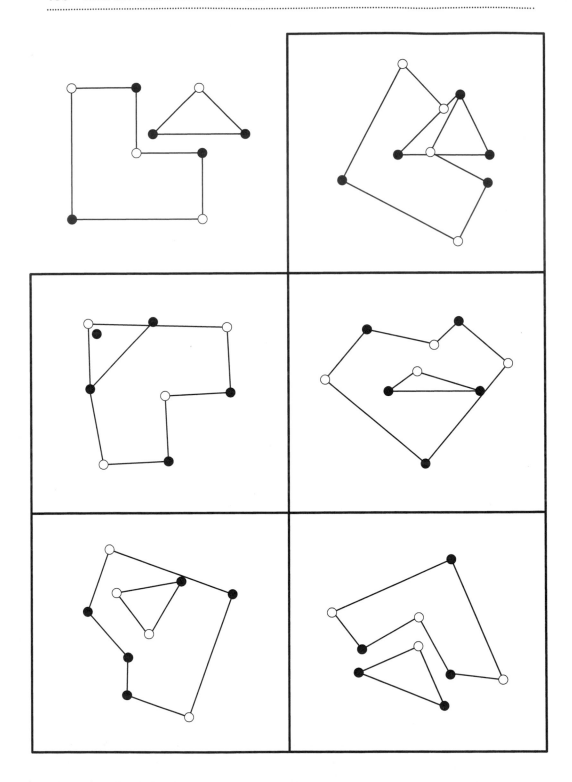

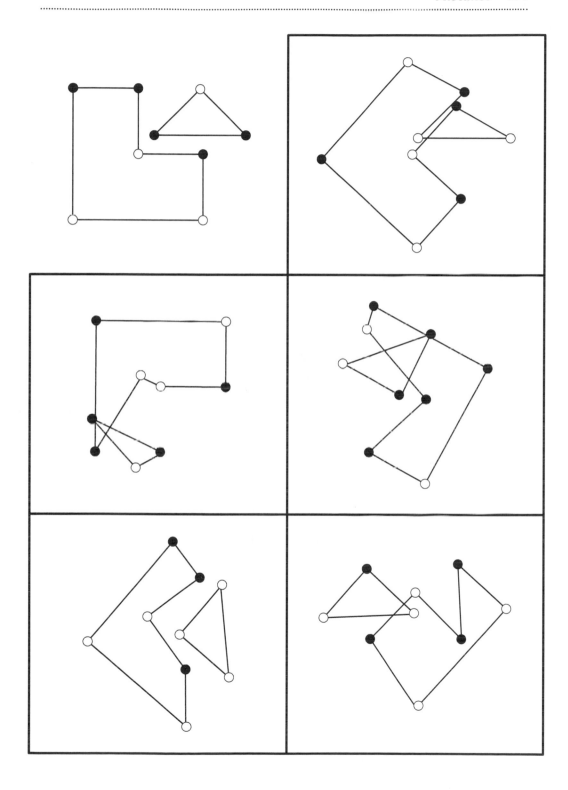

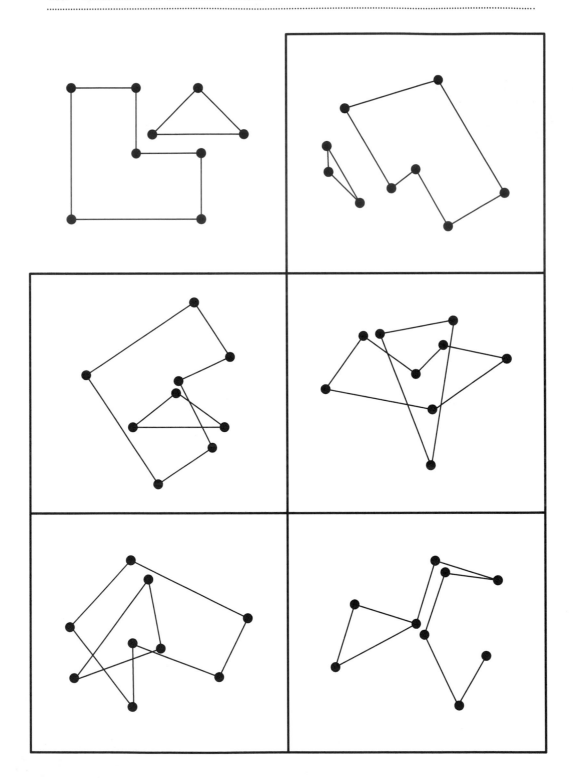

This series of puzzles was designed to remind people that sometimes the clues we mindlessly depend on to solve a problem can lead us astray. We need to keep in mind the carpenter's rule: "Measure twice, cut once." Always double-check your work.

FINDING THE LOGIC FLAW

Dot puzzles like those you just solved require the mental agility to shift between inductive and deductive thinking—sometimes you looked for specific relationships; sometimes you eliminated flawed relationships.

The following puzzle is a variation on the progressions you solved in Chapter 5. As you might expect, I embedded a mistake in the puzzle. To complete it, identify the rule, cross out the error, and select the correction.

In the lower left corner of page 134, notice that I've given you four different types of progressive relationships. Progression A is the most straightforward—the same rule applies throughout. If the rule were "Change in place," a place change would occur in each frame.

In B, you're looking for two rules. The same rule applies to every other frame. In other words, frames 1, 3, and 5 demonstrate a progression based on one rule. Frames 2, 4, and 6 demonstrate a progression based on a different rule.

Progression C is comprised of three sets of two frames. Frames 1 and 2 make up the first set; frames 3 and 4 are the second set; frames 5 and 6 are the third set. The three sets are governed by the same rule, but no relationship exists between the sets. For example, if the rule were "Change in size," then you would see a size difference between the images in frames 1 and 2, but not between frames 2 and 3. However, there would be a size difference between frames 3 and 4 but not between 4 and 5. Likewise, the images in frames 5 and 6 would be similar except for a size difference.

Like B, the rules alternate in Progression D. Notice the link between frames 2 and 3. There is also a link between frames 5 and 6. The link between frames 1 and 3 trails off to indicate that if there were a frame 7, it would follow the rule established between frames 1 and 3. In D, you are looking for three different rules.

You may be wondering why I've given you so many possible progressions. It's because I want you to become aware that sometimes things that on the surface

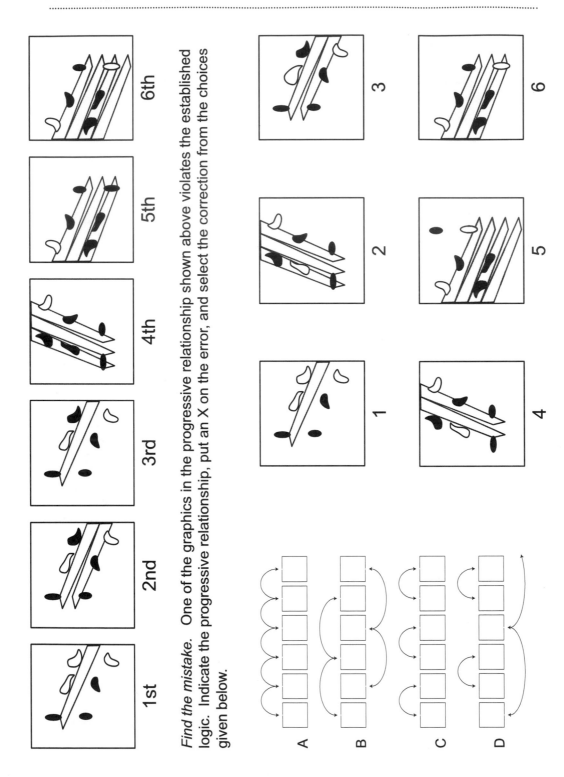

Find the mistake. One of the graphics in the progressive relationship shown above violates the established logic. Indicate the progressive relationship, put an X on the error, and select the correction from the choices given below.

look related may not be. In other words, there may be no cause-and-effect relationship between a minor disagreement you had with your boss three months ago and recently being fired. Our brains create links quite easily, so we have to be on guard against trusting superficial relationships. Mistake progressions retrain your brain by giving you practice in finding flaws in logic.

Now look at the top row of the puzzle page. Notice that the frames are numbered first, second, third, and so on. In each frame you see six small blobs of different colors. You also see long objects that resemble the tines of a fork.

A quick glance shows that the blobs in frames 1, 2, and 3 stay in the same place. However, they are rotated in frame 4 and are rotated again in frame 5 but not in frame 6. It's possible that frame 4 is a mistake. If that were the case, our progression would consist of two sets. Frames 1, 2, and 3 would belong to the first set; and frames 4, 5, and 6 would belong to the second set. Look at the progressions in the lower left corner. We don't have a sample showing two sets of three frames, so we'll have to try again.

Let's count the tines in each frame. Write each number above the corresponding frame. For example, frame 1 has one tine; frame 2 has two tines, and so on. If we just look at the numbers, we see "1, 2, 1, 3, 3, 4."

Compare these findings to Progression C. You might want to draw links between frames 1 and 2, frames 3 and 4, and frames 5 and 6 as a visual reminder. Now look for a numerical pattern. In the first and third sets, one tine is added. In the second set, two tines are added. Frame 3 should probably contain two tines because frame 4 has three tines. Then we would have the rule "Add one tine." According to our rule, frame 3 has the error.

Now look at the corrections at the bottom left of the puzzle page. Only answers 3 and 4 have two tines, so we can eliminate answers 1, 2, 5, and 6. Notice the difference between 3 and 4. The tines seem to be coming out of the right side in answer 3 and the top in answer 4.

Look at the progression on the top of the page. In the first set, the tines come out of the right side of the frame. In the third set, the tines come out of the left side. In frame 4, the tines come out of the top. If the rule is "Rotate counterclockwise," answer 4 is the correction we want.

Now, let's verify our answers. We've selected Progression C based on exploration. The third frame has the error that violates the rule "Add one tine and rotate tines counterclockwise." Answer 4 is the correction that complies with both rules.

You solved this puzzle by taking a systematic, step-by-step approach. You discovered that sometimes things can look logical at first.

You discovered that recognizing we have a problem is only the beginning. We have to take steps to find and correct it. Our first suspicions should always be tested against an established logic. Don't jump to conclusions.

We have to establish rules to achieve the results we want. Once we've established the rules, we have to play by them.

The final step is to verify that you got what you wanted. Effectiveness takes time and energy. It requires careful attention to detail and a clearly defined objective. You might as well get what you pay for—the results you want or at least what you're willing to settle for.

To be effective, we need mental agility. We have to be able to switch easily between inductive and deductive reasoning. This allows us to make educated guesses and eliminate the impossible—what doesn't fit—when dealing with complex problems.

WHAT'S WRONG WITH THIS PICTURE?

In the mistake puzzle you just completed, you had to shift your perspective to identify the hidden logic. You were given four progressions—that is, four different perspectives—as possible answers. This is similar to attending an interdepartmental meeting in which you have to understand someone else's perspective before you're able to effectively explain where the problem lies. If people think you don't understand them—that you don't see the problem from their point of view—they won't listen to you, no matter how logically you present your argument. If you can't get people to listen, you're setting the stage for a mistake to happen.

This new puzzle consists of two pages. The first page shows a mass of interconnected images; on the second page, the images are neatly separated from each other. You solve the puzzle by identifying which images on the second page are not on the first. In a sense you're looking for something that does not exist. The puzzle provides practice in verifying what *is* there so you can eliminate what *is not*.

Because our brains are so efficient at taking in a little bit of information and extrapolating assumptions, we easily lose sight of real conditions; this is especially true when a person, object, or event triggers an emotional reaction from us. How many times have your colleagues misinterpreted your suggestions or ideas because they were under deadline pressure or were dealing with a frustrating project? The emotional resonance of these situations caused them to use flawed logic; they said or did something that didn't logically flow from the integrated information. To guard against this very human tendency to jump to conclusions, we need to anchor our minds to those things we can actually prove. We need physical evidence.

In this puzzle, you're looking for specific details. Once you can identify what is real, you can eliminate what is fake.

The first rule that governs the puzzle is that an image can be a different size or can be rotated differently on the first page from the way it is on the second. For instance, the baseball is bigger on the first page than it is on the second page. According to the rule, that's okay.

The second rule is that mirror images are mistakes. In other words, if the golf flag is blowing to the right on the first page but to the left on the second page, you've found a mistake. When you find a mistake, mark it with an X.

Unless you want to do this the hard way, get some colored pencils or markers to help you remember what you've already found. Of course, you can solve the puzzle any way you want. If you find yourself getting frustrated, I suggest the following seven-step method:

1. Look at the second page and name the images you see. Not all of them are going to be found on the first page, but naming them will help you remember what you want to find.

2. Glance over the first page. Perhaps you can name some of the images here, too. Do any of the names sound familiar? Select the image that goes with that name. Compare that image with the one on the second page. Are they a match? Remember size and rotation don't matter, but reversal (mirror image) does.

3. When you find matching images, color the one on the first page red. Put a small check mark next to the image on the second page. This reminds you that you've already found it.

4. Some of the images on the first page don't have corresponding images on the second page. If you're absolutely sure the image on the first page has no match, color it blue.

5. A colored image—red or blue—can be ignored. In this way, you gradually reduce the number of images you need to look at. Eventually, every image on page 138 should be colored.

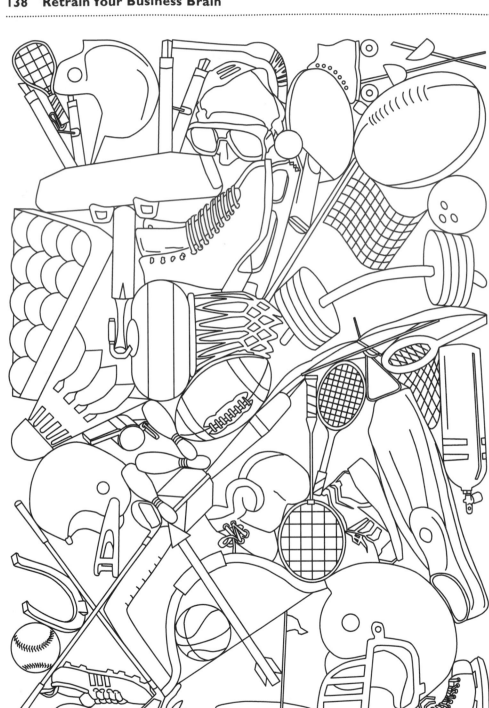

Objective: Put Xs on the images below that are not part of the big picture.

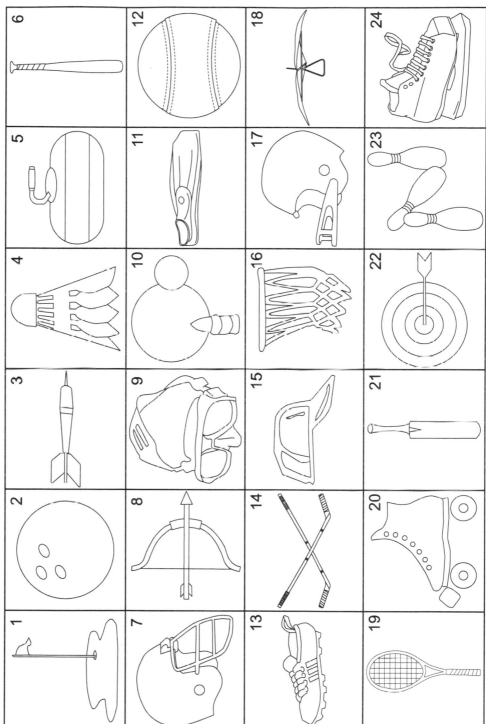

6. When you think you can't find any more matches between the first and second page, double-check the images on the second page that don't have check marks next to them. Once you're certain that an image has no match, put an X on it. You've found a mistake.
7. Continue until all the images on the second page (page 139) have either a check mark or an X.

If you feel up for a challenge, do the second puzzle on pages 142 and 143 with one or more of the following restrictions:

- Set a time limit of 10, 15, or 20 minutes to complete the puzzle.
- Don't use colored markers or pencils. Come up with another system.
- Study the images on page 143 for one to three minutes. Turn page 143 over so you can't see the images. Look at page 142. Circle all the images that don't have a corresponding image on page 143. Find as many of these as you can before you verify your answers.

Schools teach us to do things right, to look for the one right answer to any problem. Our brains have therefore been trained to think we've solved a problem once we can come up with an answer. In this way we efficiently rush through our assignments without giving much thought to whether we've achieved the results we want. In a complex world, little mistakes along the way and little errors in logic can snowball into major crises. Corporate bankruptcies and other debacles that result in massive layoffs and federal investigations begin small and grow as minor mistake piles on minor mistake. Every blizzard starts with a single snowflake. Not every crisis can be avoided, and these puzzles cannot help people fix every problem caused by their mistakes. Many times, people are unwilling to acknowledge their mistakes, especially when they result in crises. They become defensive when others suggest they did something wrong, and they may even be unwilling to admit their mistakes to themselves. The mental agility conferred here sharpens our mistake radar and helps us recognize that errors are eminently correctable, especially if we spot them early and correct them quickly.

These exercises help you decrease your mistakes by practicing mistake detection in a content-free environment. When you don't have to worry about the ramifications of your mistakes—being chewed out by your boss or costing the company money and opportunities—you're free to focus on the process of identifying and correcting mistakes. More than that, you become aware of the types of mistakes to which you are particularly vulnerable. The exercises help you to think in a mistake-detection mode. You become sensitive to the nuances of your mistake making (just as you became sensitive to the nuances of these exercises), becoming aware of the events or situations most likely to cause you to mess up. If you are aware that you are more prone to making errors at a particular time, such awareness can heighten your vigilance to review your work more carefully and even ask others to check for errors.

Just as significant, by arming yourself with a mistake-identifying process, you can fix what goes wrong before it causes much damage and even before anyone else knows you've made a mistake. If we are introspective and understand and accept our strengths and weaknesses, we can act as our own consultant.

Everybody makes mistakes. Some are correctable; some are without remedy; and some are unavoidable. Being able to recognize the difference will make you more effective at getting the results you want.

Objective: Put Xs on the images below that are not part of the big picture.

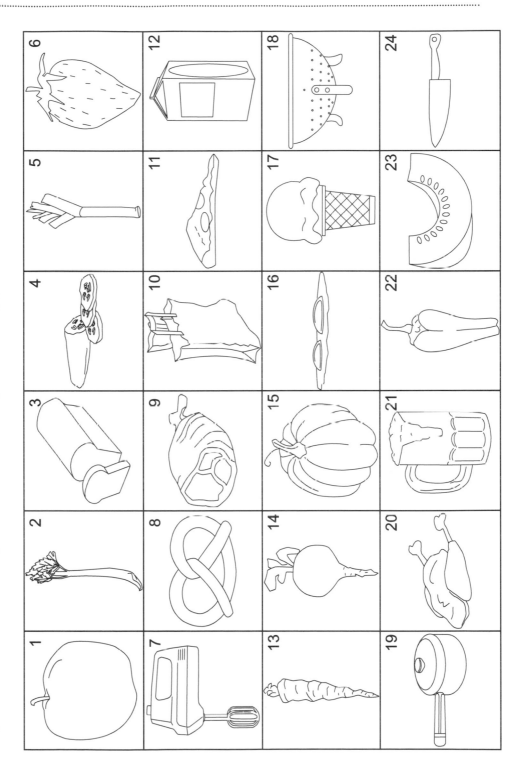

ANSWERS FOR MISTAKE PUZZLES

Page 134:
   3rd, C, 4
Page 139:
   6, 7, 10, 12, 14, 15, 19, 22, 24
Page 143:
   1, 3, 5, 9, 12, 16, 17, 19, 20, 24

Verbal Mental Agility

Words are enormously powerful tools that most organizations don't fully appreciate. Although they recognize the importance of communication skills, they don't really grasp how to help their people become more effective communicators. Training is fine—it can help people become better at writing business letters or at public speaking—but it only scratches the surface.

When people develop true mental agility in working with language, they gain a range of skills that make them more highly effective employees. **Attuned to the nuances of words, they become expert at working in teams; they can communicate clearly and translate the real meaning of what one person says to another person. They are able to separate their emotional reaction to a report from their cognitive reaction and as a result can glean what's really significant about the report.** They can "read" a customer by the words she uses and the way she uses them.

Before working with the puzzles that help develop verbal mental agility, we need to understand that there's more to language than meets the eye.

THE POWER OF WORDS

Language is a neurocognitive tool by which we can:

- Transmit and exchange information.
- Influence and control the behavior of others.
- Establish and demonstrate social cohesion.
- Imagine and create new ways of experiencing life.

To appreciate the power and majesty of words, we have to recognize that they mean more than their dictionary definitions. Words require context to make them meaningful. We understand them in relation to other words. A single word such as *light* can evoke different images and emotions at different times: *The Charge of the Light Brigade,* a light snack, the light at the end of the tunnel, lighthearted, lightweight, lightbulb, light of my life, and on and on. In *Language in Thought and Action* (Harcourt, 1990), U.S. Senator S. I. Hayakawa advised, "If we can get deeply into our consciousness the principle that no word ever has the same meaning twice, we will develop the habit of automatically examining contexts, and this enables us to understand better what others are saying."

We understand others best when we can identify the purpose that frames the words. For instance, reports are intended to help people crystalize a problem. A good report contains information that is verifiable. A good report writer carefully avoids inferences, judgments, and inflammatory language that might bias the reader and affect the quality of the work.

On the other hand, preachers, parents, teachers, propagandists, politicians, and employers use directives to influence and control the future behavior of their listeners or readers. Directives promise rewards and/or consequences. Those that have the strongest impact engage people's emotions through the dramatic application of tone, rhyme, rhythm, and repetition, devices through which the message is embedded in our memory.

Words are so much a part of our human experience that we need a way to disengage ourselves from them. We disengage by turning words into objects—by playing word games. People who play with words are more conscious of the subtleties and innuendos that conversations contain and are less likely to be swayed by emotional appeals or fall victim to their own prejudices.

At first glance the puzzles in this chapter look different from the others in the book. Instead of images, you'll encounter words. To solve my word puzzles, you have to employ the same mental agility you did for my graphic puzzles:

- Compare details.
- Separate parts from wholes.
- Identify progressions.
- Define rules.
- Establish systems.

Some people find these word puzzles much easier to solve than the graphic ones. They realize that most words have multiple meanings and are best understood in relation to other words. Other people think the puzzles in this chapter are harder. Like many of the early computer scientists who struggled with artificial intelligence programs, these people perceive words as having single meanings that can be isolated from context. Most people, however, are somewhere in between the two extremes—they enjoy a good joke but sometimes miss the innuendo of a pun.

Don't expect my word puzzles to immediately improve your vocabulary or writing skills. They don't work at that level. I designed them to enhance mental agility—to help you break away from your efficient communication style and develop an appreciation for the subtleties and multiple dimensions of language. By *playing* with words instead of *working* with them, you'll learn to disengage yourself from their emotional impact and detect the emotional value certain words have for other people. You'll be a more effective communicator when you recognize that carefully chosen words are the master keys to getting the results you want.

> **"A sense of humor is part of the art of leadership, of getting along with people, of getting things done."**
>
> —Dwight D. Eisenhower

WHAT WORDS ARE WORTH TO A CORPORATION

"Businessese," like any type of jargon, often causes confusion more than clarity. When we spend most of our time with specialists in our field, we fall into the habit of talking in a kind of code. A story told about the Friar's Club, a famous hangout for entertainers, centered on a veteran comic who one day brought a new up-and-comer to the club. During dinner someone shouted out "342." Laughter erupted around the room, and then things quieted down. Soon someone else yelled "157"; again, tumultuous laughter. This continued throughout dinner, and the new kid watched in fascination. Finally, he got up the nerve to yell as loud as he could "291." Dead silence. Even the waiters stopped serving for a moment. Then the old comic leaned forward, patted the kid on the arm and said, "It's all in the delivery."

Veteran comedians were so familiar with all the old jokes that they had numbered them for convenience. The code number reminded them of the entire joke. Of course, the new kid had no way of knowing this; to him the numbers were random and meaningless. He was so happy to be invited to the club and wanted so much to belong that he just couldn't admit he didn't know what the numbers meant. He wanted to be in on the joke. He wanted the other comics to respect his intelligence.

It is very hard for intelligent people to admit that they don't understand something. When we were in school, we quickly discovered that teachers most often called on the kids who looked as though they didn't know the right answer. So we practiced the "knowing look." We'd raise our hands with an air of confidence. We weren't confident of the right answer, but we were pretty confident we wouldn't be called on and embarrassed.

When people in organizations pretend to have knowledge they lack, they can create major problems. You've probably seen the results of managers making decisions without adequate knowledge or people losing deals because they lacked sufficient information to make a credible presentation. "Faking it" is standard operating procedure in many companies, where saying "I don't know" is considered a major blunder. Leaders often assume that they must act as if they know exactly what they're doing or their people will lose confidence in them. The result, of course, is that people eventually lose confidence in the leaders because by faking it, they actually make unnecessary mistakes.

> **"I was born not knowing and have had only a little time to change that here and there."**
>
> —*Richard Feynman*

I also want to bring out a second point in the Friar's Club story—it's not just what you say; it's how you say it. Miscommunication and/or misinterpretation are inevitably the result of misperception. The speaker perceives the problem one way, the listener another. In a matter of minutes, a part-whole speaker can lose the attention of a progression listener. Likewise, a progression speaker may seem gruff and uninteresting to an analogy listener. Understanding how you prefer to organize information is the first step to becoming a more effective communicator. Recognizing how someone else organizes information is essential to getting the results you want. Given the opportunity to intentionally practice recognizing the different communication styles in the form of these puzzles, you become more attuned to different styles of communication and less likely to misinterpret what someone else says.

WHAT WORDS ARE WORTH TO A CORPORATE CAREER

Stephanie, a financial wizard, was stuck in middle management. She knew the recreational products industry like the back of her hand, speaking quickly and to the point. She prided herself on her efficiency, but her direct reports regarded her as uninspiring and lacking empathy. She wasn't intentionally mean, but sometimes she seemed inconsiderate, particularly when a deadline was looming.

Stephanie came to me because she was getting older and was tired of "spinning her wheels." Her last performance review questioned her leadership skills. She confessed that her group noticeably lacked initiative and enthusiasm for their work.

As we discussed her job, I was impressed by how much Stephanie enjoyed her work. When I asked about her relationship with direct reports, though, her voice became monotone and staccato. She communicated with her direct reports in an efficient, no-nonsense manner, sounding almost robotic and as interesting as a laundry list. I immediately realized that Stephanie's efficient manner inevitably rubbed people the wrong way.

I told her I wasn't going to give her a quick-and-dirty course in executive leadership or teach her how to motivate people to work harder. The way I saw it was that her direct reports already were being pressed pretty hard. She had just lost two good people—one transferred out of her group and the other left the company. Stephanie didn't know why they had left her department.

As I explained my work, I could see doubt creeping into her eyes. She wasn't sure what she was getting herself into, but she had been to all the leadership seminars, listened to all the tapes, and read all the books. Stephanie regarded me as her last hope. I wasn't insulted or surprised; a lot of my corporate clients think of me that way.

We started with the complex figure, the same one I gave you in Chapter 1. As you might expect, Stephanie was a left-to-righter. I talked her through my other puzzles. She came back week after week, month after month. The puzzles didn't become easier, but she found herself enjoying them more.

Then one day at work she noticed something different about herself. Edward, a direct report, had made an expensive error. She was certain he knew better and told him so, but not in her old efficient way. Stephanie knew she needed Edward. Her group was short-staffed and crunch time was coming. She heard herself telling Edward how much she had appreciated his work in the past, that everybody had been putting in a lot of overtime lately, and that things weren't going to get easier anytime soon. She pointed out his mistake but said she knew it was unintentional. Then Stephanie said something that surprised even herself. She asked what she could do to make his work easier.

After an uncomfortable minute of silence, Edward admitted it bothered him when Stephanie looked over his shoulder when he was working. When she stood behind him, it stymied his thinking. He couldn't say for certain that was how he had made the error, but it might have been.

Stephanie now describes that moment as the turning point in her career. She started noticing the way her words affected direct reports, bosses, and others. She's out of her rut too. The last time I heard from Stephanie she had just been made a vice president of that recreational products company.

RELATIONSHIPS BETWEEN WORDS

Now that you have a strong understanding of verbal mental agility, let's get started on some puzzles.

●   ●   ●

The left column on puzzle page 151 has curved arrows that probably remind you of the progression puzzle you solved in the last chapter. On the other hand, if you read the instruction at the top of the page, you know you're looking for analogies. My word puzzle is a kind of hybrid. It looks similar to the problems you'd find on an IQ test, but appearances can be deceiving, as you learned by solving the mistake puzzles.

In IQ tests you're given three out of four words and a multiple choice to complete an analogy. Because my word puzzle provides practice in pattern detection, I've given you all four words. I want you to draw arrows to illustrate *how* the four words are related to each other.

Look at pattern A in the left column. The arrows indicate a simple progressive relationship between the words. Notice also that all the words belong to the same category. Let's label it "emotional responses to someone else." From *despise* the degree of attractiveness gradually improves until we reach *admire.* The logic progresses from the first word to the second; from the second to the third; and, finally, from the third to the fourth.

In pattern B the first word is generally associated with the third word. The second word is generally associated with the fourth word. *Pacific* is a kind of *ocean,* and *Jupiter* is a kind of *planet.*

Draw arrows as shown to best illustrate the relationships in the given analogies.

A despise : dislike :: like : admire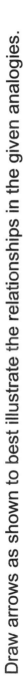

B Pacific : Jupiter :: ocean : planet

C lion : sphinx :: eagle : phoenix

D mitt : glove :: boxer : catcher

1. passenger : guest :: visitor : traveler

2. Ohio : Missouri :: Oklahoma : California

3. derby : rally :: horse : car

4. China : Australia :: panda : platypus

5. squat : bend :: stand : stretch

6. sorry : small :: sound : vigorous

7. legislator : jury :: lawyer : lobbyist

8. blemish : fault :: defect : deficiency

9. cowardly : yellow :: gloomy : blue

10. battle : rainfall :: skirmish : drizzle

For pattern C we link the first word to the second and the third word to the fourth. A *lion* is a real mammal, and a *sphinx* is a mythological mammal. An *eagle* is a real bird, and a *phoenix* is a mythological bird. Actually, there are multiple relationships here. The first one we recognize is a general category we'll call "type of animal," a category that has two subcategories—mammal and bird. Another relationship is that between fact and fantasy. Lions and eagles belong to the category of real animals, whereas the sphinx and the phoenix belong to mythological animals. The key to recognizing an analogy is that the words can be grouped in many different ways.

Pattern D also has several relationships. A *mitt* and a *glove* are both worn on the hand; *boxer* and *catcher* are both athletes. We just found two categories. Can we establish a relationship between athletes and what they wear on their hands? Catchers wear mitts. Boxers wear gloves. Is there a similarity between a catcher's mitt and a boxer's glove? Both are sports equipment worn on the hands. We have to mentally reverse the word order to solve this puzzle. The link is between the first word and the fourth, and between the second word and the third.

So how do we solve these word puzzles? Do one or more of the following:

Overlay each word series on patterns A, B, C, and D. Look at problem 1 in the middle column—"passenger : guest :: visitor : traveler."

Pattern A describes a progressive relationship within a category. Passengers, guests, visitors, and travelers are all people away from home. Is there a gradual change in degree between passenger and guest? No, the question doesn't make any sense. Therefore, we can eliminate pattern A.

What about pattern B? Do we generally associate passenger with visitor and guest with traveler? Is a passenger a kind of visitor and a guest a kind of traveler? Maybe, but the association isn't very strong. We'll hold B in reserve in case we don't find anything better.

Let's look at pattern C, remembering we are looking for multiple relationships here. C is a classic example of an analogy. Read "passenger : guest :: visitor : traveler" as "passenger is to guest as visitor is to traveler." As we already discovered, we have one category—people away from home. Are there any others? Yes, but we'd have to rearrange the order of the words. C doesn't quite work with this word series.

Pattern D also describes multiple relationships. We'll start again with the general category "people away from home." What else do we know? Passengers and travelers travel; guests and visitors visit. We have two subcategories—people who travel and people who visit. Pattern D illustrates a link between the first word *passenger* and the fourth word *traveler*. The second word *guest* and the third word *visitor* are also linked. Does D make more sense than B? I happen to think so. Not to pull rank, but I created the puzzle.

Actually, you may discover that some of my answers don't "sit right" with you. That's all right. You may have different associations and experiences with the words. It's more important that you practice detecting patterns than that we're 100 percent in agreement.

Say the words out loud as they were given and in different orders. If you just scan or speed-read the problem, you're handicapping yourself. Remember all words are made of sounds called *phonemes,* which affect us on a neuromuscular level. Every word you have ever heard or spoken has had a physical influence on you. By saying the words out loud and in different orders, you engage your muscle memory. Some words just sound and feel more right together than do others. Every word we understand has multiple associations for us—mentally, physically, and emotionally. As children we instinctively played with sounds, busily creating neuromuscular connections that stay with us throughout our lives.

Skip the tough problems and do the easier ones first. My word puzzles demonstrate different ways of organizing information. Some are progressions. Some are part-whole relationships. Some are analogies. Some are categories. Consequently, you'll find that some relationships are easier for you to recognize than are others. That's your preferred way of organizing information.

Feel free to solve the puzzles that are easiest for you first. You'll be warming up your mental muscles. As you become more familiar with the format, you'll find that the puzzles that initially stumped you gradually become solvable.

For pattern detection practice, solve the puzzles on pages 154 and 155.

● ● ●

TURNING ONE WORD INTO ANOTHER

It takes a long time to learn to read. It takes a longer time to learn to read well. Once that threshold has been crossed, we become efficient readers. We read automatically—traffic signs, cereal boxes, billboards, T-shirts, and so on.

Draw arrows as shown to best illustrate the relationships in the given analogies.

A despise : dislike :: like : admire

B Pacific : Jupiter :: ocean : planet

C lion : sphinx :: eagle : phoenix

D mitt : glove :: boxer : catcher

11. Irish : Labrador :: setter : retriever

12. relativity : Einstein :: evolution : Darwin

13. match : pencil :: broomstick : flagpole

14. measure : mix :: bake : eat

15. kangaroo : marsupial :: python : snake

16. mouse : pelican :: fish : grain

17. desert : warm :: tundra : wet

18. premise : syllogism :: hilt : sword

19. gauntlet : helmet :: hand : head

20. ballroom : court :: tennis : tango

Draw arrows as shown to best illustrate the relationships in the given analogies.

A   despise : dislike :: like : admire

B   Pacific : Jupiter :: ocean : planet

C   lion : sphinx :: eagle : phoenix

D   mitt : glove :: boxer : catcher

21.   Pacific : Atlantic :: typhoon : hurricane

22.   tenacious : stubborn :: persistent : firm

23.   starboard : left :: stern : front

24.   tongue : leg :: shoe : pants

25.   football : down :: baseball : out

26.   blood : sheep :: dog : hound

27.   old : twenty :: one : maid

28.   vocal : active :: mute : inert

29.   alert : tired :: drowsy : asleep

30.   moat : trench :: moor : heath

I designed the next word puzzle on page 157 to make you stop reading and look at the elements that make up words. You solve this puzzle by discovering the part-whole relationship between letters and words. Are you ready?

●   ●   ●

Look at the example at the top of the puzzle page. Notice the words read from left to right as follows: SEED, SEEK, PEEK, PECK, PICK. There is a little rhyme but not much reason to the order of these words, if they're looked at strictly as words. Let's look at them instead as combinations of letters.

SEED and SEEK are four-letter words that share three of the same letters—S, E, and E. Similarly SEEK and PEEK share three letters—E, E, and K. PEEK and PECK also share three letters—P, E, and K. Finally, PECK and PICK share three letters—P, C, and K. In this way, we've managed to turn SEEK into PICK.

The instructions on the top of the puzzle page explain some of the rules: change only one letter at a time; each time you have to make an American English word. By that I mean you could find the word in a good dictionary, and you can use a letter only once. There is another implicit rule, but before you read on, see if you can figure it out based on the example.

I'll tell you what the implicit rule is. You create a new word by selecting a letter from the word on the far right. The letter you select will be in the same place in the new word that it was in the old word. I know this is confusing, but look at the example. The first word is SEED. The last word is PICK. How did I turn SEED into PICK? I took off the last letter in SEED—the D. I replaced the D with the last letter in PICK—the K. The new word is now SEEK.

Let's look at the next word—PEEK. If you take the first letter—S—from SEEK and replace it with the first letter—P—from PICK, you get the word PEEK. If you take the third letter—E—from PEEK and replace it with the third letter—C—from PICK, you get the word PECK. Then all you have to do is replace the second letter—E—from PECK with an I and you have the last word—PICK.

What makes this puzzle hard is that you have to switch between thinking abstractly and concretely. The puzzle would be easy if all you had to do was randomly replace letters. By having to come up with a legitimate word each and every time you change a letter, you have to think through the words you know.

Remember this is a part-whole puzzle. The letters are the concrete parts. The words are the abstract wholes. As with my graphic part-whole puzzles, you're practicing perceiving the consequences of your actions. The puzzle demands that

Objective: Turn the word on the left into the word on the right by changing one letter at a time to spell an American-English word.

Do not change any letter more than once.

SEED	_SEEK_	_PEEK_	_PECK_	PICK
HANK	_____	_____	_____	PORT
HARE	_____	_____	_____	COOK
MAUL	_____	_____	_____	WILD
ROOD	_____	_____	_____	LICK
HELP	_____	_____	_____	ROAM
TEST	_____	_____	_____	PORE
DILL	_____	_____	_____	BOOT
TUBA	_____	_____	_____	DONE
DIVE	_____	_____	_____	HART
DUNK	_____	_____	_____	BEET
MUST	_____	_____	_____	DOCK
LIFE	_____	_____	_____	DEBT
HAIR	_____	_____	_____	DEAN
DELL	_____	_____	_____	VOTE
MITT	_____	_____	_____	PACE

you move both forward and backward to solve the problem; and many times you have more than one option available to you. In considering which option to explore, you must examine how your choice affects the sequence.

A VERBAL RUBIK'S CUBE

The exercise on page 159 is probably the most challenging of the exercises in this chapter, but it also conveys a benefit that's critical to organizations: it helps people stretch how they organize information. We take in written and spoken words and put them in little boxes. We have one box for information about companies in our industry, another box for data about other industries; we have a box for what we learn from our boss and a box for what we learn from reading. Being able to reconfigure these boxes—to create new, more diverse boxes where information from different sources commingles—allows people to reorient their perspectives. These fresh perspectives help people become more innovative as well as better able to communicate information in more compelling ways. Too often, we rely on the same old ways of introducing subjects, asking direct reports to carry out tasks, and even motivating people to perform. Putting together ideas and words in fresh ways invigorates both written and verbal communication.

●   ●   ●

To solve this puzzle (page 159) you have to perceive the depth of a word's meaning. Notice that at the top of the puzzle page I've provided a list of words. You'll use these words to fill in the blank ovals.

The lines connecting the ovals indicate a meaningful relationship between the words. For instance, look through the list and find a word that means both benevolent and just. The best match is the word *good*. Write the word *good* in the oval between *benevolent* and *just*.

You solve the puzzle by finding meaningful relationships between the words as the lines indicate. Sometimes more than one word seems to work. I recommend you do this puzzle in pencil and have a good eraser handy. You may find that you have to change your mind a few times before you get the hang of it. The following techniques may be helpful:

- **Group words with similar meanings together.** On a separate paper, list "families" of words. For instance, *good, nice,* and *pleasant* share similar

Objective: Complete the diagram by establishing meaningful relationships among the words provided below.

Hint: Lines indicate connections between words as given in a thesaurus.

scrupulous   good   rainless   benevolent

witty   faithful   nice   just

amusing   observant   pleasant   conscientious

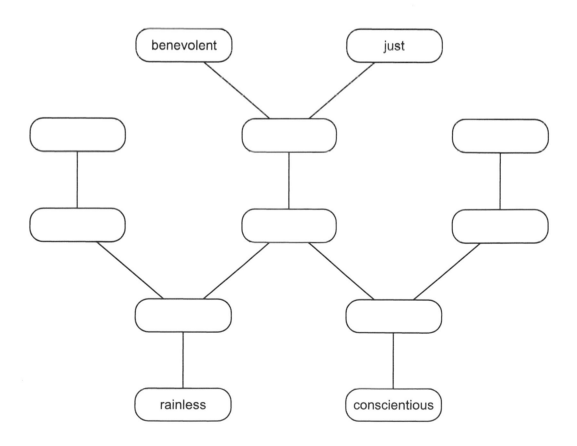

meanings. *Witty* and *amusing* also have similar meanings. Grouping words in this way helps you organize and reorganize the words as you fill in the ovals. I scrambled the list of words on the top of the page to make the puzzle more difficult. Rewriting the words in different groupings helps you engage your muscle memory.

- **Identify words with more than one meaning.** Notice that the word *pleasant* can refer to both behavior and weather. Therefore, *pleasant* might be connected to *good,* but it could also be connected to *rainless.* Be sure to make a note of this on your paper.

- **Play with the words.** If you're not in the habit of glancing through the dictionary or thesaurus, you're limiting your perception. To enhance your verbal peripheral vision, let your mind free-associate. For instance, using the word *faithful,* you might be reminded of how faithful Lassie was to Timmy. *Faithful* might also refer to religion. Is there a relationship between someone who is faithful to her religion and someone who is observant of his religion?

When you're ready to start filling in the puzzle, put your first word choice in the oval and a second choice underneath it. That way you can remind yourself you have an option. Underline your second choice. In some cases you may find your second choice works better.

If you're not sure how well two words relate, place a question mark on the line connecting them. Here again you're reminding yourself that none of your answers have been written in stone. You can always go back and change them if you find something better.

Finally, cross out words from the list at the top of the page as you write them in the ovals so you won't use any word twice. Remember that you don't have to be absolutely certain before you write a word. Just leave yourself a hint that you want to go back and look at it again.

If you're up for the challenge, solve this next verbal relationship puzzle on page 161. Notice that here you're on your own. The difficulty level has greatly increased. You have a format—the flowchart—and a list of relevant information—the words—but the rest is up to you. This is your opportunity to get creative. You may come up with an entirely different arrangement than I did. That's fine as long as you can justify your choices.

●   ●   ●

Objective: Complete the diagram by establishing meaningful relationships among the words provided below.

Hint: Lines indicate connections between words as given in a thesaurus.

abandon   knock off   pay   cease

agree   pen   complete   write

settle   correspond   discontinue accomplish

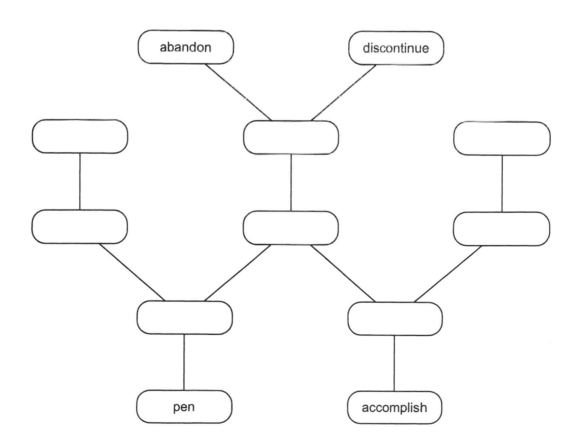

TAKING VERBAL RISKS

Just as we favor some ways of structuring information over others, we favor some communication styles over others. Although this is efficient—we don't have to give it much thought—it isn't necessarily effective for getting the results we want.

After working with me for several months, Mike, an executive, told me he found himself using a much wider vocabulary and a greater range of analogies when talking with other people. One day in particular he realized he wasn't getting through to Alex, a direct report. Mike had been trying to explain how other team members needed information that only Alex could provide, but it was of little use to them if the information arrived late.

Mike had played football when he was younger and remained a big fan of the sport. Not surprisingly, his talk was routinely and liberally sprinkled with such references as two-minute warning, fourth and one, Hail Mary pass, and the like.

Alex, on the other hand, was not athletic and rarely, if ever, listened to any sportscast. When Mike tried to explain the problem in terms of the quarterback and receiver needing to coordinate the pass and the run, he saw Alex's eyes glaze over. Then, as Mike told me later, it was as if a lightbulb went on in his head. He started talking about the concert he and his wife had attended recently, referring to how each instrument—violin, French horn, cello, harp, and others—had to come in at the right moment for maximum effect. Half a beat too soon or half a beat too late and the orchestra's reputation would be damaged. People would remember the mistake even if everything else was perfect.

Before that day Mike had never thought of an orchestra as a team, but the analogy made sense to him. More important, the analogy made sense to Alex. Mike got the result he wanted.

ANSWERS FOR VERBAL PUZZLES

Draw arrows as shown to best illustrate the relationships in the given analogies.

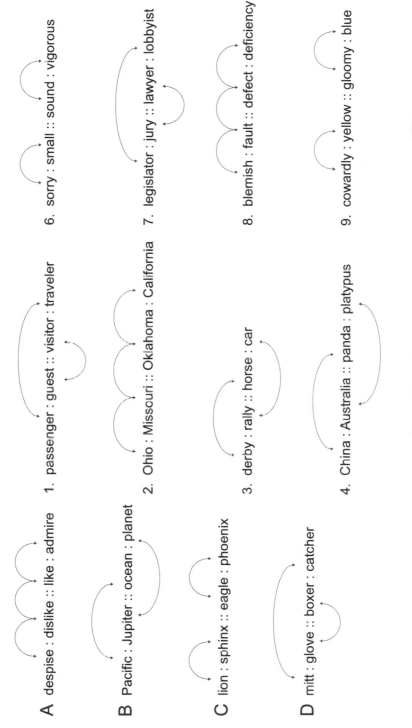

A despise : dislike :: like : admire

B Pacific : Jupiter :: ocean : planet

C lion : sphinx :: eagle : phoenix

D mitt : glove :: boxer : catcher

1. passenger : guest :: visitor : traveler

2. Ohio : Missouri :: Oklahoma : California

3. derby : rally :: horse : car

4. China : Australia :: panda : platypus

5. squat : bend :: stand : stretch

6. sorry : small :: sound : vigorous

7. legislator : jury :: lawyer : lobbyist

8. blemish : fault :: defect : deficiency

9. cowardly : yellow :: gloomy : blue

10. battle : rainfall :: skirmish : drizzle

Draw arrows as shown to best illustrate the relationships in the given analogies.

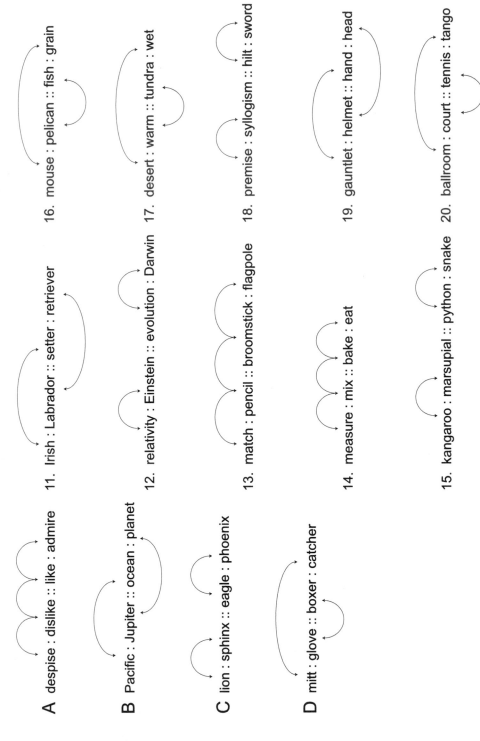

A despise : dislike :: like : admire

B Pacific : Jupiter :: ocean : planet

C lion : sphinx :: eagle : phoenix

D mitt : glove :: boxer : catcher

11. Irish : Labrador :: setter : retriever

12. relativity : Einstein :: evolution : Darwin

13. match : pencil :: broomstick : flagpole

14. measure : mix :: bake : eat

15. kangaroo : marsupial :: python : snake

16. mouse : pelican :: fish : grain

17. desert : warm :: tundra : wet

18. premise : syllogism :: hilt : sword

19. gauntlet : helmet :: hand : head

20. ballroom : court :: tennis : tango

Draw arrows as shown to best illustrate the relationships in the given analogies.

A despise : dislike :: like : admire

B Pacific : Jupiter :: ocean : planet

C lion : sphinx :: eagle : phoenix

D mitt : glove :: boxer : catcher

21. Pacific : Atlantic :: typhoon : hurricane

22. tenacious : stubborn :: persistent : firm

23. starboard : left :: stern : front

24. tongue : leg :: shoe : pants

25. football : down :: baseball : out

26. blood : sheep :: dog : hound

27. old : twenty :: one : maid

28. vocal : active :: mute : inert

29. alert : tired :: drowsy : asleep

30. moat : trench :: moor : heath

Verbal Part-Whole Relationships—Answer Sheet

SEED	SEEK	PEEK	PECK	PICK
HANK	HARK	PARK	PART	PORT
HARE	CARE	CORE	CORK	COOK
MAUL	MALL	WALL	WILL	WILD
ROOD	ROOK	ROCK	LOCK	LICK
HELP	HEAP	REAP	REAM	ROAM
TEST	PEST	POST	PORT	PORE
DILL	DOLL	BOLL	BOLT	BOOT
TUBA	TUBE	TUNE	TONE	DONE
DIVE	HIVE	HAVE	HATE	HART
DUNK	BUNK	BUNT	BENT	BEET
MUST	DUST	DUSK	DUCK	DOCK
LIFE	LIFT	LEFT	DEFT	DEBT
HAIR	HEIR	HEAR	DEAR	DEAN
DELL	DOLL	DOLE	DOTE	VOTE
MITT	MITE	MICE	MACE	PACE

Objective: Complete the diagram by establishing meaningful relationships among the words provided below.

Hint: Lines indicate connections between words as given in a thesaurus.

scrupulous   good   rainless   benevolent

witty   faithful   nice   just

amusing   observant   pleasant   conscientious

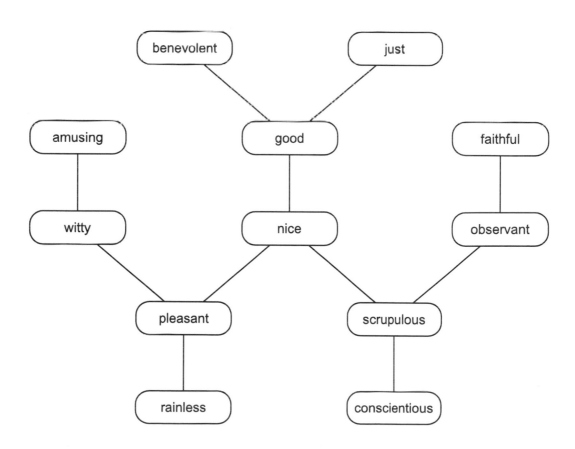

Objective: Complete the diagram by establishing meaningful relationships among the words provided below.

Hint: Lines indicate connections between words as given in a thesaurus.

abandon   knock off   pay   cease

agree   pen   complete   write

settle   correspond   discontinue   accomplish

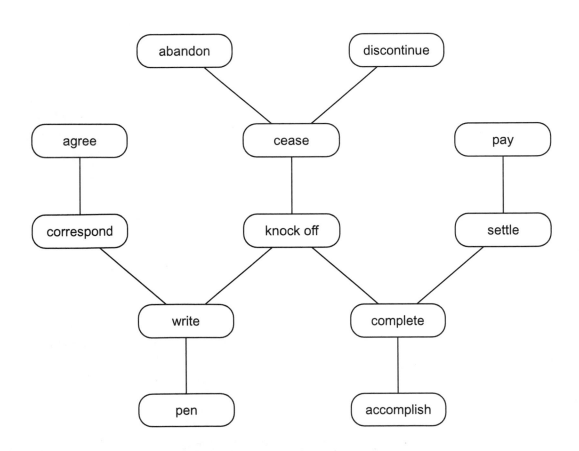

Connecting the Dots

If you're feeling a bit overwhelmed by all the reports, memos, letters, pamphlets, periodicals, and books—not to mention e-mails, voice mails, and old-fashioned phone calls—that come your way, you're not alone. Yet as much as we gripe about being inundated with information, nobody is suggesting we put an end to it or even set limits on it in some way. Without a sufficient amount of data, we would make poor decisions.

Access to information, though, isn't enough. This became painfully clear after September 11, 2001. Follow-up investigations indicated that the FBI had adequate information to deter, if not prevent, the destruction of New York's World Trade Center. The information, however, was not structured in a timely and useful manner; it was not turned into knowledge. Knowledge enables us to make decisions and take the actions necessary to get the results we want.

You probably have many smart people in your organization, but they often don't make good decisions that help the company or team achieve goals. As we'll see, they possess all the information they need to make good decisions, but they simply haven't *linked* the disparate pieces of information. **The people in your**

company need to learn to connect the dots. Unfortunately, sometimes their education and training predispose them to separate the dots.

FOCUSING ON THE FACTS

Throughout our life, people have given us all kinds of information. We're given historic dates, chemical formulas, calorie counts, sports scores, weather reports, stock market averages, interest rates, and on and on. Much of the information we receive has little personal significance, which is why it's so hard to remember. Nevertheless, we try to remember as much of what we hear or read as possible because we think we should.

We've been trained to think that smart people remember tons of information. After all, the smartest kid in the class always knew the right answer to any question the teacher posed. People with facts and figures "at their fingertips" seem so much on top of things that we may hesitate to question the relevance of their statements. Information is relevant when it is personally significant to us. We make our best decisions when we understand their personal significance—how and why the results matter to us.

> **"Information is the oxygen of the modern age."**
>
> —*Ronald Reagan*

Our perceptions enable us to intuitively distinguish relevant information from irrelevant information. In our mind's eye we can "see" how the pieces fit together; we can also eliminate the pieces that don't fit. The point I've been making throughout the book is that having many different ways of arranging information allows us to be more effective decision makers and problem solvers. Consequently, we are more likely to achieve the results we want. If we intuitively—and therefore efficiently—view every event through the lens of one perception, we can be quickly overwhelmed by the vast amount of information available to us.

As you work through my puzzles, you become increasingly proficient in shifting perceptions. So far you've had practice with analogies, progressions, and part-whole relationships. You've also practiced detecting mistakes and exploring the same perceptual processes on a verbal level.

These connect-the-dot puzzles give you practice in selecting relevant information. Of course, in real life what is relevant to one person may be completely irrelevant to another. These puzzles teach you the process of distinguishing relevant information from information that is useless to you at the moment. This is important:

Sometimes information that is useless today is vital tomorrow.

Knowing when information matters and when it doesn't distinguishes the bona fide expert from the merely competent.

In *Sources of Power: How People Make Decisions* (MIT Press, 2001), Gary Klein explored "natural decision making" in real-life situations. He and his research team interviewed "firefighters [who] make life-and-death decisions under extreme time pressure . . . pilots, nurses, military leaders, nuclear power plant operators, chess masters, and experts in a range of other domains." The experts themselves credited their successful decisions to intuition. Klein and his researchers determined that to get the results they wanted, the experts intuitively looked for:

- Connections and meanings to establish relationships.
- Essential characteristics that were not altered by circumstance.

In addition they:

- Could compare past memories to the present circumstance.
- Were concerned with accuracy and precision.
- Defined the problem clearly in their own mind.
- Planned their behavior.
- Suppressed their impulsivity.
- Confirmed their inferences before they took action.

Although it sounds complex, all of these behaviors occurred within a matter of seconds. They are also behaviors you'll learn as you practice solving the connect-the-dots puzzles. Now practice connecting the dots.

THE MOUSE AND THE SIDEWAYS BOWL

In Chapter 7 you solved some connect-the-dots puzzles by first disconnecting them. All the lines you see connecting the dots on puzzle page 172 are correct; I put them there to give you a head start.

Connect the dots to make four of each of the figures shown in the square.

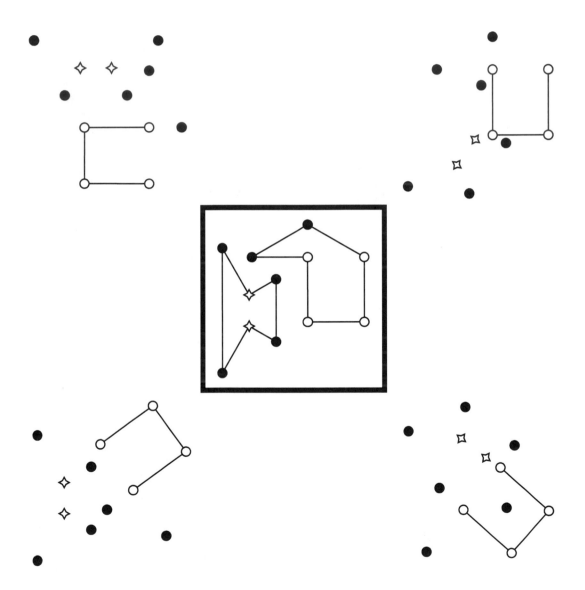

In the center of the puzzle page is a square drawn with a thick line. Inside the square are two complex figures comprised of lines, dots, and stars. The figure with the two white stars looks something like a bowl turned sideways, so I'll refer to it as a *bowl*. The figure with the four white dots reminds some people of a very abstract drawing of a mouse, so I'll call it a *mouse*. The bowl and the mouse are the sample figures I want you to replicate by drawing lines connecting the dots and stars. Use a pencil and have a good eraser handy.

Surrounding the center square are four groups of three lines, ten dots, and two stars. Each group contains the information you need to replicate the bowl and the mouse found in the center square. All that's missing are the other lines. You solve the puzzle by drawing the missing lines.

Look at the group in the upper right corner. Notice the four white dots that are connected by the three lines. The orientation of this set is the same as the bottom of the mouse in the center square. In the other groups the mouse's bottom has been rotated. Actually, the whole mouse has been rotated. The bowl has also been rotated in some of the groups. Occasionally, the mouse and the bowl overlap.

You may feel tempted to rotate the puzzle page to make it easier to see the mouse and bowl. PLEASE DO NOT GIVE IN TO TEMPTATION! One of the skills you're practicing with this puzzle is learning to rotate images in your mind—to perceive them in different ways. It is important to keep the entire page oriented so that *the instructions are always on top.*

By the way, I gave the figures in the center square the names *bowl* and *mouse* for two reasons: First, so I can easily refer to them; second, because we can imagine the abstract more clearly if we can relate it to something concrete.

Now, cover the bowl in the center square so you can't see it. Look at the mouse. It can be taken apart and described in several different ways, making what I call a *parts list:*

- A square topped by an isosceles triangle
- Two black dots and four white dots
- Two groups of three equidistant dots (one black and two white)
- One black dot and two white dots aligned horizontally
- One black dot and two white dots aligned vertically

Turn the puzzle page facedown so you can't see the dots or anything else. On another piece of paper, draw the mouse from memory. Include the white and black dots if you can.

Turn the puzzle page faceup again and compare your drawing with my mouse. How accurate were you? Is your drawing the same size as mine? Are the white and black dots in the same place? Are they the same distance apart? Is the mouse's nose pointing in the same direction?

Make a mental note to yourself about the difference(s) between your drawing and mine. Be as detailed as you can, as this will help you remember the result you want.

Turn the puzzle page facedown again. On another piece of paper, draw the mouse again, but this time refer to the parts list I provided, you using any or all of the information to improve your drawing. Take your time to make it as accurate and precise as you can.

Once again turn the puzzle page faceup and compare your new drawing with my old mouse. Is it more accurate? Look at your first drawing. Make a mental note of the differences between your first drawing, your second drawing, and my mouse.

What you're doing is embedding the result you want in your visual memory. There is a theory that says we never really succeed at anything until we can envision it in our mind's eye.

Look at one of the groups on the puzzle page. Find the mouse's bottom. Pick the group that is easiest for you. Can you find the two black dots that would complete the mouse's nose?

You've just separated relevant information from irrelevant information. Remember, sometimes information that is useless today is vital tomorrow, so let's look at the useless information.

Go back to the puzzle on page 172. This time cover the mouse in the center square. Look at the bowl, which can also be taken apart and described in several different ways:

- Four black dots and two white stars
- Two parallel lines that you can see—if you connected the two white stars, you'd have three parallel lines
- Two sets of two black dots and one white star that form right angles and are mirror images of each other
- Two black dots make the top of the bowl, two black dots make its base, and two white stars form the waist.

Now that we have a parts list, turn the puzzle page facedown so you can't see the dots or anything else. On another paper, draw the bowl from memory. When you're through drawing, turn the puzzle page faceup. Compare your drawing with my bowl and make a mental note of the differences.

Turn the puzzle page facedown again. This time draw the bowl and use the parts list to help you improve your drawing. When you're finished, turn the puzzle page faceup. Compare your second drawing with my bowl. Also, compare your first drawing to your second. Make a mental note of all the differences you can identify.

Look at the puzzle page. See if you can find a bowl in one of the groups. Remember the bowl has two white stars on its waist.

Now you're ready to solve the puzzle. You may start with either the mouse or the bowl, whichever you find easier. Start with any group. Connect the dots and the stars to form the mice and bowls. When you've finished solving this puzzle, you'll have drawn four mice and four bowls in various relationships to each other.

Some people have difficulty separating the relevant information—for example, the dots that make up the mouse—from the temporarily useless information—for example, the dots and stars that make up the bowl. If you're having difficulty, use a marker with your favorite color (except black or white) to fill in the white dots to help distinguish the mouse's bottom and anchor the image for you.

Another technique is to refer to your parts list. For instance, you know that the two stars form the bowl's waist. You also know that the top and base of the bowl are parallel lines. You could make a third parallel line by connecting the two stars.

Please remember to keep the puzzle page oriented so that the instructions are always on the top. By rotating the image in your head instead of rotating the paper, you're retraining your brain to perceive things differently. This is important to getting the results you want.

To solve the connect-the-dots puzzle on page 172, you needed mental agility. Your mind constantly shifted between inductive and deductive reasoning. You mentally projected images of the mouse and the bowl onto the dot groups. You segregated parts from wholes to locate the figures. Then you integrated the parts into wholes to verify the accuracy of your drawing. You had to plan ahead and inhibit the impulse to draw a line if you didn't know why you were drawing it. You also had to practice connecting the dots precisely so the lines didn't extend into empty space.

This is how an expert processes information. Don't worry if you couldn't solve this puzzle immediately or perfectly. Practice is necessary before you reach an expert level, and the next puzzle will give you further practice.

WORKING WITH A LOSS OF ORIENTATION

In the previous connect-the-dots puzzle, I included some lines to help you get started, a situation similar to receiving an assignment at work that already has an operating procedure. You have some guidelines to help orient yourself, so you can't stray too far from the results you want.

In the following puzzle on page 177, I've taken away the guidelines but not all the cues. This is similar to getting an assignment that requires you to establish a procedure. As before, you'll need to distinguish relevant information from temporarily useless information.

One of the complex figures in the center square probably looks familiar to you because it's our old friend the bowl. Notice the changes. The two white stars are now two white circles. The bowl is on the right side of the square and has been rotated so its top is to the right. Other than these minor changes, our parts list stays pretty much the same:

- Four black dots and two white dots
- Two parallel lines that you can see—if you connected the two white dots, you'd have three parallel lines
- Two sets of two black dots and one white dot that form right angles and are mirror images of each other
- Two black dots make the top of the bowl, two black dots make its base, and two white dots form the waist

The other figure in the square reminds some people of an upside-down recliner chair, although I always thought it looked like a sock with its toe pointing down. How you identify it isn't important, but naming it after something concrete is. This helps you remember the result you want.

Let's make a parts list for the chair or sock. It includes the following:

- Three white dots and two black dots
- Three white dots aligned on the same axis and equidistant
- A right angle made up of two black dots and one white dot; two right angles made up of two white dots and one black dot

You may find other relationships that I haven't included in the parts list.

Connect the dots to make four of each of the figures shown in the square.

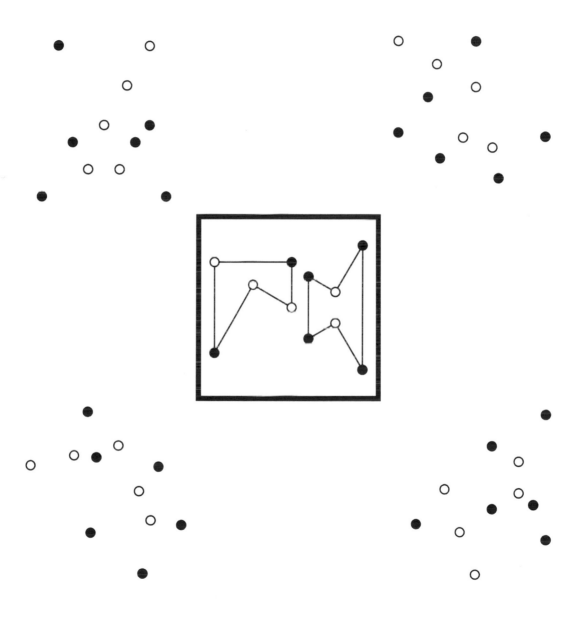

As you did for the first puzzle, practice drawing the bowl and the chair/sock from memory. Then compare your drawings with mine, and make a mental note of the differences. Use the parts list to help make your drawings more accurate, taking as much time as you feel you need. Then look at the four groups of dots on the puzzle page to see if you can locate one bowl and one chair/sock anywhere on the page.

When you're ready, solve the puzzle by connecting the dots. Many people look for the bowl first because they are already familiar with it. Experts use this technique to solve real-life problems; they look for something familiar when they confront unusual situations. Sometimes minor pieces of information can turn chaos into order.

Of course, you can start with either the bowl or the chair/sock. Select the group that seems the easiest for you. Remember that the images have been rotated and may overlap. Do not rotate the page—it defeats the purpose of the puzzle.

If you're having difficulty separating the relevant dots from the useless information, color the three white dots that are on the same axis—just don't color them black or white. Use the parts list to help you talk your way through the problem. Remember the bowls and chairs/socks in the four groups will be the same size as the samples in the center square.

Take your time and verify your solutions. When you're finished, you'll have drawn four bowls and four chairs/socks.

NEGOTIATING SHADES OF GRAY

At first glance the puzzle on page 177 may look more difficult than the previous ones you solved. There are only two white dots in each group. Look at the top figure in the center square. Does it seem familiar? It's our little old mouse with its nose pointing down. Of course, it's a little different; now its bottom is made of black dots instead of white ones, but everything else is the same. Let's check our parts list:

- A square topped by an isosceles triangle
- Six black dots
- Two groups of three equidistant dots
- Three black dots aligned horizontally
- Three black dots aligned vertically

Look at the bottom figure in the center square. Notice the two white dots in the middle. Notice also that the top and bottom lines are parallel. If you drew lines connecting the left top dot with the left bottom dot and the right top dot with the

Connect the dots to make four of each of the figures shown in the square.

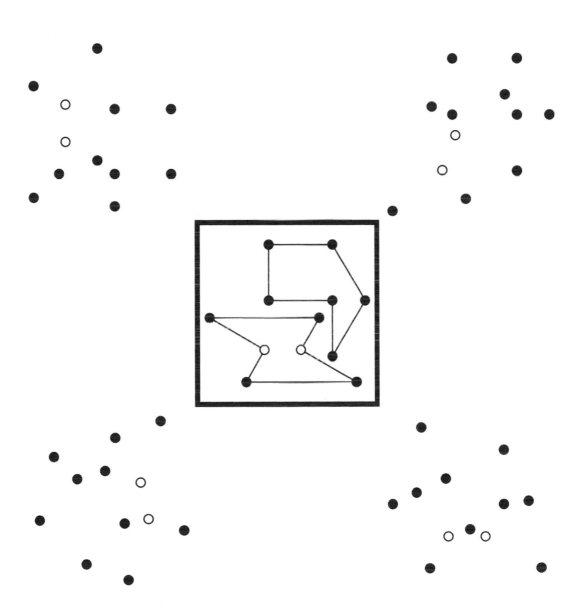

right bottom dot, you would create two more parallel lines. As it is, the two white dots kind of pinch the waist of the parallelogram. For now, I'll refer to the bottom figure as a parallelogram. Perhaps you can think of a better name—one that means something to you. In the meantime, let's create a parts list:

- Four black dots and two white dots
- Two parallel lines made by the four black dots—connect the white dots and you'd make a third parallel line
- Two right angles each made by two black dots and one white dot

Perhaps you can think of some additional relationships. For now, draw the mouse from memory again. Do the comparisons between your drawing and my mouse. By now you probably know the routine.

Next, draw the parallelogram from memory—and so on. Then look at the four groups of dots and decide if you want to find the mouse or the parallelogram first. Choose the group that is easiest for you to solve.

Some people start with the two white dots that form the pinched waist of the parallelogram. Remember that the white dots are in the middle of the two right angles. Draw a line very lightly between the two white dots. You can locate the four black dots by drawing two lines that are parallel to the line you drew between the white dots. You can erase the line between the white dots later.

Some people like to start with the mouse because they are already familiar with its shape. They envision the four black dots that make up the mouse's bottom as a square. Once they find the square in the group of dots, they can add the triangle that makes up the mouse's nose.

You may need to erase some of the lines you've drawn when they don't quite work. That's all right because this is a learning process. Make use of the parts list if you need it. Remember you can always color in the two white dots to make them stand out for you. And also remember not to rotate the puzzle page.

As you work this puzzle, you may find it easier to solve parts of the mouse and then parts of the parallelogram. As in real life, sometimes all the pieces don't come together immediately. If you know the result you want and can envision it in your mind's eye, you'll eventually achieve it.

When you've solved the puzzle, you'll have drawn four mice and four parallelograms. One mouse will overlap each parallelogram. All the figures you draw should be the same size as the ones in the center square, but they will not have the same orientation. Here are some additional puzzles to give you practice in separating relevant from temporarily useless information.

Connect the dots to make four of each of the figures shown in the square.

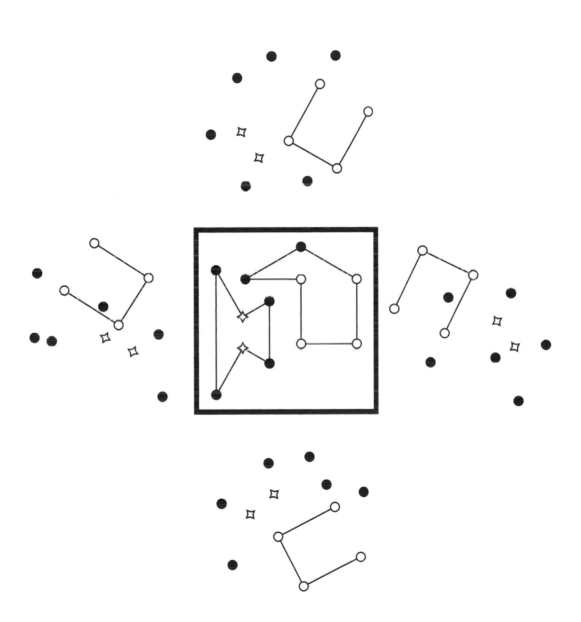

Connect the dots to make four of each of the figures shown in the square.

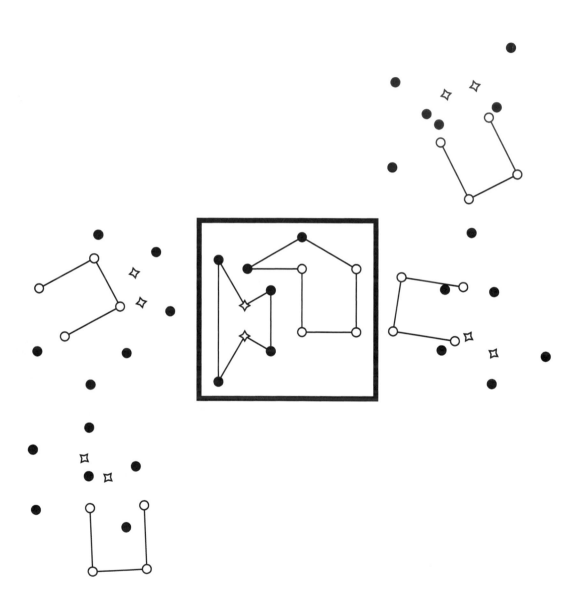

Connect the dots to make four of each of the figures shown in the square.

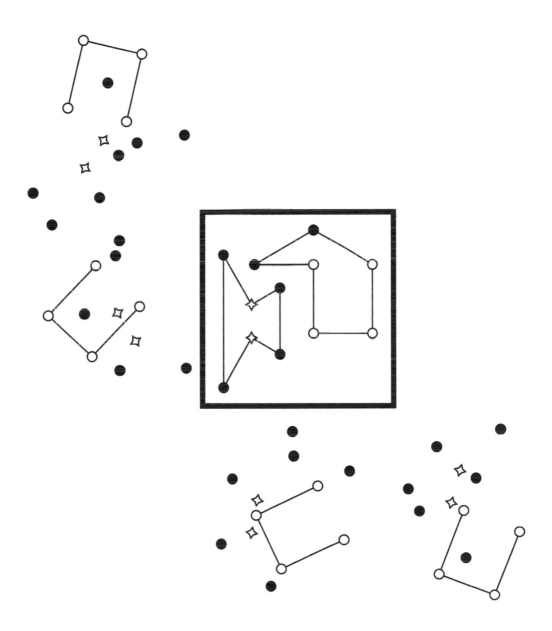

Connect the dots to make four of each of the figures shown in the square.

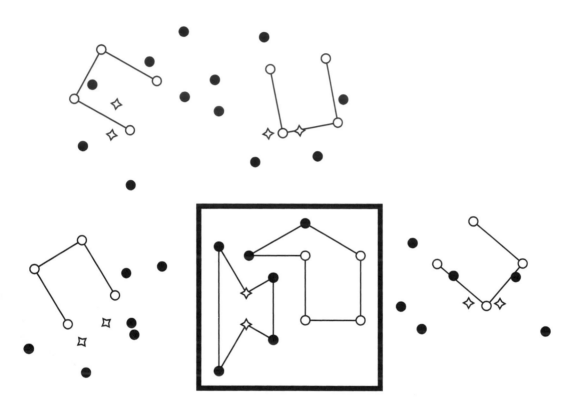

Connect the dots to make four of each of the figures shown in the square.

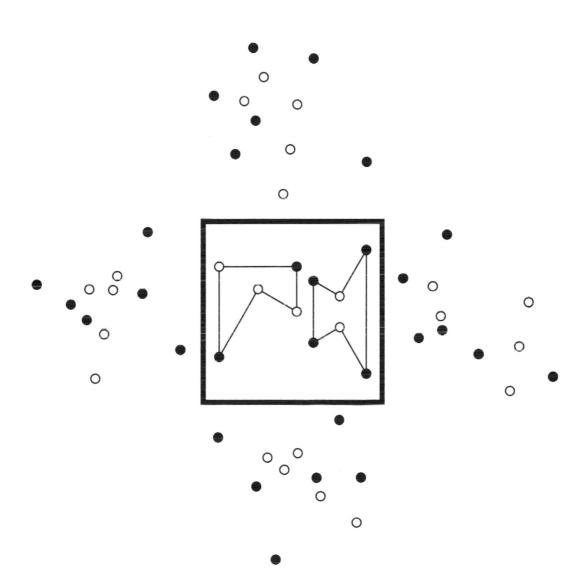

Connect the dots to make four of each of the figures shown in the square.

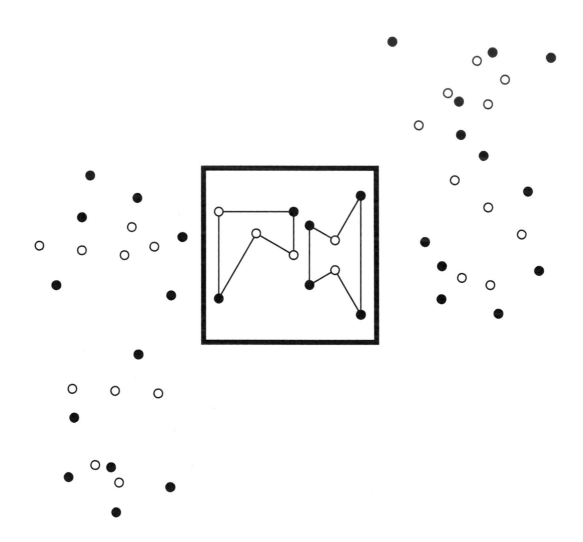

Connect the dots to make four of each of the figures shown in the square.

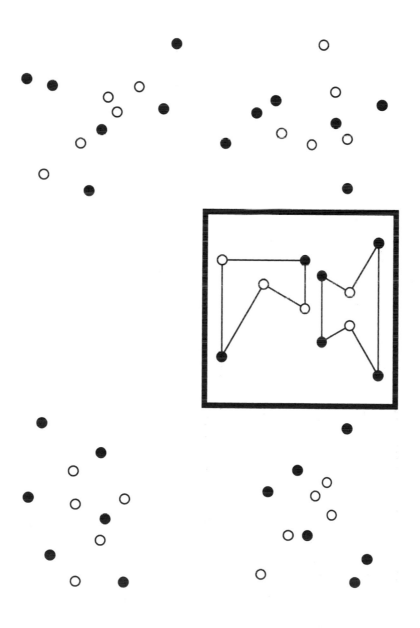

Connect the dots to make four of each of the figures shown in the square.

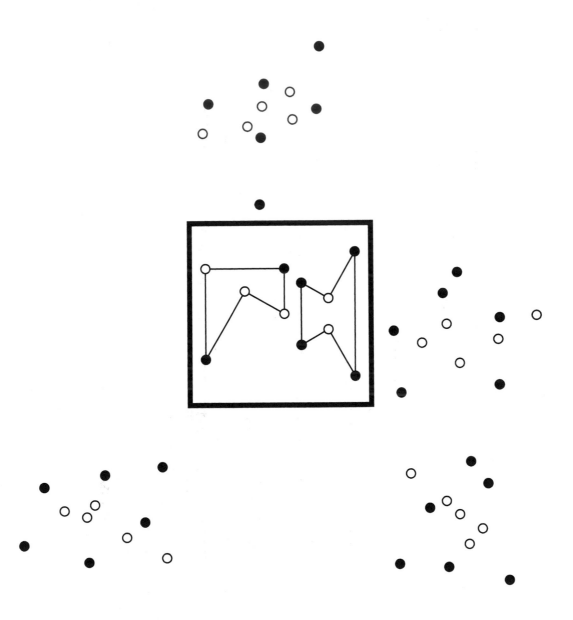

Connect the dots to make four of each of the figures shown in the square.

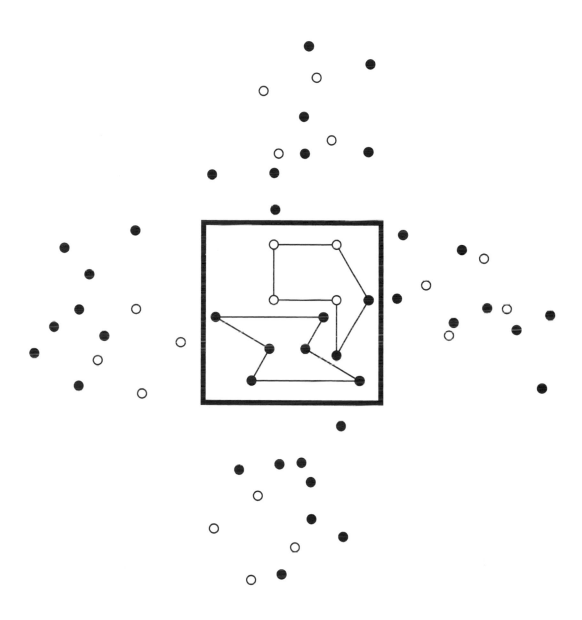

Connect the dots to make four of each of the figures shown in the square.

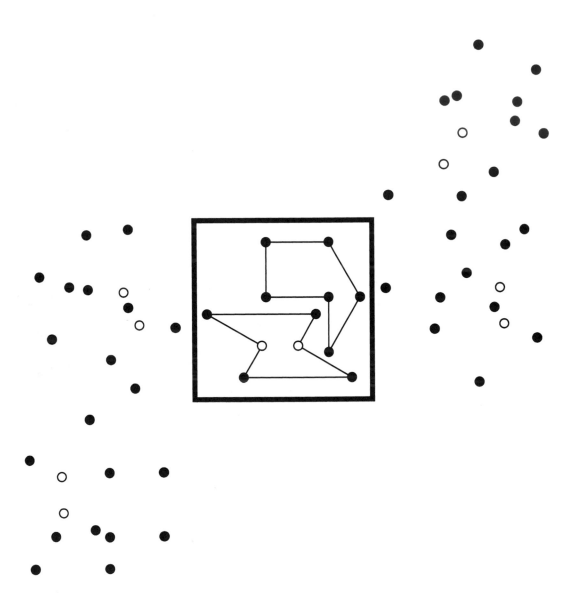

Connect the dots to make four of each of the figures shown in the square.

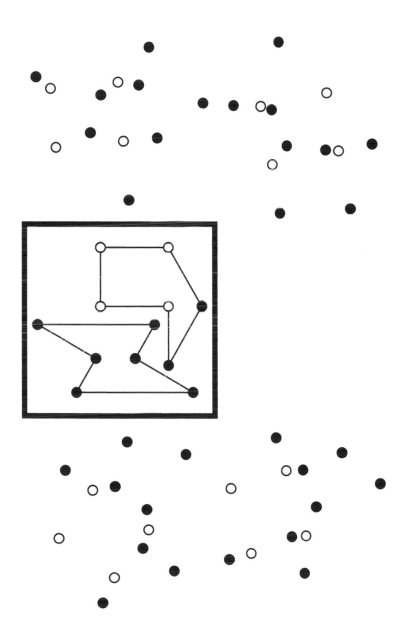

Connect the dots to make four of each of the figures shown in the square.

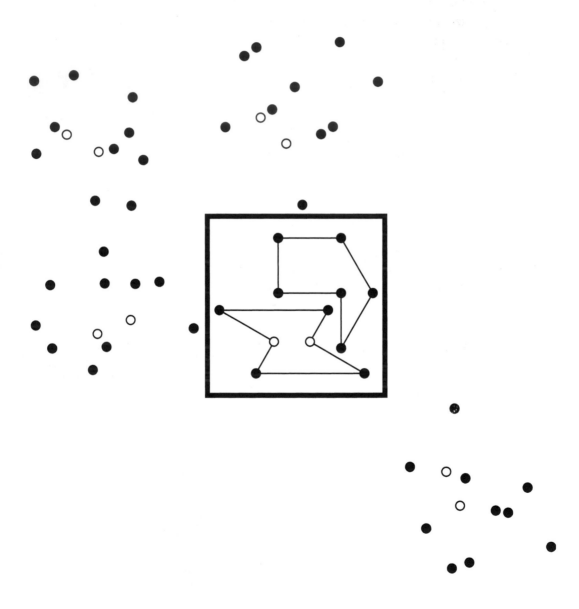

NO PAIN, NO GAIN:
Why These Puzzles Are Worth the Effort

I often receive highly diverse reactions to connect-the-dots puzzles, so you shouldn't be surprised if some people love them and others hate them. For individuals who don't organize information in a connect-the-dots kind of way, these puzzles can be quite challenging. On the other hand, I've found them to be enormously effective, in part because they give people practice in a wide variety of thinking skills, including the following:

- Selecting relevant information amid chaos
- Projecting the desired result, which minimizes ambiguity
- Manipulating information mentally
- Planning behavior and confirming inferences before taking action
- Verifying results
- Changing strategies as needed to attain desired results

In organizations where knowledge workers are at a premium, these skills are crucial. Remember that information has no value unless we can turn it into knowledge. Knowledge has value when we use it effectively to get the results we want.

ANSWERS FOR CONNECT-THE-DOTS PUZZLES

Connect the dots to make four of each of the figures shown in the square.

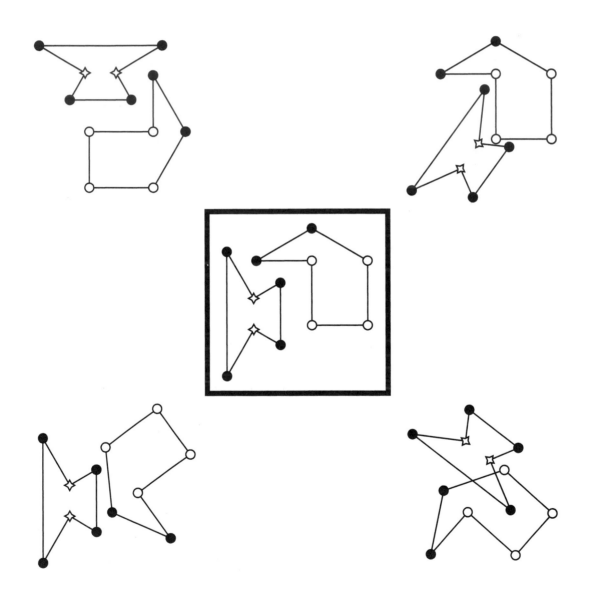

Connect the dots to make four of each of the figures shown in the square.

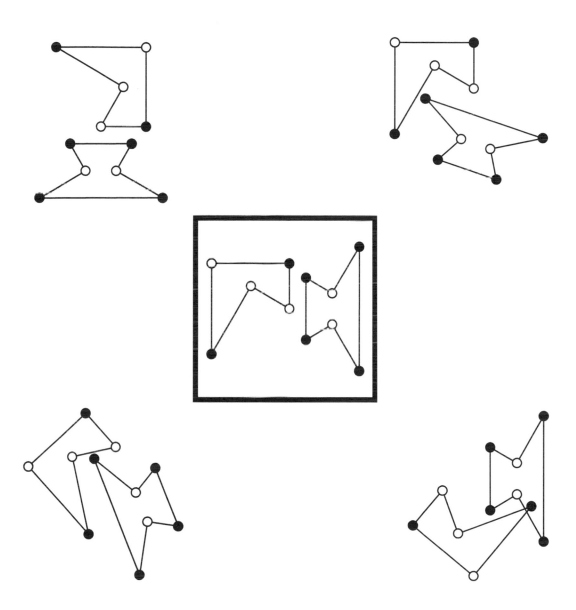

Connect the dots to make four of each of the figures shown in the square.

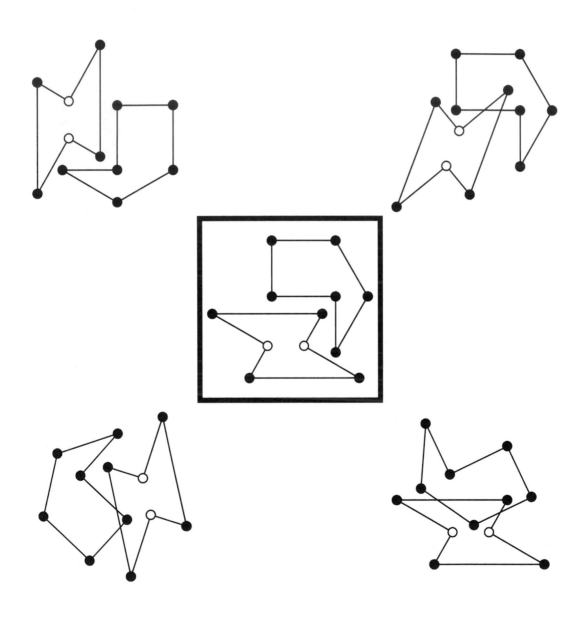

Connect the dots to make four of each of the figures shown in the square.

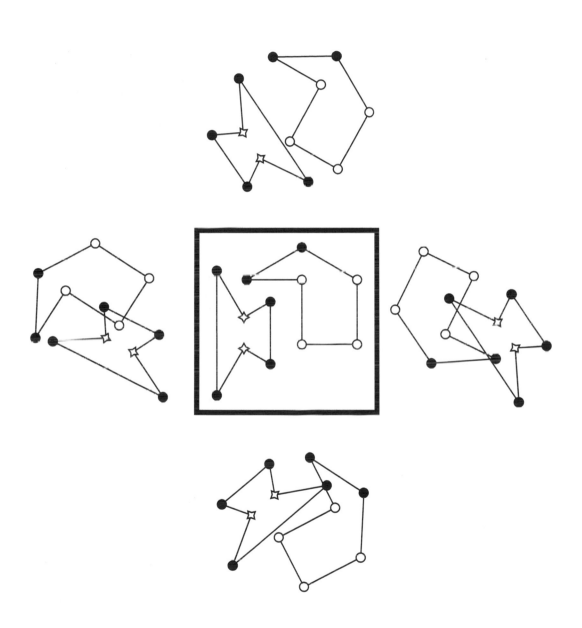

Connect the dots to make four of each of the figures shown in the square.

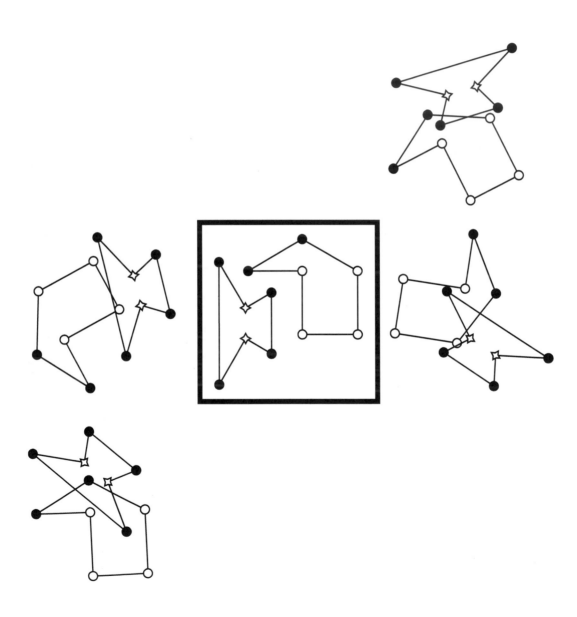

Connect the dots to make four of each of the figures shown in the square.

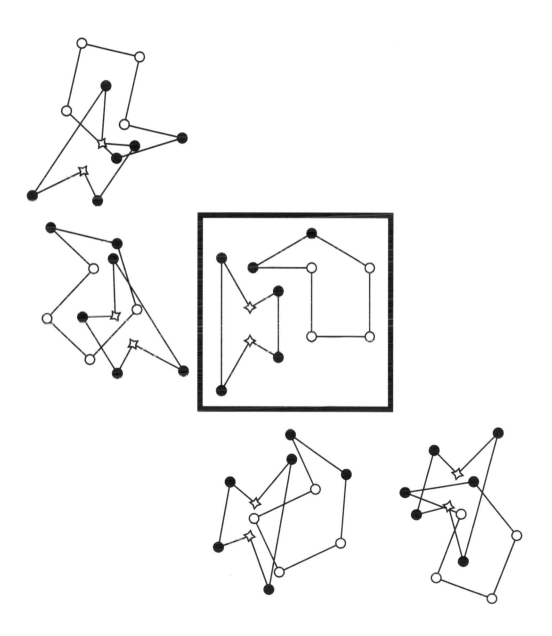

Connect the dots to make four of each of the figures shown in the square.

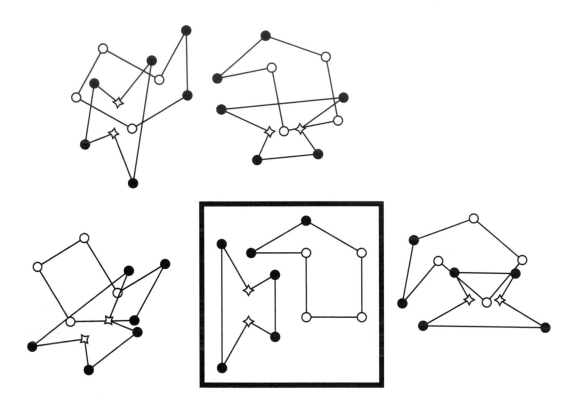

Connect the dots to make four of each of the figures shown in the square.

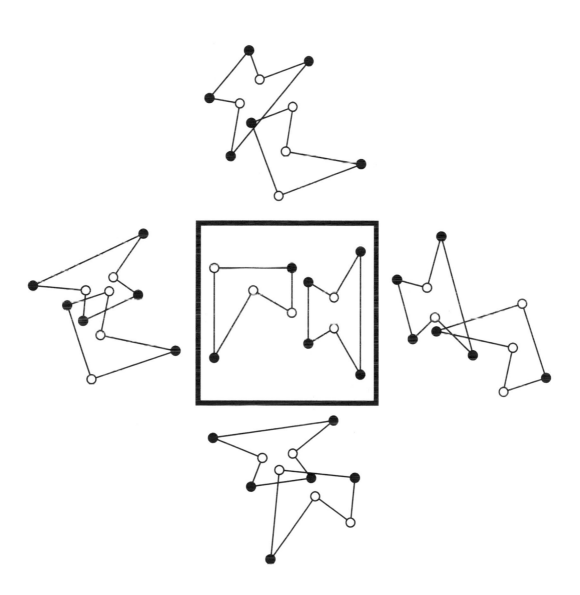

Connect the dots to make four of each of the figures shown in the square.

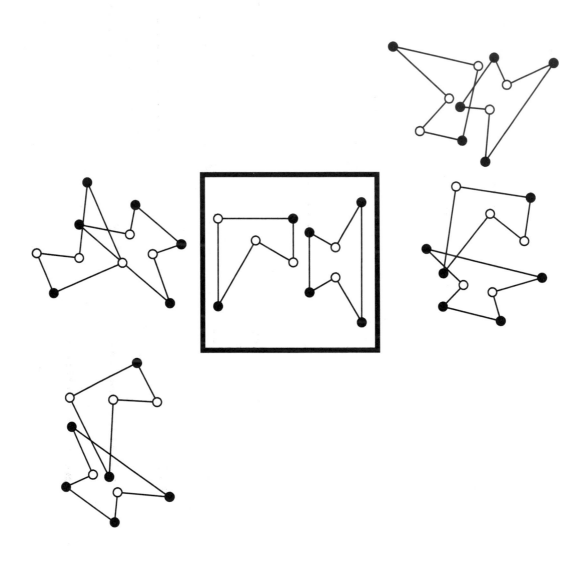

Connect the dots to make four of each of the figures shown in the square.

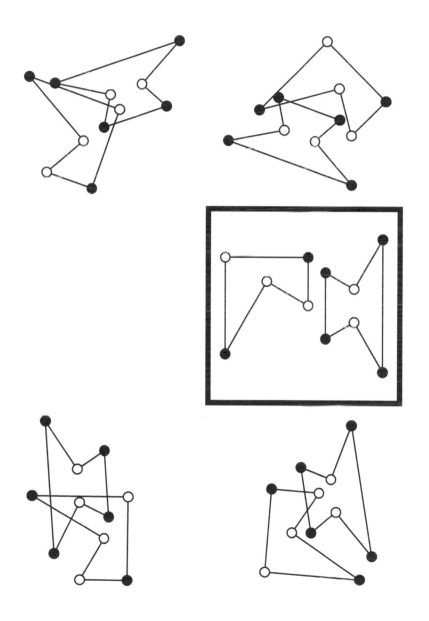

Connect the dots to make four of each of the figures shown in the square.

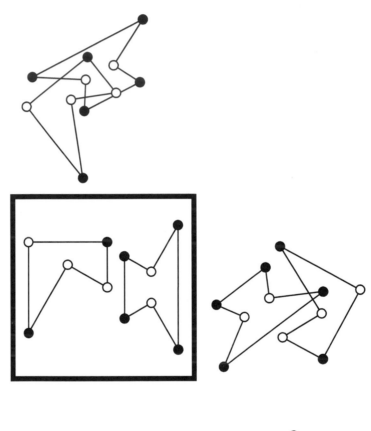

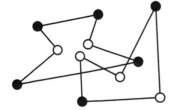

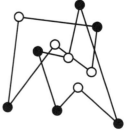

Connect the dots to make four of each of the figures shown in the square.

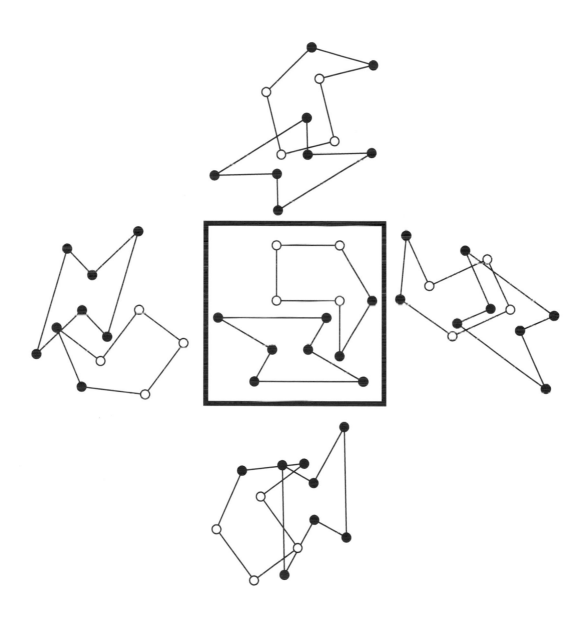

Connect the dots to make four of each of the figures shown in the square.

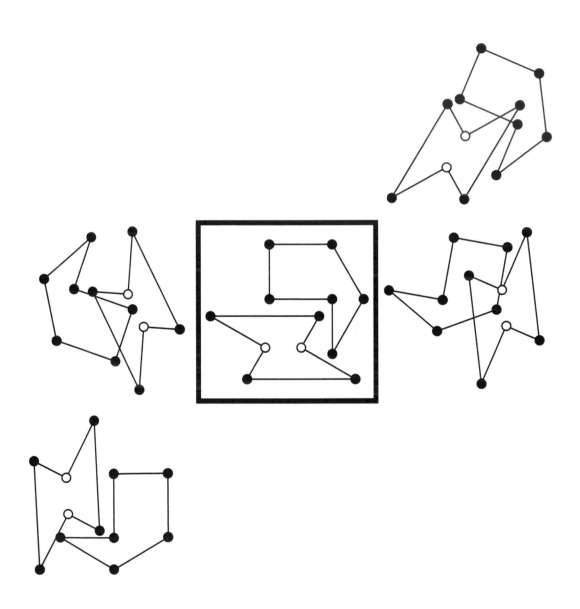

Connect the dots to make four of each of the figures shown in the square.

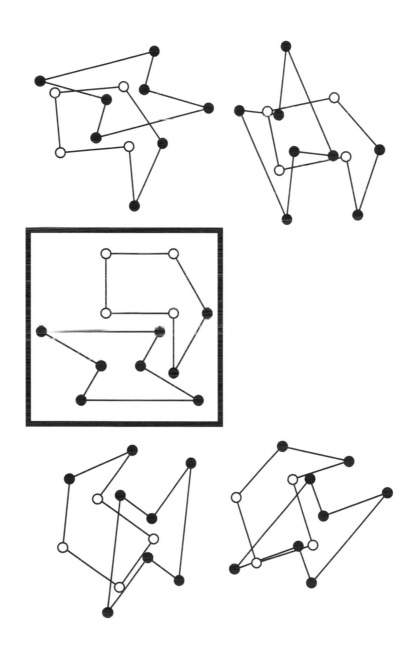

Connect the dots to make four of each of the figures shown in the square.

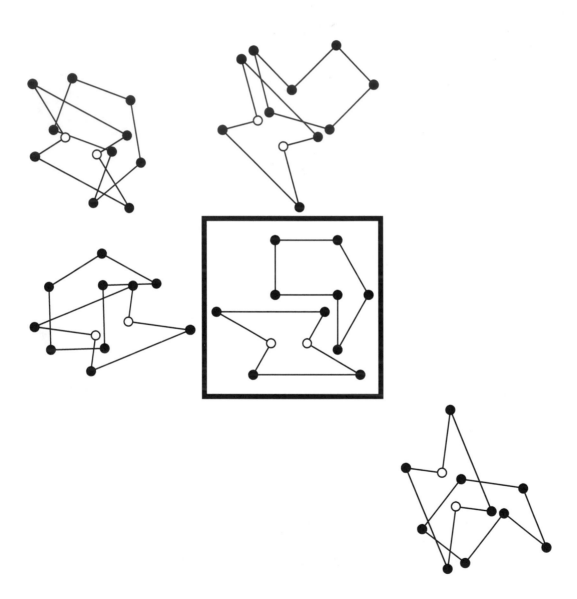

Categories

Most of us categorize at work in the same way we categorized at school. At a very young age, we learned how to place things in boxes: Big things go in the red box, little things go in the green box. Essentially, we were *sorting,* the most basic form of categorization.

At work, this sorting function is important for efficiency, if not effectiveness. We must file reports alphabetically. We have to group assignments according to dates due. We also sort people in a similar manner. Everyone in a given function belongs to a certain group—in our minds, marketing people are in one box and financial people in another. We also sort people according to departments, divisions, titles, and so on.

There's nothing wrong with this, except that it doesn't make us more effective. In fact, it can limit our effectiveness, causing us to think in very narrow ways. We're not just putting facts and people in boxes, but we're placing our own thinking process in the same type of confining space. Organizations that are highly effective have a critical mass of people who categorize on a higher level.

DEVELOPING HIGH-LEVEL THINKING

At the most basic level, words refer to people, places, and things: mommy, playground, kitty, and the like. We learn that one word can refer to many similar things—Bobby's house is different from mine, but they're both houses. This ability to move swiftly from the specific to the general—from the concrete to the abstract—takes us to a second level that research indicates most animals never achieve. Abstraction allows us to infer and predict.

Most people don't reach the third level, though the ones who do are the most effective at getting the results they want. The third level is commonly called *insight,* or *reflective thinking.* Essentially, it means the ability to *unlearn efficiency.*

Remember that efficiency gets in the way of effectiveness. At best, it helps us do things right. But it frequently interferes with our ability to do the right things—the things that get us the results we want.

The chapters in this book are organized in hierarchical order, which means that the skills developed in previous chapters build on one another to provide a strong framework for highly analytical problem solving. In order to categorize, we need to draw on the skills developed in previous chapters. Let's review what we have learned and how this learning applies to categorizing information, relationships, and problem solving.

As you solved the previous puzzles, you've been retraining your brain to become more effective. In Chapter 4 you practiced predicting results through analogies. When you're faced with unusual, unique, or simply unfamiliar circumstances in the real world, your ability to form an analogous relationship gives you an edge. It allows you to treat the unknown as though it were known.

A well-constructed analogy takes into account multiple variables. It focuses attention on the similarities and differences, enabling adjustments in real time. With good analogies you can function where others falter.

Chapter 5 taught you to think about change over time through progressions. To solve my progression puzzles, you had to discount similarities and focus on subtle differences. You had to pay excruciating attention to detail.

Crisis analysis inevitably reveals that the accumulation of minor errors in judgment leads to major disasters. Both God and the devil are said to be in the details.

My part-whole puzzles in Chapter 6 gave you practice inferring relationships. Through inference we learn to see the big picture and the consequences of our actions.

Chapter 7's mistake puzzles gave you the opportunity to fine-tune your new skills by exploring ways things can go wrong and correcting them.

My verbal puzzles in Chapter 8 turned words into objects that you could visually manipulate. My purpose was to free you from viewing words strictly in the abstract—to give you a more concrete command over them.

By connecting the dots in Chapter 9, you practiced shifting between deductive and inductive reasoning. We solve problems deductively by eliminating the irrelevant. We solve them inductively by selecting the relevant.

By exploring and rehearsing new perspectives, you primed your mind for insight. In *The Symbolic Species: The Co-evolution of Language and the Brain* (W.W. Norton, 1997), Terrence Deacon wrote, "A propensity to search out new perspectives might be a significant advantage for discovering symbolic relationships." The discovery of symbolic relationships generates new knowledge, enabling us to discard old assumptions and envision new possibilities. In this way, we *unlearn* efficiency and become more effective in communicating and getting the results we want.

"The use of symbols has a certain power of emancipation and exhilaration for all men."

—Ralph Waldo Emerson

When we categorize something, we are engaging in third-level, or symbolic, thinking. With categories we cluster information and quickly form general impressions, using past experiences and streamlining decision making. Categorization lets us bypass analytical thinking, particularly when a logical process isn't evident. This is a much more sophisticated thinking process than the sorting I referred to earlier. Many people confuse the term *categorization* with *sorting*. Of course, categories require some type of sorting; we make distinctions and apply labels, and we pigeonhole information and experiences. The difference is that sorting is static, whereas categorization is dynamic. To understand this last point, let's take a quick look at the differences between the two skills.

In our first years in school, we learned to sort by color—red M&Ms in this group, green M&Ms in that group. We learned to sort by size—big buttons here, little buttons there. Perhaps even by shape—triangles in this box, rectangles in that box. Sometimes we sorted by multiple characteristics, also called variables—little red buttons here, big green rectangles there. Once we separated things into their correct group, we didn't do anything else with them, except put them away as we got ready for the next lesson or for lunch.

Sorting was supposed to teach us to identify salient characteristics that diverse objects shared. For most kids the lesson was little more than busywork. It was not endowed with any significant meaning.

Sorting became more significant in high school biology. There we learned the principles of taxonomy. All living things can be classified by kingdom, phylum, class, order, family, genus, and species. We learned how salient characteristics infer relationships, the basis for Charles Darwin's *Origin of Species*. Darwin set in motion the concept of evolution—progressive change over time. No longer did diversity among plants and animals seem arbitrary or the whim of a Creator. Life possessed a perceivable logic. The interrelationships among plants, animals, and environments were complex but decipherable.

As with sorting and classification, we begin to categorize things by giving them labels. When we categorize something, unlike when we sort and classify, we establish a personal—and therefore dynamic—relationship with it.

The process of categorization employs what scientists call *fuzzy logic*. Instead of absolutes, fuzzy logic allows us to organize information in terms of degree. We use modifiers: usually or rarely; likely or unlikely; many, several or few; possible or improbable.

Fuzzy logic might not seem particularly businesslike, but it's the way our brains work. Our brains filter the world through our emotional experiences. How we categorize something determines how we will behave toward it. Categories that are formed during intense emotional experiences tend to be either positively or negatively prejudicial. Someone who was once bitten by a dog may categorize all dogs as dangerous, even if future encounters with dogs are uneventful. On the other hand, someone who has had dogs for pets may view all dogs as loving companions and excuse an occasional nip as accidental roughhousing. Once established, categories usually stay intact despite evidence that they're not valid.

All the puzzles in this book were designed to utilize what your brain already does naturally and efficiently. By becoming aware of the perceptual processes, you gain control over them. Then you can incorporate them effectively into intentional actions. Although categorization works on a quicker and more subliminal level than do the other processes, it is still controllable when we understand what's going on inside our heads.

At work, people are generally good at sorting and bad at categorizing. Or to put it another way, they're good at placing information in files but bad at juxtaposing the filed information and creating innovative, new categories. This is one reason people have so much difficulty working in cross-functional teams; they've sorted themselves into one function and can't think of themselves as a part of a multifunctional group.

Another problem is that people miscategorize all the time because of emotional experiences vis-à-vis a category. You probably have a direct report who hates the category of technology. Most likely, he had a negative emotional experience early on with computers—he couldn't get the hang of using a piece of software years ago—and it has caused him to categorize technological tasks as bad.

The puzzles here help people get out of thinking ruts. As you go through them, you'll find that they help you unlearn your assumptions. By making you more conscious of how you arrive at category conclusions, you'll become much more astute about evaluating whether they're effective conclusions. To solve the puzzles, you use many of the perceptual skills you've already acquired, including these:

- Comparing similarities and differences between objects
- Breaking down complex images into simpler parts
- Distinguishing relevant from irrelevant information
- Determining which parts belong to which wholes

What you're really learning is to think about how you think—which is how we gain insight.

DEVELOPING A CATEGORY VOCABULARY

Look at the category puzzle on page 214. You see three circles labeled 1, 2, 3. In each circle are three objects. Some of them may remind you of nothing in particular and are, therefore, more abstract. Other objects look like things you've seen before and could be called more concrete.

Each circle represents a different category. Determine what all three objects in a circle have in common. To solve this puzzle, select descriptive words from the list of variables at the bottom of the puzzle page. Write your answers on the lines under the circles.

Look at the list of words at the bottom of the puzzle page. You may be familiar with the meaning of some of them. I'll give you some general explanations to get you started.

- Color—Some objects contain large areas of black and white within their borders. Other objects are outlined in black but are white inside.
- Number—Each object in the circle has the same number of parts.

Objective: Determine the variable(s) that the group of pictures in a circle share.

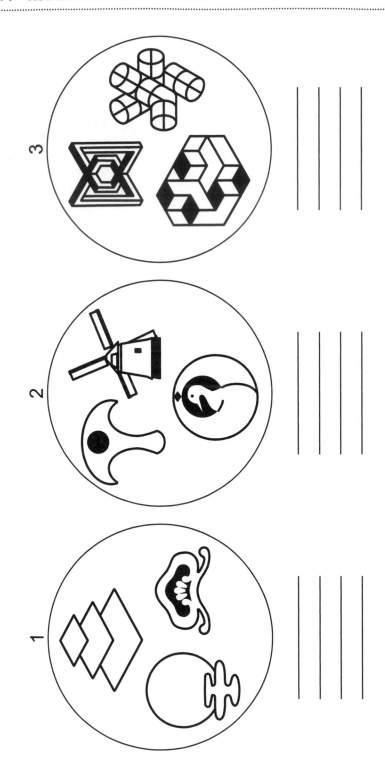

Hint: The pictures may share one or more of the variables listed below.

Abstract	Color	Linear	Shape	Symmetry
Asymmetry	Concrete	Curved	Number	Size	Texture
	Dimension			

- Shape—The objects have similar outlines.
- Size—The objects are similar in height and width.
- Abstract—You can neither recognize nor name the object.
- Concrete—You can recognize and name the object.
- Asymmetry—If you split the objects vertically or horizontally down the middle, one side looks different from the other.
- Symmetry—If you split the objects vertically or horizontally down the middle, one side is a mirror image of the other.
- Curved—The object is composed almost entirely of curved lines.
- Linear—The object is composed entirely of straight lines.
- Dimension—If an object looks flat, it is two-dimensional. If an object seems to project off the page, it is three-dimensional.
- Texture—A pattern is repeated inside the object—for example, stripes or polka dots.

The explanations I've provided are not absolute, so you don't have to take them literally. It's more important that you recognize how you use a word and that you use it consistently. A word may apply to more than one category.

If you do this puzzle with other people, you may find that they interpret the objects differently from the way you do. For instance, some people think the top object in Circle 1 looks like a stack of papers. Other people see it as entirely abstract; to some people, it is two-dimensional; to others, it is three-dimensional.

An answer is wrong only if you cannot explain why you used it. Consistency is more important here than consensus. I want you to think about what words mean to you—how you usually use a particular word.

If you're having trouble getting started on this puzzle, cover Circles 2 and 3 so you can't see them. Then ask yourself if the objects in Circle 1 look abstract to you. Look at each object individually. Does the word apply to each specific object? If you answered yes three times, write the word *abstract* on a line under Circle 1.

Go through all 12 words in the list. Not all of the words will apply. Something cannot be abstract and concrete at the same time—at least not in this puzzle. If you're not sure if a word applies, don't write it down. Remember that you have to justify your use of the word, and you have to be consistent. Find at least three variables per category.

When you're through with Circle 1, cover it and look at Circle 2. Go through the word list again. Use your experience with Circle 1 to help you determine what traits the objects in Circle 2 share.

When you're through with Circle 2, cover it and look at Circle 3 and so on.

After you've determined all the variables in Circle 3, uncover Circles 1 and 2. Read the words you've written. Did you use them the same way for all three categories? Remember the object of this puzzle is to give you insight into how you use words to describe things. If you're inconsistent, you won't communicate effectively. You won't get the results you want.

See some possible answers on page 220. Yours may differ.

CIRCLES WITHIN CIRCLES

Remember that one of the strengths of categorization is that it allows us to engage in fuzzy logic. We don't have to think in absolutes but can categorize things by degree.

To solve the first category puzzle on page 214, you had to evaluate the variables. To solve this next puzzle on page 217, you have to prioritize variables. You have to determine which are relevant and to what degree.

●   ●   ●

Look at the puzzle on page 217. Notice we're using some of the same objects we used in the previous puzzle, although some objects are new. Notice that now the three circles are overlapping each other. Where the circles overlap, you see horizontal lines. Write your answers on these lines.

As before, the three circles indicate three categories. Now they are not entirely distinct from each other. Each category has objects with variables in common with the other two. The three categories have one object with a variable that is common to them all.

If you cover the objects in the top two circles, you see the bottom circle already has two objects in it. It also has three horizontal lines indicating that three more objects belong to this category. The left line indicates an object with a variable that is common to the top left circle and the bottom circle. The right line indicates an object with a variable that is common to the top right circle and the bottom circle. The middle line indicates an object with a variable that is common to all three circles.

Look at the row of objects at the bottom of the puzzle page. Notice that the objects are numbered 1 to 5. These are the answers you use to solve the puzzle. Write the number that corresponds to the object on the appropriate horizontal line.

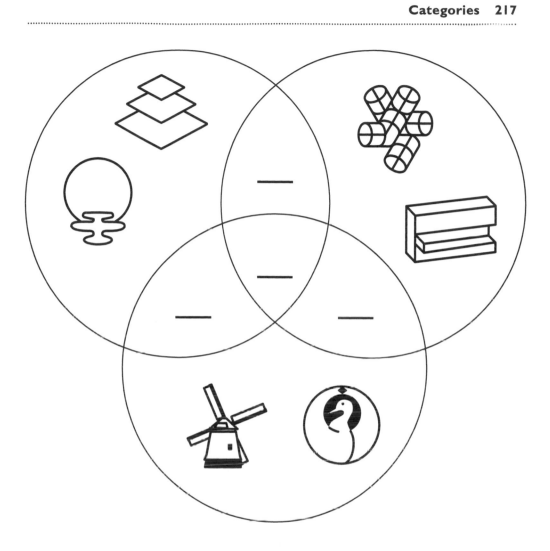

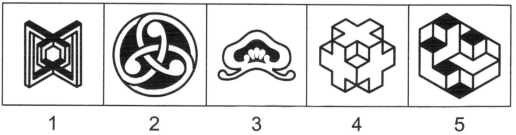

1   2   3   4   5

As before, you may want to cover the objects in two of the circles so you can focus your attention on the salient characteristics of one category at a time. Use the list of words from the previous puzzle to help you describe what you see. Either in or next to the circle write the word(s) that best describe(s) the category. You'll find that several answers seem to fit. Write the numbers of the possible answers under the horizontal lines for ready reference.

After you've looked at each category individually and have written your possible answers under the appropriate lines, cover the objects in the bottom circle. Be sure you don't cover the row of answers on the bottom of the puzzle page because you'll want to refer to them.

Compare the variables you've listed for the top left circle and the top right circle. One thing they have in common is color. None of the objects in either group have large black areas. Look at the row of answers at the bottom of the puzzle page. Only number 4 lacks large black areas. So number 4 is a possible answer. Let's see how well it fits.

The two objects already in the top left circle are symmetrical—so is number 4. The two objects already in the top right circle are four-dimensional—they seem to project off the page and confuse the eye. Number 4 fits there also. Write 4 on the topmost horizontal line.

Continue comparing the variables in two circles at a time. Remember to verify your answers, making sure they fit neatly into each category. You must be able to defend your answer by naming specific variables; otherwise it is wrong.

When you're through comparing the variables in two circles at a time, compare the variables in all three. Use the same method to systematically select your answer.

Remember to verify. Cover the objects in the top right and bottom circles. Can you logically defend your choices by naming the variables all five objects share in the top left circle? Do the same for the other circles.

If you do this puzzle with other people, you may find that they come up with answers different from yours. **Remember consistency in the way you use words is more important than consensus.** You have to be able to logically defend your choice by specifying the variables you selected.

See some possible answers on page 220.

CATEGORY BENEFITS

The previous category puzzles offered you the chance to become more insightful, which may seem a small thing from a business perspective but is actually a big thing. Insight is akin to the X-ray vision Superman possessed, except that instead of seeing through objects, you see through false assumptions and distracting variables. As a result, you can make better decisions faster.

Consider some of the skills you used in working on the category puzzles. You had to infer relationships between diverse elements, prioritize efforts, and envision consequences. You had to distinguish the relevant detail from the irrelevant one. And you had to understand how all the pieces fit within the larger whole.

Even though you may use some of these skills at work, they're not habitual. The exercises, when practiced consistently, make these skills intuitive.

Your organization can benefit in many ways if a critical mass of employees practice these skills regularly. To give you a sense of how these puzzles translate into real work advantages, following are just some possibilities.

They help to prioritize the *big* picture. At this level, people are able to organize their work according to a series of goals. They categorize tasks for themselves and others based on what's the most important thing they (their group or the company as a whole) need to achieve, the second most important, and so on. Although this type of prioritizing might sound relatively easy to do, in fact it's quite difficult. Caught up in the daily routine of organizational life, goals—like the circles in our exercise—overlap. Not only don't we stop and think if a given task is helping us achieve our primary goal, but we're not always sure of the answer even if we do. Typically, we're involved in so many projects simultaneously that it's tough to know if we're really focusing our efforts on the right things. Big-picture prioritizing helps us make that determination.

They help to identify the problem. When people possess the thinking skills to organize information in new ways, it becomes much easier to see what's wrong in a given situation. Recall the 12 variables in the circle exercises. They provide practice in looking for different ways of grouping items based on shared characteristics. When you see the variables that justify a grouping, it's an ah-ha moment. The same ah-ha occurs when you frame a problem in a new way, finding the variable that creates the new frame (or the new category). Suddenly, this new perspective reveals what's wrong. Looking at a situation from a different angle reveals flaws that were hidden by other perspectives. It's like looking at a jewel in a dull light; to the inexperienced eye, it seems perfect. But when the jewel is rotated in a better light, the flaws are revealed. It's been said that in organizations, it's easy to solve problems. What's difficult is identifying them.

They help to allocate resources. At the very least, these category exercises should help people make better use of their time and energy. As you probably know all too well, many employees have sloppy work habits. They waste time and energy because they take on jobs they should delegate or because they're focused on doing a job perfectly that doesn't need to be done 100 percent correctly. By categorizing their work in new ways, they become aware of the assignments they should delegate and those they should handle on their own. It becomes clear that certain tasks demand error-free implementation and others don't.

To use time wisely, we have to think effectively. We have to do the right thing at the right time. We have to be skilled in inferring relationships between diverse elements, prioritizing efforts, and envisioning consequences. We have to distinguish those things that are relevant to achieving the results we want—and be willing to ignore those things that are irrelevant, however appealing they might be. We also have to understand where we fit into the big picture. When we can do all of these things intuitively, we've become insightful.

The following pages—221 through 227—allow you additional practice for category exercises.

● ● ●

A, B, C at the top are complex geometric figures. The designs numbered 1-12 were derived from Figures A, B, or C.

Objective: Match the designs to their original geometric figures. Write your answers on the space provided under the appropriate figure.

A, B, C at the top are complex geometric figures. The designs numbered 1-12 were derived from Figures A, B, or C.

Objective: Match the designs to their original geometric figures. Write your answers on the space provided under the appropriate figure.

A	B	C
1	**2**	**3**
4	**5**	**6**
7	**8**	**9**
10	**11**	**12**

A, B, C at the top are complex geometric figures. The designs numbered 1-12 were derived from Figures A, B, or C.

Objective: Match the designs to their original geometric figures. Write your answers on the space provided under the appropriate figure.

A, B, C at the top are complex geometric figures. The designs numbered 1-12 were derived from Figures A, B, or C.

Objective: Match the designs to their original geometric figures. Write your answers on the space provided under the appropriate figure.

A	B	C
1	2	3
4	5	6
7	8	9
10	11	12

A, B, C at the top are complex geometric figures. The designs numbered
1-12 were derived from Figures A, B, or C.

Objective: Match the designs to their original geometric figures. Write your
answers on the space provided under the appropriate figure.

A, B, C at the top are complex geometric figures. The designs numbered 1-12 were derived from Figures A, B, or C.

Objective: Match the designs to their original geometric figures. Write your answers on the space provided under the appropriate figure.

A, B, C at the top are complex geometric figures. The designs numbered 1-12 were derived from Figures A, B, or C.

Objective: Match the designs to their original geometric figures. Write your answers on the space provided under the appropriate figure.

ANSWERS FOR CATEGORY PUZZLES

Page 221:
    a. 5, 7, 9, 11
    b. 1, 3, 8, 12
    c. 2, 4, 6, 10
Page 222:
    a. 1, 3, 5, 11
    b. 2, 6, 7, 9
    c. 4, 8, 10, 12
Page 223:
    a. 1, 6, 7, 11
    b. 3, 5, 9, 10
    c. 2, 4, 8, 12
Page 224:
    a. 3, 5, 10, 12
    b. 1, 7, 9, 11
    c. 2, 4, 6, 8
Page 225:
    a. 3, 5, 9, 10
    b. 1, 4, 6, 8
    c. 2, 7, 11, 12
Page 226:
    a. 1, 6, 7, 11
    b. 3, 5, 9, 10
    c. 2, 4, 8, 12
Page 227:
    a. 1, 5, 9, 11
    b. 3, 4, 8, 10
    c. 2, 6, 7, 12

CHAPTER

Decoding a System

Technology can make us more efficient but not more effective. Our complex brains make us effective. Unfortunately, most of the time we don't make good use of our ability to think; thinking takes practice. Our brains are so good at extrapolating information that it takes intentional effort to slow down and think about what we're doing and why we're doing it.

The puzzles in this chapter were designed to give you an opportunity to rehearse complex problem solving in a situation where you are forced to design a system. In many instances, the first system you design won't work. You'll be forced to review the problem again along with your newfound understanding of the variables and refine your system appropriately.

In the following pages, you're going to decode the Babylonian, Egyptian, Greek, and Mayan numerical systems. This may strike you as an impossible task initially, but believe me, it's not. Though these systems may seem literally and figuratively foreign, you're well prepared for the challenge. If you're skeptical, consider that you've already learned how to:

- Compare similarities and differences.
- Discover analogous relationships.
- Divide wholes into parts and reunite them.
- Recognize how values progressively changed.
- Practice switching between deductive and inductive thinking.
- Determine when information was relevant and when it was irrelevant.

These critical thinking skills will facilitate your work on the decoding puzzles. When you first look at the puzzles, don't be put off if you can't see a starting point immediately. Too often, when we don't get something right away, we become frustrated and assume we're dumb. In our society, we assume that people who finish tests first, snap off ten ideas in ten seconds, and raise their hands before anyone else are the smartest. The truth is that smart, effective people put a lot of time and effort into thinking through a problem. It's only when they've decided on the results they want and determined how to achieve them that they think fast.

Therefore, give yourself permission to think through the ancient numerical systems and give your mind a chance to use all the great new skills you've acquired.

WHAT AN ANCIENT NUMERICAL SYSTEM HAS TO DO WITH THE MODERN WORLD OF WORK

Try to see the world of written language through the eyes of kindergarteners. At first, all the words in a book look like gibberish. Before they know the alphabet, all the markings on the page are completely meaningless. Even after they learn their letters, most kids still have to make considerable effort before they master reading. Eventually, though, they do master it. If children can decode this complex system, people in organizations can achieve similar feats.

When children learn to read, they're absorbing a lot of information, filtering it through their mind, comparing and contrasting and finding a way into what at first must seem like a closed system. It opens up through little clues—saying letters out loud, recalling how a simple word is pronounced and seeing it on the page, using knowledge of how to read a simple word like *cat* to figure out how to say a slightly more complicated word like *catsup*.

Almost everyone has had some experience decoding different types of systems. Learning the Arabic numerical system, a foreign language, a computer system, the customs of another country, and the way a new team operates are just some examples of how we decode systems in order to operate effectively within them. Most people can decode at least parts of a system. It's the rare individual who can't learn even a little of a foreign language or is incapable of doing basic functions on a computer. Many individuals, however, either take a long time to decode a system or decode too small a piece of it to derive a meaningful benefit.

Think about what happens when someone joins a team in your organization—someone who is new either to the team or to the company itself. The new member knows little about the team's history. Each member, too, has a history, a way of interacting in team settings that will be unfamiliar to the rookie. Policies and procedures have been put in place, and there's probably also an informal agreement about how the team works. The new member can't absorb everything at once and decode the system instantly. Instead, she needs to make mental connections based on bits and pieces of information. Using this information, she can take incremental steps toward understanding the system, starting small and working her way toward a larger understanding. When she first joins the team, she will be disoriented by the new system; things don't work the same way that they did on a previous team. Initially, she must tolerate a great deal of ambiguity, uncertainty, and complexity until she gets her bearings. But she must decode the system if she is to become a productive member of the team.

People who are new to various organizational systems—whether teams, partnerships with outside groups, foreign offices—typically have problems adapting, preventing these systems from functioning optimally. Here are the usual reactions when people are thrust into unfamiliar systems:

- **They try to impose their own perspective and their own will.** Having only one perspective can make simple problems seem extremely complex.
- **They become flustered.** If people don't understand how the information was organized, they won't see even the most obvious solution.
- **They become slaves to routine.** People adhere rigidly to routines when they don't know how to effectively get the results they want.

The puzzles in this chapter help people develop alternatives to these reactions. As you'll discover, you can react to complexity and chaos with intelligence rather than illogic.

DECODING THE BABYLONIAN NUMBER SYSTEM

Long ago, people all over the world looked up at the night sky and saw an orderly system. Through observation they learned to predict lunar and solar eclipses and seasonal changes. Celestial pattern detection led to agriculture, astrology, and astronomy. *Pattern detection is the basis of all knowledge.*

My designing-a-system puzzles give you practice in generating knowledge from unknown systems. Let's work on some of these puzzles.

●   ●   ●

Look at the puzzle on page 233. On the right side of the page under the heading "Column B," you see an assortment of familiar Arabic numbers. Under the heading "Column A," you see an assortment of hash marks. These are ancient Babylonian numbers. To solve the puzzle, write the Arabic number on the horizontal line next to the corresponding Babylonian number.

Start by thinking about some of the things you already know about number systems. They have a:

- Hierarchical order (smaller values to larger)
- Consistent set of rules
- Recognizable pattern
- Multiple base—for example, the number 25 actually means 2 multiplied 10 times plus 5 multiplied 1 time ($2 \times 10 + 5 \times 1$)

Look at the puzzle page again. Under Column A, I numbered the hash marks "1, 2, 3 . . ." for easy reference. These numbers indicate that there are 20 problems in this puzzle.

Remember that Column A has the Babylonian numbers. Notice that each Babylonian number consists of vertical and horizontal marks, and some numbers have more marks than others.

On the left side of the puzzle page, I've given you some hints. Just as with the Arabic numbers you've been using since grade school, in the Babylonian system the smallest valued numbers are on the right. In other words, in the number 862, the 8 represents 8 hundreds; the 6 represents 6 tens; and the 2 represents 2 ones.

The second hint—"The base changes"—tells you that you won't be able to solve the problems simply by counting the number of vertical and horizontal

Objective: Match the Arabic numerals in Column B to their Babylonian equivalents in Column A.

Hints: 1. Like Arabic numerals, in the Babylonian system the smallest valued numbers are on the right.

2. Unlike Arabic numerals, in which the base stays constant, the base changes within a Babylonian number.

	Column A		Column B
1.	`--- ||| ||| `	_____	862
2.	`| -- |`	_____	790
3.	`-- ||| |`	_____	112
4.	`| - |||`	_____	242
5.	`| === ||`	_____	59
6.	`--- ||'`	_____	209
7.	`| --- |''`	_____	100
8.	`||| === ||`	_____	1,000
9.	`- ||| - ||`	_____	163
10.	`' ===`	_____	73
11.	`||| -- ||| |||`	_____	732
12.	`---	- ||`	_____	35
13.	`- |`	_____	11
14.	`-- ||' - ||`	_____	27
15.	`|| === |||`	_____	1,152
16.	`--	-`	_____	81
17.	`' === ||| |||`	_____	94
18.	`|| - ||| |`	_____	129
19.	`-- || -- ||`	_____	1,032
20.	`-- |'' ===`	_____	137

marks. Sometimes you'll have to multiply. For example: in the number 862, 8 actually means 800 or 8 times 100.

Look at the Babylonian numbers in Column A again. Think about what you know now. A group of marks on the right of a Babylonian number represent a lesser value than the group of marks on the left. Also, the Babylonians used groups of vertical and horizontal lines, so the change in a mark's direction must have some significance.

It seems logical to assume that smaller numbers will have fewer marks. Remember this is just an assumption and is something we'll have to test later. For now, look at Column A, line 13. The Babylonian number there has one horizontal mark and one vertical mark. Line 13 has the fewest marks of all, so let's assume it represents the smallest number.

Look at Column B. The smallest number there is 11. If this is a match for line 13, then a vertical mark on the far right of a Babylonian number represents a value of 1. A horizontal mark to the immediate left represents a value of 10. We know that $10 + 1 = 11$. Write "11" on the horizontal line that corresponds to Column A, line 13.

Starting with this basic knowledge, let's find the other Babylonian numbers that have only vertical marks on the right and horizontal marks to their immediate left. Notice that only lines 1, 3, and 6 qualify.

Look at line 1. If a horizontal mark represents the number 10, then the five horizontal marks must mean 5×10 or 50. Also, if the vertical marks represent the number 1, then the nine vertical marks must mean 9×1 or 9. Line 1 would equal $50 + 9$ or 59. There is a 59 in Column B we can use. Write "59" on the horizontal line that corresponds to Column A, line 1.

Now solve lines 3 and 6 on your own.

Notice that most, but not all, of the Babylonian numbers have a group of vertical marks on the far right. The maximum number of vertical marks in the far right group is nine. We can start doing some educated guessing.

Look at Column A, line 2. Reading from left to right, it has one vertical mark, two horizontal marks, and again one vertical mark. The vertical mark on the far right equals the number 1. Look at Column B. We've already used "11." You can cross that out to remind yourself you're not going to use it again. The only other number with a 1 in the "one's column" is "81." Let's see if it works.

Look at line 2 again. Notice the two horizontal marks. They equal 2×10, or 20. If we assume that line 2 equals 81, then the vertical line to the immediate left would have to equal 60. This is because $81 - 21 = 60$. Let's test this theory on line 4.

The three vertical marks on the far right of the Babylonian number equals 3. The one horizontal mark equals 10. So far we have 10 + 3 or 13. If the vertical line on the far left equals 60, we would have 60 + 10 + 3, or 73. Look in Column B. We have a 73 we can use. Write "73" on the horizontal line that corresponds to Column A, line 4.

Solve as many of the problems as you can with the knowledge you have acquired so far. Remember to cross off the numbers in Column B as you use them.

Notice that the maximum number of horizontal marks in the second from the right group is six. Therefore, the maximum number that group can equal is 60.

Let's recap. We can have a maximum of nine vertical marks in the far right group. A horizontal mark in the next to the right group equals ten. To indicate 20 we would use two horizontal marks. We can only have six horizontal marks in the second from the right group. So six horizontal marks means 6 × 10, or 60. So far, so good.

A vertical line in the third group from the right represents 60—the same value as six horizontal lines. Why did the Babylonians have two different ways of representing the same number? Because they didn't have a mark to represent zero and couldn't have a group with nothing in it.

Look at Column A, line 10. Notice that the marks on the far right are horizontal not vertical. That means the "one's column" is equal to 0. The four horizontal marks mean 4 × 10, or 40. The vertical mark to the immediate left equals 1 × 60, or 60. So 40 + 60 equals . . . well, you can figure that one out.

So far we've covered the first three groups beginning on the far right. Look at Column A, line 9. Reading from the right, we have two vertical marks, one horizontal mark, six vertical marks, and one horizontal mark. The maximum number of vertical marks in the third group from the right is six. A single vertical mark there equals 60. Therefore, the maximum number that group can equal is 60 × 6, or 360. Because the Babylonians had two ways of representing 60, let's assume they also had two ways of representing 360. If this assumption is valid, then a horizontal mark in the fourth group from the right would equal 360. Do the math for line 9 and see if Column B has an Arabic equivalent you can use.

Using all the new knowledge you've acquired about Babylonian numbers, solve the rest of the problems on the puzzle page. **Remember to use each Arabic number in Column B only once.** After you've verified your answers, check them against mine.

TRANSLATING GREEK INTO EGYPTIAN

This next puzzle also consists of ancient number systems—specifically Greek and Egyptian. However, we're going to take a little break from math. You don't have to translate the numbers in Columns A or B into Arabic. All you have to do is match the numeric equivalents. I gave you two examples to get you started.

● ● ●

Look at Column A, line 7 on puzzle page 237. The early Greek symbol looks like a backward 7 or a hook. Let's call it a *hook*.

As we learned from decoding the Babylonian number system, the smallest numbers are the simplest. Therefore, we can conclude that number 7 in Column A corresponds to letter D in Column B. Notice also that in Column B the vertical marks are either alone or to the right of the other symbol groups. The symbols also change size.

Look at Column A. The symbols change size here too. Perhaps we can assume that size is irrelevant in both ancient Greek and Egyptian numbers.

Again look at Column A. Our hook occurs in lines 1, 4, 5, 7, and 8. However, it is not always on the far right. The hook is only on the far right in lines 7 and 8.

We know from the example that the hook represents five vertical marks. Looking at Column B, we see that the Egyptian number in line G also has five vertical marks. All the other answers in Column B have more than or fewer than five vertical marks.

Let's compare line 8 and line G again. In the Greek number, to the left of the hook we see seven triangles. In the Egyptian number, to the left of the five vertical marks we see seven upside-down Us. What else? In line 8 the Greek number has two Hs. In line G the Egyptian number has two curly-Qs. Using this knowledge, solve the remaining problems on the puzzle on page 238.

BRUSHING UP ON YOUR ANCIENT MAYAN

Archeologists have discovered only two ancient cultures that employed zero as a placeholder in their number system—the Muslims who gave us the Arabic numbers and the Mayans of Mexico and Central America. After solving my Babylonian puzzles, many people have a greater appreciation for the lowly zero.

● ● ●

Objectives: Match the figures in Column B to their numeric equivalents in Column A.

Column A (Early Greek)		Column B (Egyptian)

1. ΧΓΙΙ ___

A. ∩∩ ¦ ¦ ¦

2. ΗΗΗ △△△ △△△ △△△ ___

B. � ∩∩∩ ∩∩∩ ∩∩ |

3. Χ △△△ △△△ △△ | ___

C. ℮ ∩∩∩ ∩∩∩ |

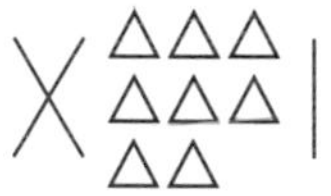

4. △△Γ ___

D. | | | ¦

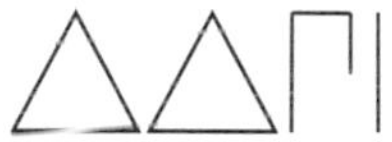

5. Η Η Η Η Γ || ___

E. ↆ | | | | | | |

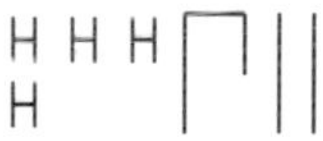

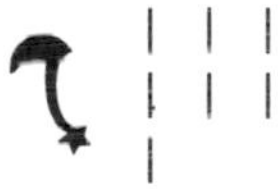

6. Η △△△ △△△ | ___

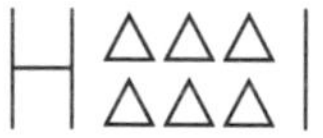

F. ℮℮℮ ∩∩∩ ∩∩∩ ∩∩∩

7. Γ ___

G. ℮℮℮ ∩∩∩∩ | | | ∩∩∩∩ | | ∩

8. ΗΗ △△△ △△△ △ Γ ___

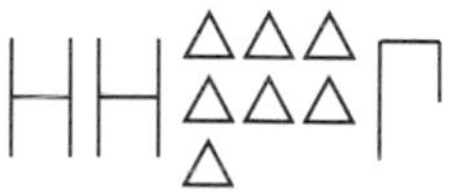

H. ℮℮℮ ℮ | | | | | | |

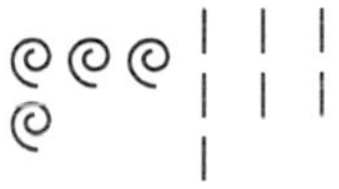

Objective: Match the Arabic numbers in the far right column to their Mayan equivalents.

Hints: 1.  represents zero value.
2. • represents a single unit which may or may not be equal to 1.

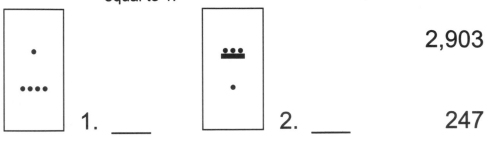

2,903

247

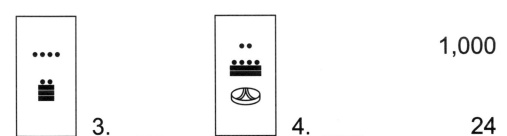

1,000

24

161

240

60

97

Look at the designing-a-system puzzle on page 238 and notice I've provided you with two hints. The first hint informs you that the picture that looks like a peace symbol or a button represents zero. As such it can be used as a placeholder. The second hint says a black dot is a single unit but is not always equal to 1. In other words, where the dot is placed will affect its value. For example: in the number 51, the 1 means just 1. In the number 15, the 1 means 10. In the number 150, the 1 means 100, and so on.

Look at the puzzle page and notice that on the far right I've given you an assortment of Arabic numbers. Solve the puzzle by matching the Arabic numbers to their Mayan equivalents.

Let's start with something we know. The peace symbol/button equals zero. There are three Mayan numbers with zero in them that I've labeled #4, #5, and #8. Also, I've given you three Arabic numbers that end in zero. Could there possibly be some connection here? The Arabic numbers are 1,000, 240, and 60.

Number 8 is the simplest of the three Mayan numbers containing zeros. The lowest Arabic number that ends in zero is 60. The Mayan number in #8 has three dots. Divide 3 into 60 and we get 20. We can probably assume that in #8 a single dot equals 20. Is that always the case or does its place have some significance?

We've already assumed a hierarchy in the Mayan number system—the lower the symbol, the lesser its value. We read our peace symbol/button as being in the "one's column." Let's look more closely at the other Mayan numbers.

In addition to the peace symbol/buttons and dots, we see horizontal bars. Let's just ignore the bars for now since we can't immediately relate them to anything.

Besides #8, the only other Mayan number without bars is #1. We see one dot on top and four on the bottom. If we assume that the top dot equals 20, what could the bottom dots equal? Let's look at our Arabic numbers. The only choice that contains a 20 is the number 24. Look again at #1. Could the 4 bottom dots equal 4? In that case, a dot in the bottom row means 1, but a dot in the row immediately above it means 20.

Because we're assuming that the bottom row indicates the lowest value, it makes sense that a single dot there could equal 1. Everybody starts counting from 1.

At this point you can write "60" next to #8 and "24" next to #1. Remember to cross off these numbers in the far right column.

Now we have to look at the Mayan numbers that contain horizontal bars. Let's make it easy on ourselves. What do we already know? A single dot in the bottom row equals 1. Number 2 has a single dot in the bottom row. Look at the Arabic number choices. Do we have any number that ends in 1? Of course we do—161.

Look at #2 again. You see three dots over a bar in the top group. If we assume that each dot still equals 20, then the three dots mean 20 × 3 or 60. With the bottom dot we now have 60 + 1 or 61. However, the number we're looking for is 161. If we subtract 161 − 61 we get 100. Could the bar equal 100? Maybe, but how can we verify that assumption?

Look at the other Mayan numbers. The bars vary in length. Is that significant? Closer examination reveals that the length of a bar is somehow related to the number of dots above it. A bar's length may be more aesthetic than numeric.

Look at #4. The maximum number of dots over a bar appears to be four. Look at #1 and #3. The maximum number of dots in a row appears to be four. In this case we can reasonably argue that a bar could equal five dots.

Let's go back to #2. We've already determined that the bottom dot equals 1 and the three top dots equal 3 × 20 or 60. So we have 60 + 1, or 61, and we need 161. If the bar equals 5 dots and each dot equals 20, then 5 × 20 equals 100. We now have 100 + 60 + 1, or 161—just what we need. Write "161" next to #2 and cross off the Arabic number in the far right column.

What else can we do with the knowledge we've acquired? Let's look at our zero placeholders again. We said #8 is equal to 60. We're through with that problem. Look at #5 and #4. They're the only other Mayan numbers with zeros in the "one's column." We've also got two Arabic numbers with zeros in the "one's column"—1,000 and 240. Because #4 has more levels than #5, we can assume that it's the higher number—1,000. What else can we learn from it?

We said that in the second from the bottom group, a dot equals 20 and a bar equals 5 dots. In other words, a bar equals 20 × 5, or 100. Notice that #4 has 4 dots and 2 bars in the second from the bottom group. The four dots mean 4 × 20, or 80. The two bars mean 2 × 100, or 200. So now we have 80 + 200, or 280.

Remember we want to prove that #4 equals 1,000. The peace symbol/button in the bottom row means zero in the "one's column." We don't really have to do anything with it as the Arabic number 1,000 also has zero in the "one's column."

Getting back to the math, we subtract 1,000 − 280 and get a remainder of 720. Look at the top row of dots in #4. There are two of them. Divide 720 by 2. The answer is 360. Can we assume that a dot in the third group from the bottom equals 360? Let's try it.

Besides #4, there is only one other Mayan number that has three groups of dots/bars. Look at #7. The bottom-most group of dots tells us to look for an Arabic number that has 3 in the "one's column." The only available number is 2,903.

Look at #7 again. The second row from the bottom has one dot. That one dot equals 20. So far we have 20 + 3, or 23. If a dot in the top group equals 360, then the three dots must equal 3 × 360, or 1,080. If a bar equals five dots, then the bar in the top group equals 5 × 360, or 1,800. Now we have 1,800 + 1,080 + 20 + 3 or 2,903—exactly what we want.

Finish solving the rest of the problems on the puzzle page. Remember to cross off the Arabic numbers in the far right column as you use them. Also, remember to verify your work.

PREPARING YOURSELF FOR THE UNKNOWN

Learning how to function effectively in confusing, overwhelming environments can give your organization a competitive edge. The majority of your people don't function effectively in these environments. Instead, they look at a project as you looked at the Mayan numeric system and say, "This can't be done." They complain that they don't have enough information, time, or resources to meet the project goal. They protest that they don't understand the new technology or are bewildered by the changing global market. All this may be true, but it's still possible—and necessary—to decode this perplexing new system.

Doing these exercises increases people's tolerance for change, complexity, and ambiguity. With rehearsal, these exercises don't cause as much stress and anxiety. They're still difficult to do, but you're in a better state of mind to do them. For many people, the ambiguity involved when facing a "foreign" system is what throws them; they desperately want things to be in black-and-white and to anchor themselves in certainties. In the same way, they hate to work on tasks that lack clear objectives or where the borders of responsibility for a project are unclear. Decoding the systems here demonstrates to people that ambiguity doesn't have to be the enemy. After some practice, they will find that they can tolerate a very high degree of ambiguity and still work on the exercises productively.

Decoding these systems also calls on our ability to hold multiple variables in our mind simultaneously. As you probably discovered, you need to keep track of many keys to unlock each numerical code. As soon as you gain one key that unlocks part of the code, you run right into another closed door and have to start searching for a second key, keeping the first key in mind as you solve the puzzle. In work situations, we often become frustrated when there are too many variables flitting about our heads. How many times have you quit on a project or problem because you were overwhelmed by details, when there were so many things going on it was impossible for you to concentrate? Decoding systems helps increase people's tolerance for multiple variables, giving them the capacity to juggle different facts and ideas without becoming overwhelmed.

Finally, breaking these system codes helps people tolerate feeling stupid. This doesn't mean it makes them feel they *are* stupid. Instead, it helps them realize there are times when it's okay to look at a problem and be completely bewildered. It's not a fatal feeling. Nonetheless, many executives refuse to allow themselves to feel stupid, believing that it somehow diminishes them as managers and leaders.

An unwillingness to feel stupid is one of the biggest deterrents to learning among high-functioning people. Refusing to admit you don't know prevents you from looking at a problem in a new way. Instead, you're more likely to "fake" knowledge and take a wild guess about the correct way to do something. To avoid admitting you don't get it, you'll avoid taking problem-solving risks. You'll be terrified of exploring an idea that might lead you nowhere.

When you look at these ancient numerical systems and admit you don't have a clue, this admission provides a basis for learning. By admitting your ignorance and then moving forward, you're demonstrating to yourself that a lack of comprehension can be a catalyst to greater knowledge. When you say, "I don't have the foggiest notion what these Mayan symbols mean," you're giving yourself permission to be temporarily ignorant, which frees your mind. It allows you to explore in new directions, since the old direction is not getting you anywhere.

The new world of virtual teams, global marketplaces, and cultural shifts should make us feel stupid. **Once we admit that we're bewildered, we can start decoding these systems and learning and growing within them.**

Objective: Decode the Babylonian number system.
Write the Arabic equivalents in the space provided.

1.  ⎯⎯ ||| ⎯⎯⎯   _____

2.  || ⎯⎯ || _____

3.  ⎯⎯ ||| ⎯ ||| _____

4. 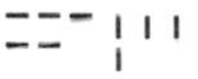 ⎯⎯⎯ ||| _____

5.  || ⎯⎯⎯ ||| _____

6.  ⎯ || ⎯⎯⎯ || _____

7.  | ⎯⎯   _____

8.  ||| ⎯ ||| _____

9. 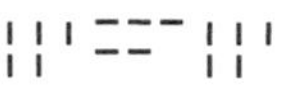 ||| ⎯⎯⎯ ||| _____

10.  ⎯⎯⎯ ||| ⎯ ||| _____

11.  ||| _____

12.  | ⎯ || _____

13.  ||| ⎯⎯ ||| _____

14. 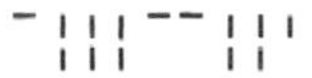 ⎯ ||| ⎯⎯ || _____

15.  ⎯⎯ ||| _____

16.  ⎯ ||| ⎯ ⎯ ||| _____

17. 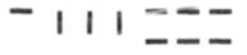 ⎯ ||| ⎯⎯⎯   _____

18.  || ⎯⎯⎯ || _____

19.  ⎯ | ⎯ | _____

20.  | ⎯⎯⎯ | _____

Objectives: Match the figures in Column B to their numeric equivalents in Column A.

Column A (Early Greek)		Column B (Egyptian)
1. △△△ / △△△ / △ ⌐ ¦ ¦ ¦	___	A. ℮℮℮∩ ⅃⅃⅃
2. H H H / H	___	B. ℮ ¦
3. HHH△ ⅃⅃⅃	___	C. ⌇⌇⌇ ⌇⌇ ∩
4. △△△ / △△ ⌐¦	___	D. ℮℮℮ ∩∩∩ ⅃⅃⅃ / ℮℮ ∩∩∩ ⅃⅃ / ∩∩
5. H ¦	___	E. ∩∩∩ ⅃⅃⅃ / ∩∩∩ ⅃⅃⅃ / ∩ ⅃⅃⅃
6. H H H △△△ / H H △△△ ⌐ / △△	___	F. ∩∩∩ ⅃⅃⅃ / ∩∩ ⅃⅃⅃
7. X X X / X X △	___	G. ℮℮℮ / ℮
8. △△⌐¦ ¦ ¦	___	H. ∩∩ ¦¦¦ / ¦¦¦

Objective: Match the Arabic numbers in the far right column to their
Mayan equivalents.

Hints: 1. 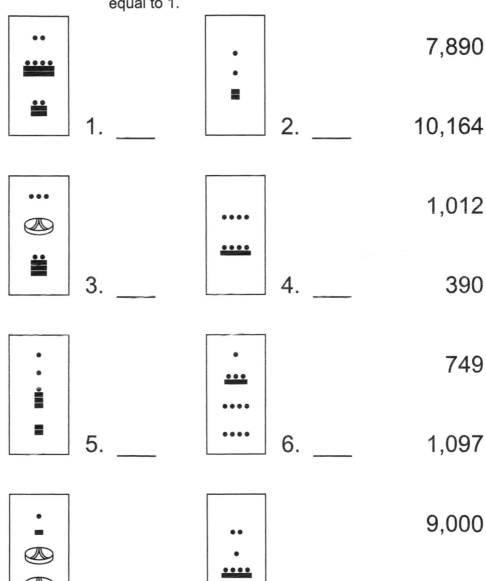 represents zero value.
2. • represents a single unit which may or may not be
equal to 1.

1. ___   2. ___   7,890

10,164

3. ___   4. ___   1,012

390

5. ___   6. ___   749

1,097

7. ___   8. ___   9,000

89

Objective: Match the Arabic numbers in the far right column to their Mayan equivalents.

Hints: 1. 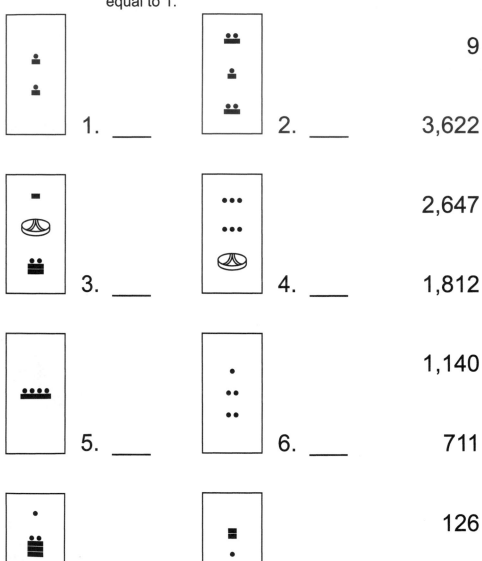 represents zero value.
2. • represents a single unit which may or may not be equal to 1.

9

1. ___   2. ___   3,622

2,647

3. ___   4. ___   1,812

1,140

5. ___   6. ___   711

126

7. ___   8. ___   402

Objective: Match the ancient Greek numbers to their Mayan equivalents.

A	B	C	D	E
				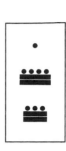

F	G	H	I	J
	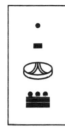	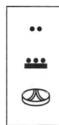		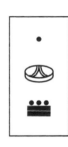

1. HHH ΔΔΔ/ΔΔΔ/Δ |||

2. HHH ΔΔΔ / HHH ΔΔΔ / HH ΔΔ

3. HHH / HHH △

4. ΔΔΔ/ΔΔΔ/ΔΔ ||

5. XXI

6. XXX/XXX/X HH|||

7. XXX/XXX/XXX △|||

8. HHH ΔΔΔ| / HHH ΔΔ|||

9. HΛΔ△Γ'''

10. ΔΔΔ/ΔΔΔ/ΔΔ Γ|||

Objective: Fill in the blanks with numbers from the required numerical systems.

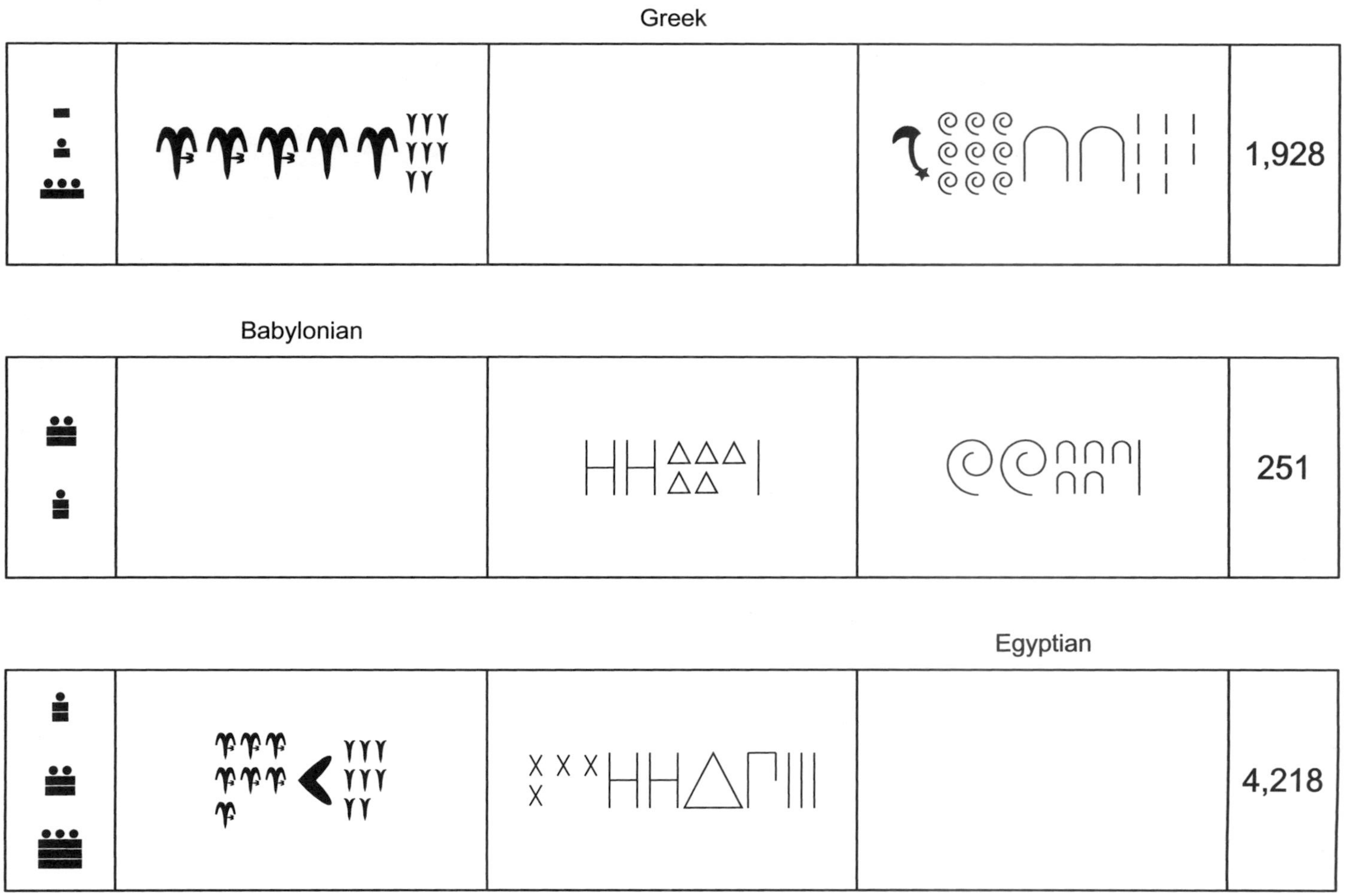

Greek

1,928

251

Egyptian

Babylonian

4,218

Objective: Fill in the blanks with numbers from the required numerical systems.

Babylonian

3,286

Arabic

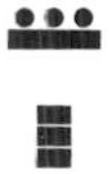

Greek

1,332

ANSWERS FOR DESIGNING-A-SYSTEM PUZZLES

Page 233
1. 59
2. 81
3. 27
4. 73
5. 112
6. 35
7. 94
8. 242
9. 732
10. 100
11. 209
12. 1,152
13. 11
14. 1,032
15. 163
16. 790
17. 129
18. 137
19. 862
20. 1,000

Page 237
1. E
2. F
3. B
4. A
5. H
6. C
7. D
8. G

Page 238
1. 24
2. 161

3. 97
4. 1,000
5. 240
6. 247
7. 2,903
8. 60

Page 243
1. 920
2. 142
3. 1,039
4. 54
5. 173
6. 522
7. 110
8. 193
9. 355
10. 1,397
11. 7
12. 72
13. 234
14. 745
15. 23
16. 646
17. 600
18. 132
19. 431
20. 101

Page 244
1. E
2. G
3. A
4. F
5. B

6. D
7. C
8. H

Page 245
1. 1,012
2. 390
3. 1,097
4. 89
5. 7,890
6. 10,164
7. 9,000
8. 749

Page 246
1. 126
2. 2,647
3. 1,812
4. 1,140
5. 9
6. 402
7. 711
8. 3,622

Page 247
a. 10
b. 3
c. 6
d. 5
e. 8
f. 4
g. 7
h. 2
i. 9
j. 1

Objective: Fill in the blanks with numbers from the required numerical systems.

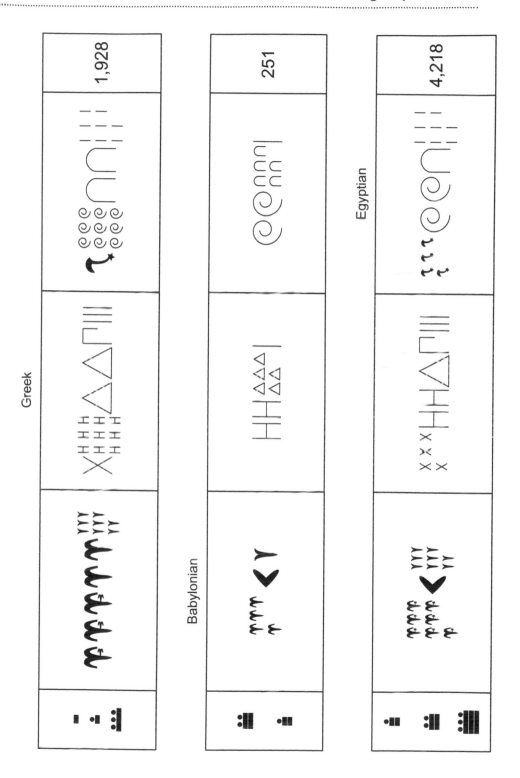

Greek

Babylonian

Egyptian

...tive: Fill in the blanks with numbers from the required numerical systems.

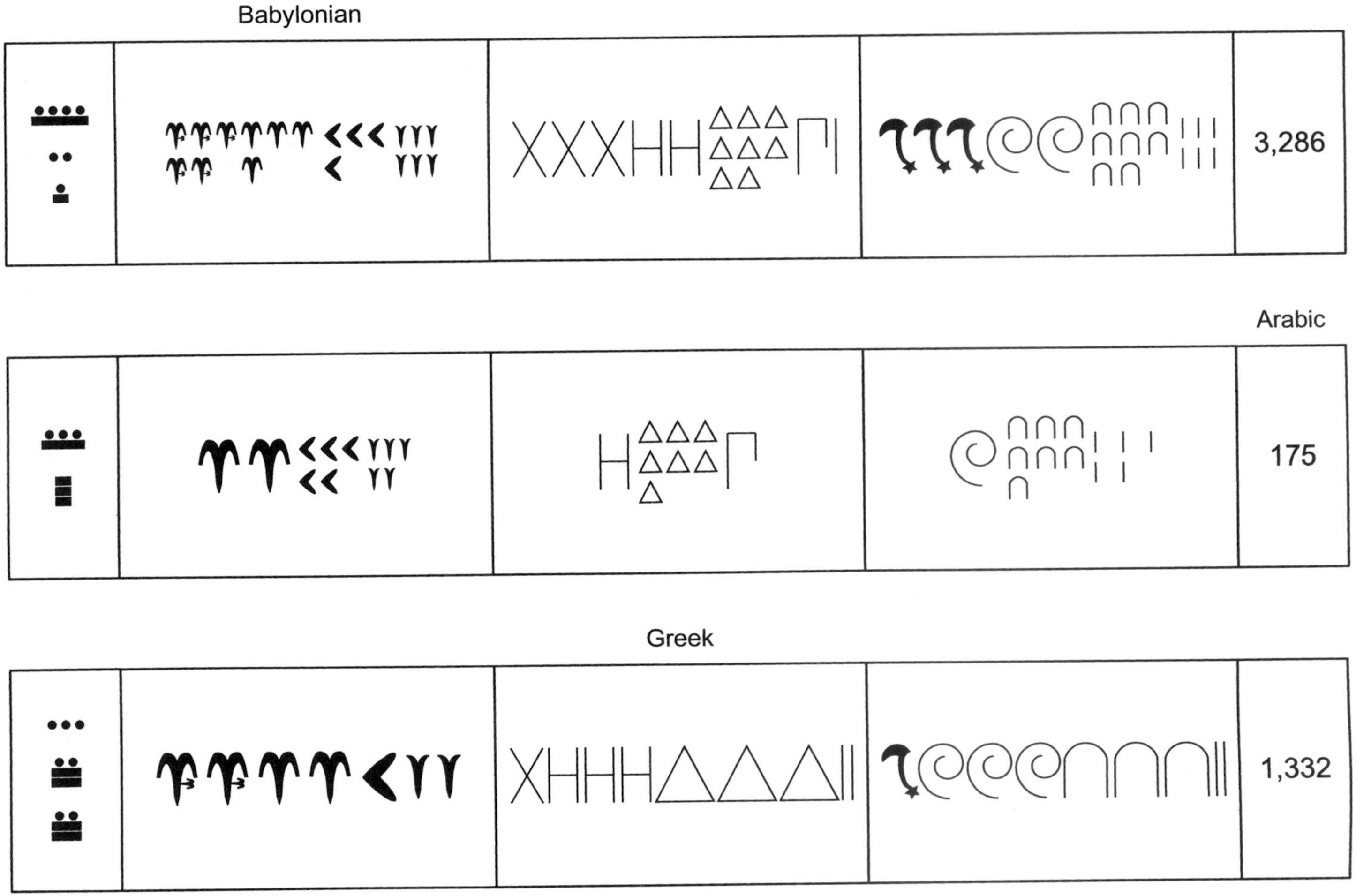

Babylonian

3,286

Arabic

175

Greek

1,332

Getting the Results You Want

Efficiency is limiting. It may help us get things done, but it doesn't help us get big things done in big ways. By choosing to be effective, we are more likely to achieve the goals that really matter to us. No matter what our goals are as leaders, managers, and individual contributors, the puzzles in this book make our goals more attainable because they make us more effective. I designed the puzzles to help you make the most of the parts of your brain that generate, analyze, and implement knowledge. My puzzles progressively stretch and strengthen your mental muscles. They give you the agility to:

- Assess the present situation in terms of a defined goal.
- Acquire the resources needed to achieve that goal.
- Shift gears or even change course when setbacks occur.
- Redefine the goal if the initial one proves unattainable.

Unless you were extraordinarily lucky, your formal education focused on teaching you routine tasks that, once learned, required little thought. You probably were lulled into believing that efficiency was the epitome of achievement.

After all, smart people seemed to know automatically what to do and when to do it. You couldn't see the gears turning in their head. You only saw the results.

Consequently, you may have inadvertently limited yourself as well as those who work for you. By assuming that only efficiency was possible, you never aspired to be effective. You assumed that people were either born to be high achievers or they weren't, that fixed intelligence was a fact of life. In reality, the human brain's natural plasticity makes it possible to move from efficiency to effectiveness. As you worked on the puzzles, you experienced this plasticity. You retrained your brain by:

- **Providing the opportunity for failure.** Success is a temporary "head trip." It makes us feel good by releasing pleasurable chemicals in our brains. Success is highly addictive. It can make us fear failure, although failure allows us to change, learn, and grow. Everyone fails at these puzzles, but it's productive failure. You realize that you can rebound from it. You discover that failure is a catalyst for new ways of thinking about problems. You also realize that failure provides the opportunity to reassess your goals—you change your mind about how quickly you're going to solve the puzzle, for instance.
- **Creating disequilibrium.** When we do only the things we already know, we develop a pseudo–self-confidence. Until we're tested, we don't really know what we can achieve or when we'll fail. Because my puzzles simulate a pressurized, confusing environment, they prepare you mentally and emotionally for higher levels of stress and chaos than you would ordinarily encounter.
- **Offering alternatives.** Having just one perspective is like having tunnel vision. It prevents us from recognizing and effectively taking advantage of opportunities. Just knowing there may be other ways of doing something gives us the ability to reorganize and rebound when other people are stymied by failure.
- **Strengthening cognitive weaknesses.** Most people don't know what they don't know. Experts recognize where their knowledge stops. They are not afraid to admit ignorance or risk failure because they know that's where learning begins. My puzzles provide people with the opportunity to discover what they don't know without personal embarrassment or professional disgrace. They also provide the opportunity to develop new cognitive awareness on a neural level.

By retraining your brain to function effectively, you avoid the pitfalls common mental rigidity, including the following:

- The unwillingness to take risks
- Taking foolish risks
- Alienating other people
- Refusing to work within established processes or systems
- The inability to manage a diverse team or function effectively within one
- The inability to think outside the box
- The inability to adapt well to change
- Ineffective prioritizing time and/or other resources

As you discovered by diagnosing drawings of the complex figure in Chapter 2, even highly intelligent and accomplished people can adhere rigidly to weakening perceptions. This discernment allows you to appreciate how other people process information. With this knowledge, you can more effectively communicate.

Different disciplines (engineering, science, management, etc.) employ different mental models. It is these mental models that interfere with communications between disciplines. As we become more specialized, our mental models become more rigid, and we need to develop the communication skills of a generalist. As we advance further in the organization, we must learn to explain our work to individuals outside our discipline. Both the art and the skill of an expert communicator is to be aware of the mental models of their audience. **The puzzles in this book unveiled the mental models that underlie various disciplines. By making mental models explicit, you now have a tool to explore your own assumptions and experience how you organize information differently from others.**

One of the quickest and most effective ways to improve mental agility is by practicing mediation. It gives us the opportunity to step outside our own head and experience how other people think.

Unlike mentoring—a method that imposes a structured behavior on someone else—mediation requires a willingness to consider alternative perspectives. By carefully listening to someone else's logic, we develop the skills necessary to:

- Make new connections.
- Generate new ideas.
- Think faster.
- Organize information in new ways.
- Achieve higher levels of creativity and innovation.
- Communicate more effectively.

Mediation is an effective method for learning to get the results you want by teaching others how to get the results they want. Though the mediation tools and techniques presented here were designed to facilitate the puzzle process, they can be adapted and applied to managing and coaching responsibilities. Suggesting someone cover up a part of the puzzle to eliminate distracting variables is not that much different from suggesting that a direct report stop trying to look at all the data and focus on one key area in order to solve a problem.

RULES TO KEEP IN MIND

You've probably noticed that throughout this book I've been fond of repeating certain critical thinking rules. These rules should be the mantras of smart organizations, providing them with guidance as they attempt to help individuals within their organization retrain their brains. In the previous section, I looked at how these rules impact an individual's thinking process. Let's review five of these rules and the implications for an organization that adopts them.

Increase Mental Agility

Companies exacerbate problems and miss opportunities because their people are locked into positions from which they refuse to move, despite information that, if properly analyzed, would cause them to move. For many reasons—training, experience, psychological makeup—people have rigid mind-sets and don't integrate new information into their thinking. This isn't a conscious rejection; their minds simply aren't flexible enough to accommodate the new input and reorganize their perspective on a given issue.

The puzzles in this book are the enemy of rigid thinking. They forced you to explore other options and entertain a range of alternatives. As you can imagine, companies with employees who can generate options and see things from new perspectives are much more likely to find innovative answers to problems; they're also much more likely to see a market everyone else has missed or find other opportunities beneath the radar.

Slow Down Before You Speed Up

People in corporations are like children who gobble their food, unable to savor anything because they're in such a hurry to finish. Understandably, employees work fast because they are under pressure to meet deadlines. What they don't realize is that if they want to accelerate their work pace, they first have to slow down their thinking process. As you saw from the exercises, the use of color slows down thinking and enables you to consider details you might have missed and compare and contrast more variables simultaneously. In other words, it facilitates better analysis. As a result, you end up on the right track and can quickly speed up once you're heading in the right direction. All the exercises are designed to slow people down; you can't do most of them unless you put on the mental brakes and start comparing and contrasting all the different images. Once you learn to slow down in this "practice" environment, you can transfer this ability to your work.

Recognize That There Are Shades of Gray

Organizations are still filled with people who want things to be black or white. They want to make unequivocal decisions and leave nothing to chance. Before making important decisions, they try to gather every piece of data that exists and delay action until all the evidence is in.

This attitude is an anachronism. There's too much information to gather enough for a "perfect" decision. People postpone and procrastinate to the point that they lose their advantages in key business situations.

Just as significant, many business issues are clouded by ambiguity, uncertainty, and complexity. Definitive solutions often don't exist, and the best managers are able to choose the best of many alternatives rather than the "right" one. To function effectively in this environment, people need to negotiate the gray areas. Instead of being discombobulated by unclear and difficult situations, they must keep their wits about them and analyze logically and insightfully.

The exercises are filled with gray areas, from problems with more than one solution to problems that seem impossible to solve. When the best answer was unavailable, you were forced to consider what the second, third and even fourth best answers were and learn how to work in the gray, the area of uncertainty.

Practice to Habituate

Retraining your brain requires practice. I hope you communicate to the people you share these puzzles with that they need to work on a lot of them if they hope to see a benefit. Just doing one exercise in each chapter won't have much impact on how you work. It's only after doing a number of each type of exercise that neural pathways open up and people begin to develop increased cognitive abilities.

Making the implicit explicit takes a certain amount of rehearsal time. As you've discovered, it frequently involves a series of steps:

1. Try the first time and fail.
2. Try again and start to get the hang of it.
3. Try a third time and start to develop a process orientation.
4. Try again with a more difficult exercise and repeat the previous three steps.

After a certain period, you started to develop a method of approaching the exercises. Instead of randomly trying this and that, you developed a process for doing the puzzles. You acquired tools and techniques that became second nature. With sufficient practice, your mind is able to apply these exercise-based cognitive skills to work issues. This book contains about 90 exercises. My Web site contains many more that people can use for practice. Therefore, I encourage you to visit <www.designsforstrongminds.com> as often as necessary to develop and maintain your cognitive skills.

When in Trouble, Mediate

These exercises are challenging. People can easily become frustrated and give up or do the exercises improperly and not gain the cognitive benefits. Therefore, make sure the mediation techniques suggested in Chapter 3 and throughout the book are used liberally. Sometimes, people develop a weird sort of machismo and believe they can handle these exercises without help. This is a mistake. Mediation is necessary for everyone to a greater or lesser extent.

Whether you're doing the mediating or someone else in your company assumes this role, the key is to intervene when people ask for help or you see they're growing increasingly frustrated. Although you don't want to give too much help too early—it's the cognitive struggle that helps build mental muscles—you also shouldn't be stingy about dispensing tips and techniques. Encourage people to work with pencil and colored markers; have them make notes on the exercises; show them how they can cover part of an image to eliminate distracting variables; let people help each other if they're doing the exercises in a group setting.

Because of the nature of this medium, you've been self-mediating. That's fine, though one-on-one interaction has obvious advantages. Once you've completed the book, you should be able to do a good job of mediation. And that's great for your organization. Companies could use more mediators and fewer mentors.

Here is a list of other critical thinking rules to be aware of as you're helping an organization retrain its collective brain:

- **Look at the big picture.**
- **Break the whole into its parts.**
- **Connect the dots.**
- **Find the pattern.**
- **Admit mistakes.**
- **Create categories.**
- **Allow yourself to feel stupid.**

BECOME AN ADVOCATE FOR CRITICAL THINKING

If you use this book throughout your organization and impact a critical mass of people, you will have a dramatic effect on how your company does business. But even if only a small cadre of people are exposed to these puzzles, it can have a positive effect on productivity, innovation, and decision making. Even five or ten people in key positions who have improved their capacity for critical thinking can provide a competitive advantage.

You can transmit critical thinking to your organization if you're a good mediator. Armed with the exercises and the mediation techniques in this book (plus the additional exercises on my Web site), you can retrain many brains. If you choose to take on this role, I would advise you to be patient with people as they learn to exercise their cognitive muscles. Remember that you're now operating at a level that others in your organization haven't yet reached, and as a result they're going to struggle with the exercises. When they have difficulty, you need to mediate constructively: Ask them what they see when they look at the images, give them hints, encourage them to make mistakes, and explain that it's more important for them to engage in the problem-solving process than solve each puzzle correctly.

Your reward for successful mediation will be a group of people who:

- Work more effectively and confidently under stress.
- Analyze problems and opportunities logically, insightfully, and quickly.
- Demonstrate creativity.

The puzzles give participants a window into their thinking process. Participants become more conscious of how they come up with new ideas, make decisions, and go about other tasks. This window makes them aware of how they think—the strengths and weaknesses of their reasoning—and enables them to correct flaws on the fly. They become their own consultants, engaged in an analytical dialogue with themselves about how they're thinking about business issues.

In organizations where I've worked with a number of leaders and executives, I often notice that people develop a shared language based on these exercises. When a customer gives them a difficult assignment, they talk about how "it's the same feeling as when we did that part-whole exercise." When they're trying to create a unified plan or strategy, they discuss the need to "connect the dots." When they run into an obstacle, they say they should look at the situation from another perspective—that they need to "rotate" the situation or "cover up" distracting details. In other words, they develop a shared framework that facilitates communication and analysis.

If I can leave you with anything that summarizes how significant these puzzles can be for your company, I would refer you to how you felt when you first opened this book. If you're like most people, when you were first introduced to these puzzles, you skimmed through the pages, examined the various puzzles, and thought that most of them seemed impossible. They made you uneasy and uncertain.

"Man's mind stretched to a new idea, never returns to its original dimensions."

—*Oliver Wendell Holmes*

Now, you can look at these same exercises with confidence. You have a sense of calm when you do them, a feeling that you now possess the skills necessary to understand and solve them.

Most people can transform their thinking in a similar way, and as a result they become infinitely more effective and productive. Just as important, they're much more confident in their ability to get any job done. This combination of superior cognitive skills and positive attitude makes for great employees and great organizations.

By retraining your brain to think more effectively, you develop insight into how and why people behave the way they do. This enables you to outthink your corporate competition and get the results you really want.

INDEX

A

Abstract concepts, analogies and, 50
Act of Creation, The, 37
Allman, William F., 2
Alternatives, 254
Ambiguity, 241, 257
Amiel, Henri Frédéric, 37
Analogical thinking, 50
Analogies, 49–79
    analogy puzzles, 53, 58–60, 62–67, *I-4–I-8*
    boundary spanning and, 60–61
    finding/applying the rule, 62–67
    learning from mistakes, 50–53
    making work fun with, 67–68
    new perspectives and, 61–62
    object of, 53–60
    recognizing false assumptions and, 61
    verbal puzzles, 150–55
Aristotle, 102
Assumptions, recognizing false, 61

B

Babylonian number system, decoding, 232–35,
    243, 248, 249
Behavioral options, increasing, 15
Bell, Alexander Graham, 49–50
Boredom, 68
Boundary spanning, 60–61
Brain plasticity, xvi
Burns, David M., 18

C

Campbell, Jeremy, 50

Case histories, use of, 120
Categories, 209–28
    benefits of, 218–20
    category puzzles, 213–18, 221–27
    circles within circles, 216–18
    reflective thinking and, 210–13
    vocabulary for, 213–16
Chance, Paul, xvi
Churchill, Winston, 15
Clock puzzles, 39–42, 43–44, *I-3*
Cognitive restructuring, xvii
Cognitive style, recognizing, 23
Cognitive weaknesses, 23
    strengthening, 21, 254
Coloring, 38
Communication, between disciplines, 255. *See
    also* Verbal mental agility
Concentration exercises, 31
Conflict management, 106
Connecting the dots, 169–208
Covering, 39
Creativity, failure and, 20
Critical thinking
    advocating, 259–60
    rules, 256–59
    skills, xvii–xviii

D

Danesi, Marcel, 3
Darwin, Charles, 212
Deacon, Terrence, 211
DeBono, Edward, xvii
Decision making, progressive thinking and, 89,
    97–98